SPORTS STARS

STARS

SERIES 2

SPORTS STARS
SERIES 2

volume 1
a–k

Edited by
Michael A. Paré

U·X·L®
AN IMPRINT OF GALE

SPORTS STARS, SERIES 2

Edited by *Michael A. Paré*

Staff

Julie L. Carnagie, *U·X·L Assistant Developmental Editor*
Carol DeKane Nagel, *U·X·L Managing Editor*
Thomas L. Romig, *U·X·L Publisher*

Margaret A. Chamberlain, *Permissions Associate (Pictures)*
The Graphix Group, *Typesetting*

Shanna P. Heilveil, *Production Assistant*
Evi Seoud, *Assistant Production Manager*
Mary Beth Trimper, *Production Director*

Cynthia Baldwin, *Product Design Manager*
Michelle Dimercurio, *Art Director*

Paré, Michael A.
    Sports stars II / Michael A. Paré.
       p.   cm.
    Includes bibliographical references and index.
    Contents: v. 1. A-K — v. 2. L-Z.
    Summary: Contains sixty biographical sketches of popular athletes active in a variety of sports.
    ISBN 0-7876-0867-X (set). — ISBN 0-7876-0868-8 (v. 1). — ISBN 0-7876-0869-6 (v. 2)
    1. Athletes—Biography—Juvenile literature.   [1. Athletes.]
I. Title.
GV697.A1P325   1996
796' .092' 2—dc20   96-10646
[B]   CIP
                                                      AC

This publication is a creative work fully protected by all applicable copyright laws, as well as by misappropriation, trade secret, unfair competition, and other applicable laws. The editors of this work have added value to the underlying factual material herein through one or more of the following: unique and original selection, coordination, expression, arrangement, and classification of the information. All rights to this publication will be vigorously defended.

Copyright © 1996

U·X·L

An Imprint of Gale Research

All rights reserved, including the right of reproduction in whole or in part in any form.

Cover photographs (clockwise from top left): Mary Pierce, Grant Hill, Drew Bledsoe and Gail Devers, reproduced by permission of AP/Wide World Photos.

∞™ This book is printed on acid-free paper that meets the minimum requirements of American National Standard for Information Sciences—Permanence Paper for Printed Library Materials, ANSI Z39.48-1984.

Printed in the United States of America

Contents

Biographical Listings
VOLUME 2: L-Z

Athletes by Sport

Italic numerals indicate series.

AUTO RACING

BASEBALL

BASKETBALL

BICYCLE RACING

BOXING

FIGURE SKATING

FOOTBALL

Reader's Guide

Sports Stars, Series 2, presents biographies of sixty amateur and professional athletes, including Grant Hill, Michael Irvin, and Michelle Kwan, as well as two sports teams, the Colorado Silver Bullets and the *Mighty Mary* yachting team. Besides offering biographies of baseball, basketball, and football sports figures, *Sports Stars,* Series 2, provides increased coverage of athletes in a greater variety of sports, such as swimming, gymnastics, and yachting, and features biographies of women, including Sheryl Swoopes, Manon Rheaume, and Picabo Street, who have broken the sex barrier to participate in the male-dominated sports of basketball, hockey, and skiing.

Athletes profiled in *Sports Stars,* Series 2, meet one or more of the following criteria. The featured athletes are:

- Currently active in amateur or professional sports
- Considered top performers in their fields
- Role models who have overcome physical obstacles or societal constraints to reach the top of their professions.

Format

The sixty profiles of *Sports Stars,* Series 2, are arranged alphabetically over two volumes. Each biography opens with the birth date and place of the individual as well as a "Scoreboard" box listing the athlete's top awards. Every essay contains a "Growing Up" section focusing on the early life and motivations of the individual or team and a "Superstar" section highlighting the featured athlete's career. The profiles also contain portraits and often additional action shots of the individual or group. A "Where to Write" section listing an address and a list of sources for further reading conclude each profile. Additionally, sidebars containing interesting details about the individuals are sprinkled throughout the text.

Additional Features

Sports Stars, Series 2, includes a listing by sport of all the athletes featured in Series 1 and Series 2 as well as a cumulative name and subject index covering athletes found in both series.

Acknowledgments

The author would like to thank the U·X·L staff, especially Julie Carnagie, for her hard work and patience in helping finish *Sports Stars,* Series 2. Special thanks also to Daniel Power, who provided invaluable assistance in determining who would be profiled in *Sports Stars.* Finally, the author would like to thank his wife, Ellen, who made innumerable sacrifices so this project could be completed on time, and his daughter, Chloe, who will be a star in whatever she decides to do when she grows up.

Comments and Suggestions

We welcome your comments on this work as well as your suggestions for individuals to be featured in future editions of *Sports Stars.* Please write: Editor, *Sports Stars,* U·X·L, 835 Penobscot Bldg., Detroit, Michigan 48226-4094; call toll-free: 800-877-4253; or fax toll-free: 800-414-5043.

Photo Credits

The photographs featured in *Sports Stars,* Series 2, were received from the following sources:

AP/Wide World Photos: pp. 1, 11, 17, 21, 26, 32, 41, 48, 50, 59, 64, 67, 71, 73, 80, 88, 92, 97, 100, 109, 116, 124, 126, 133, 146, 148, 159, 163, 166, 189, 201, 203, 210, 217, 219, 227, 233, 235, 281, 283, 287, 290, 316, 318, 322, 325, 331, 333, 342, 348, 351, 359, 361, 369, 381, 389, 398, 401, 413, 415, 422, 425, 445, 450, 459, 462, 477, 484, 486, 493, 495, 504, 506, 512, 515, 524, 528, 536, 538; **Photograph by Scott Olson. Reuter/Archive Photos:** p. 9; **Reuters/ Bettmann:** pp. 24, 56, 245, 442, 452, 522; **Photograph by Gary Hershorn. Reuter/Archive Photos:** pp. 35, 182, 212; **UPI/Bettmann:** p. 82; **Photograph by Peter Jones. Reuter/Archive Photos:** p. 107; **Photograph by Tami L. Chappell. Reuter/Archive Photos:** p. 114; **Photograph by Jeff Christensen. Reuter/Archive Photos:** p. 136; **Photograph by Tony Quinn. Courtesy of ALLSPORT Photography USA Inc.:** p. 141; **Photograph by Rebecca Cook. Reuter/Archive Photos:** p. 159; **Reuters/Bettmann Newsphotos:** p. 174; **Photograph by Wolfgang Rattay.**

Reuter/Archive Photos: p. 183; **Photograph by Blake Sell. Reuter/Archive Photos:** p. 191; **Photograph by Fred Prouser. Reuter/Archive Photos:** p. 243; **Photograph by Brent Smith. Reuter/Archive Photos:** p. 307; **Photograph by Ray Stubblebine. Reuter/ Archive Photos:** p. 314; **Photograph by Masaharu Hatano. Reuter/ Archive Photos:** p. 340; **Photograph by Sue Ogrocki. Reuter/Archive Photos:** p. 371; **Photograph by Jack Dabaghian. Reuter/Archive Photos:** p. 379; **Courtesy of the Milwaukee Bucks:** p. 406; **UPI/Corbis-Bettmann:** p. 433, 435; **Courtesy of Texas Tech Sports Information. Used with permission:** p. 468; **Courtesy of Texas Tech University. Used with permission:** p. 470; **Photograph by: Susumu Takahashi. Reuters/Archive Photos:** p. 475; **Bettmann Newsphotos:** p. 531.

Michelle Akers

1966—

In 1991 soccer forward Michelle Akers was on the top of the world. She had led the U.S. women's national soccer team to the first-ever World Women's Soccer Championships and experts called her "the Michael Jordan of women's soccer." Then, mysteriously, Akers began to feel exhausted. Unable to play the game she loved, she went to doctor after doctor looking for answers. Finally, she discovered she suffered from Epstein-Barr syndrome, a disease that drained her energy and made it difficult for her to complete even the easiest tasks. Through patience and hard work, Akers has learned to deal with the disease and again has taken her place as the best female soccer player in the world.

"It's a tremendous honor to be thought of as the best player in the world."
—Michelle Akers

Growing Up

MOMMA'S GIRL. Michelle Anne Akers was born February 1, 1966, in Santa Clara, California. Akers grew up in the Seattle,

SCOREBOARD

ALL-TIME LEADING SCORER IN U.S. WOMEN'S INTERNATIONAL SOCCER COMPETITION (85 GOALS).

SCORED BOTH U.S. GOALS IN 2-1 VICTORY OVER NORWAY IN 1991 WORLD WOMEN'S SOCCER CHAMPIONSHIPS FINAL GAME.

WON FIRST-EVER HERMANN AWARD IN 1984, GIVEN ANNUALLY TO NATION'S BEST COLLEGIATE SOCCER PLAYER.

AKERS OVERCAME A SERIOUS DISEASE TO AGAIN PLAY THE GAME SHE LOVES.

Washington, area along with her younger brother, Michael. Her mother, Anne, earned her living as a firefighter and ambulance driver. Akers credits her mother with teaching her determination and coolness under pressure. "My mom was a pioneer," Akers related in *People* magazine. "She's a spirited lady."

DEALING WITH DIVORCE. Akers's father, Robert, was a supermarket meat department manager. Her parents divorced when Akers was 13 years old. Akers had a hard time dealing with her parents' breakup. She slept in her brother's room for a month after receiving the news. "It wasn't a friendly split, but afterwards they got more involved in my sports," Akers told *People* magazine. "They wanted Michael and me to be sure we knew they loved us." Although Akers wanted her parents to get back together, she soon realized they never would.

SHOOTING STAR. Akers first took up soccer when she was ten years old. "I played mostly with the boys," Akers recalled in *People* magazine, "and it was tomboy soccer—skinned knees and getting in fights." Akers became a star at Shorecrest High School, where she earned All-American honors for three consecutive years. Her talent landed her a scholarship in 1984 to the University of Central Florida, where she continued to shine. Akers established herself as the finest player in the United States, four times earning All-American recognition at Central Florida. She also won the first Hermann Award in 1984, now given annually to the nation's best collegiate soccer player.

FIGHTS TO PLAY. After graduating from college, Akers earned a spot on the U.S. women's national team. She played for the love of the game, not the money. National team members made only $10 a day, plus room and board. Akers dedicated her body to the sport. Seven times she had surgery on her knees, and she had to fight the U.S. Soccer Federation to play despite her injuries.

In 1990 Akers married Roby Stahl, a former soccer pro whom she had met at his soccer camp. Her marriage also took a back seat to soccer. Akers spent months away from her husband, playing on a semiprofessional team in Sweden and in international competition for the United States.

Akers's early experiences with the national team proved disappointing. She realized after a trip to Italy that the national team had a long way to go in terms of talent and image. "We didn't look like a national team," Akers admitted in *Sports Illustrated*. "All we had were these lime-green and purple uniforms. No one was fit. It just felt like we were off to Italy on a vacation. We were just a bunch of kids, we didn't know what we were getting into." Akers and her teammates, playing four matches, tied with one opponent and lost to the others.

BEST IN WORLD. Slowly the U.S. team began to come together. "Our national-team mentality is that we're not gonna wear down," Akers explained in *People* magazine. "We're gonna beat you if it takes all day." Anson Dorrance, coach of the powerful University of North Carolina women's soccer team, coached the U.S. squad. In qualifying for the first-ever world championships in 1991, the U.S. team blew out five opponents by a combined score of 49-0.

By the time of the World Women's Soccer Championships, held in November 1991 in the People's Republic of China, Akers had arrived as a dominant force. Twice experts named Akers soccer's Female Athlete of the Year. "The reason she is so feared all over the world is that she has so many

COWBOY KICKER

In 1988 the Dallas Cowboys invited Akers to try out as a kicker for their team. "All these Cowboy fans came around, and they were just acting like idiots," Akers recalled in *People* magazine. "Their attitude was, 'You should still be in the kitchen baking cookies.'" Akers silenced the fans by making 90 percent of her kicks inside of 40 yards and blasting a 52-yard field goal. "Considering she had never kicked a football before, she picked up the technique real fast," Cowboys consultant Ben Agajanian told the *Tampa Tribune*. "If she's into it, I'd definitely like to see how good we could make her." Akers has not ruled out playing football when her soccer career is over. "If I decide to do it, I'll take it seriously," Akers explained in the *Tampa Tribune*. "It would be my focus and I would train for it on the same level as I do everything. I wouldn't be there as a joke or a female Bozo for the media. I'd be out there because I was a good field goal kicker worth taking a look at."

dimensions to her game," Dorrance stated in *People* magazine. "She is a nightmare matchup for a defender."

Superstar

WORLD CHAMPS. The American women peaked at the world championships. They defeated Sweden, Brazil, and Japan. The U.S. team then defeated Taiwan 7-0 behind five goals by Akers. In the semifinals, the Americans defeated Germany, 5-2, earning a place in the finals against Norway. Some 65,000 spectators filled the stadium for the championship game, providing Akers with her most glorious stage ever.

Akers scored the game's first goal for the Americans on a brilliant header (shooting the ball with the head). Norway came back to tie the game 1-1. The score remained 1-1 with less than three minutes to play. Both teams played tough defense, and it appeared the game was going into overtime. Just then a Norwegian player made a weak pass back to her goalie. Akers pounced on it, stole the ball, and drove home the winning goal into an open net. The victory gave the United States its first world soccer championship. Dorrance told *People* magazine that Akers was "the best female soccer player in the world—no question about it."

The performance sealed Akers's reputation as the game's number one player. Despite being double- and triple-teamed, Akers scored ten goals in the six games of the tournament. "I like her because she is intelligent, has presence of mind and is often in the right position," the legendary Pele, Akers's soccer idol, told *Sports Illustrated* after the final game. "She's fantastic." Akers won the Golden Boot Award as the tournament's leading scorer and the Silver Ball Trophy as the second-best player in the world championships.

MYSTERIOUS DISEASE. Shortly after returning from China, Akers began to feel tired. At first doctors said she suffered from exhaustion, had heart problems, or had mononucleosis. Despite feeling exhausted, Akers led all scorers—men and women—in Sweden's professional leagues in 1992, with 43 goals. It took four years for doctors to diagnose Epstein-Barr syndrome, otherwise known as chronic fatigue syndrome, as the cause of Akers's illness.

The virus slowly dissolved Akers's strength. By the spring of 1994, the illness forced her to sit on the sidelines, sometimes for entire games. "Every day I felt as if I had just flown to Europe, not gotten any sleep or anything to eat, gotten right back on the plane, flown to the U.S. and then trained," she recalled in *Sports Illustrated*. "When it was bad, I couldn't sit up in a chair. All I could do was lie in bed. At night I sweated so much I went through two or three T-shirts. And the migraine headaches pounded. Boom! Boom! Boom!" During one game teammates had to help her off the field because she became delirious, drooling and wandering around the field.

Even the most simple tasks became hard for Akers. She had difficulty taking a shower or brushing her teeth and often was in a bad mood. "But on the field she still was the same dominating player," teammate Julie Foudy recalled in *Sports Illustrated*. "She just couldn't go 90 minutes. It was a factor of time, how long she could play and not be wiped out for the next game." Akers conserved her energy on the field, not running hard down the field on defense. "I have only so much in the gas tank now," Akers related in the *Seattle Times*. "I have to choose when to run, and when not to run. Mentally, it's exhausting."

NEVER QUIT. Akers refused to quit. In August 1994 she played for the United States in the CONCACAF Qualifying Championship, the tournament that determined which teams from North and Central America and the Caribbean would play in the 1995 World Women's Soccer Championships. "My challenge was to help us win, whether or not I was playing," Akers told *Sports Illustrated*. Unbelievably, Akers scored six goals in four games and tournament officials named her the Most Valuable Player. The U.S. won the tournament and the right to defend their world title.

GETTING PRIORITIES STRAIGHT. Returning to the U.S. after the tournament, Akers was an emotional and physical wreck.

Trying to improve her health, she transformed her life. As a first step, Akers divorced her husband in early 1995, asserting that the relationship had failed and was not worth trying to save. "I had been unhappy for a while," Akers admitted in *Sports Illustrated*. "It was the hardest decision I've ever had to make in my life."

Akers also worked on other parts of her life. She told the *Trenton Times* that religion helped get her through the tough times. Akers initially embraced Christianity as a sophomore in high school, but drifted away from religion during college. Besides her spiritual well-being, Akers also tended closely to her body, improving her diet and restricting her tough training program.

After a difficult six-month spell between the spring and summer of 1995, Akers's health improved. Despite being limited because of her illness, she remained a key offensive weapon for the U.S. team. "Out of hard times comes maturity," Akers told the *Tampa Tribune*. "These last couple of years have been really tough in a lot of ways. I think I've been able to grow up and I've learned a lot. All of that was hard until I got my priorities straight."

DEFENDING TITLE. Although she doubted she could do it, Akers's recovery allowed her to again be a dominant player leading up to the 1995 World Women's Soccer Championships. "To me, Michelle is just so courageous to be out there playing with an illness that makes it hard for some people just to get out of bed," teammate Carla Overbeck told the *Tampa Tribune*. "Even when she's not 100 percent, she has such a huge presence out there on the field. She's a fighter and wants to be out there."

Akers worked her way back to playing full games and looked forward to the challenge of defending the world title. "This is really different than '91 because we were rookies at that World Cup," Akers explained in the *Washington Post*. "Now we're a little more in the spotlight and people know who we are. The rest of the world is gunning for us, and I really like it that way. It's going to be a real challenge, a real test, on how tough we are mentally and how much we're willing to give up in order to win. I really like these kinds of tests."

Unfortunately for Akers, an injury in the first game of the world championships limited her play. She received a concussion and injured her knee when she collided with another player. With their main scoring threat injured, the United States lost 1-0 in the semi-finals to Norway. The U.S. team then defeated China, 2-0, to win the bronze medal. Akers did not score in the tournament.

OLYMPIC CHALLENGE. For the 1996 games, the International Olympic Committee approved women's soccer as a medal sport for the first time. Akers, a member of the U.S. team, hopes the Olympics, held in Atlanta, Georgia, will help popularize women's soccer. She works hard to promote the game, answering fan mail and making public appearances. Through 1995 Akers had averaged almost a goal per game in international competition (85 goals in 92 games). This is an amazing feat considering her illness restricted Akers to part-time duty for several years. "It's a tremendous honor to be thought of as the best player in the world," Akers explained in the *Trenton Times*. "You work toward something your whole life and then all of a sudden the title is there for you. You step on the field and already there's an amount of respect from your opposition."

OFF THE FIELD. Akers lives in Oviedo, Florida. She likes to read Stephen King novels and scuba dive. Akers is a spokesperson for Umbro soccer shoes, the first woman to receive such a contract. In 1989 she earned her bachelor's degree in liberal studies and health. Working so hard has often made life difficult for Akers. "I feel sometimes I'm missing out," Akers stated in *People* magazine. "But I know in the future I'm going to be able to do all the things I want."

Akers admits she is a perfectionist. "In everything I did, I wanted to be the best at it," Akers said in *People*. She hopes

ROLE MODEL

When Akers started playing soccer, there were no female soccer role models for her to look up to. Now Akers is a role model to younger players. "In high school our coach showed us tapes of the 1991 World Cup," U.S. midfielder Tiffany Roberts explained in *Sports Illustrated*. "She [Akers] was the best player I had ever seen. I was in awe."

to continue playing soccer until the 1999 Women's world championships. She stated in the *Trenton Times,* "My guideline for myself is as long as I'm healthy, as long as I'm enjoying myself, which is the number one thing, I'm going to keep playing."

Sources

Chicago Tribune, July 9, 1994.
Christian Science Monitor, August 12, 1994.
Newsweek, June 5, 1995.
New York Times, June 15, 1995.
People, November 25, 1991.
Seattle Times, August 19, 1984; May 12, 1995.
Sports Illustrated, December 9, 1991; June 5, 1995.
Sports Illustrated for Kids, December 1995.
Tampa Tribune, May 2, 1995.
Trenton Times (New Jersey), August 2, 1995.
USA Today, December 2, 1994.
Washington Post, May 4, 1995.
Additional Information provided by U.S. Soccer Federation.

WHERE TO WRITE:
U.S. SOCCER FEDERATION,
1801-1811 SOUTH PRAIRIE AVE.,
CHICAGO, IL 60616.

Albert Belle

1966—

Albert Belle is the best home run hitter in the American League in the 1990s. He has hit 186 home runs in just five seasons, an average of more than 35 per year. Belle was the main man in the 1995 Cleveland Indians lineup, which powered the team to 100 victories and the highest team batting average in 45 years. Despite his success, very little is known about the Indians' slugger. A powerhouse on the field and a private person off it, Belle promises to continue to send baseballs into orbit.

"Albert doesn't hit singles anymore. Albert only hits bombs."
—Cleveland Indians' manager Mike Hargrove

Growing Up

BELLE BORN. Albert Jojuan Belle was born August 25, 1966, in Shreveport, Louisiana. His father, Albert, is a football coach, and his mother, Carrie, is a math teacher. Belle has a twin brother, Terry. His parents stressed education, and Belle and his brother took 15 hours of college computer courses during his senior year in high school. "How many other major

SCOREBOARD

FIRST PLAYER IN MAJOR LEAGUE HISTORY TO HIT MORE THAN 50 HOME RUNS AND 50 DOUBLES IN THE SAME SEASON (1995).

LED MAJOR LEAGUES IN HOME RUNS IN 1995 (50).

LED MAJOR LEAGUES IN RUNS BATTED IN (RBI) IN 1993.

BELLE HAS OVERCOME ALCOHOLISM AND A FIERY TEMPER TO BECOME THE BEST POWER HITTER IN THE MAJOR LEAGUES.

leaguers know [computer languages] BASIC and FORTRAN?" Terry Belle asked in the *Sporting News.*

Belle was a good student and a gifted athlete. One year with his Little League team, he hit 21 home runs and was 8-0 as a pitcher—in 16 games. Belle was also an Eagle Scout and performed community service in Shreveport.

TIGER TERROR. Belle and his family thought he would be offered a minor league baseball contract when he graduated from high school. No offer came, so Belle enrolled at Louisiana State University (LSU). He majored in accounting and starred on the LSU Tigers baseball team. During his three seasons at LSU (1985-87), Belle set university records in seven offensive categories, including home runs (49), runs batted in (172), runs (157), hits (194), and at-bats (585). Belle hit 21 home runs in his junior season at LSU. "He could hit with a matchstick," his LSU coach Skip Bertman recalled in the *Sporting News.* "He was a hard worker."

His time at LSU was not always happy, however. Fans repeatedly yelled racial slurs at him from the stands. During the 1987 Southeastern Conference Baseball Tournament, Belle jumped into the stands trying to catch a racist fan. His teammates tackled him and the fan escaped.

CLEVELAND PICK. The Cleveland Indians drafted Belle in the second round of the 1987 major league draft. He quickly worked his way through the minors, joining the major league Indians in July 1989. Belle started fast in Cleveland, hitting .311 with two home runs in his first dozen games. One of the home runs was a grand slam against the New York Yankees.

Soon, however, the rookie began to struggle. Belle slumped and lost his temper several times. "I was sure I'd be a superstar by the time I was 21," Belle admitted in *Sports Illustrated.* "Baseball messed up my plan of life. When I fail, I get

upset. Sometimes I get upset too quickly, without thinking of the consequences."

Belle hits a home run against the California Angels in 1995.

GETS HELP. Belle started slowly in 1990 for the Indians. Before long Cleveland demoted him to the team's AAA minor league team in Colorado Springs, Colorado. Soon after arriving in Colorado Springs, Belle checked himself into the Cleveland Clinic for treatment of alcohol abuse. "Some people like to sip a drink and enjoy it," Belle explained in *Sport* magazine. "But I got to the point where I didn't feel like waiting around. I wanted to relax. I wanted to get drunk. As fast as possible." He added that his admission of alcoholism was hard for his whole family. "One of the bad things about being an alcoholic is that your parents think they did something wrong bringing you up," he said. "I was raised the best way they knew how. Whatever the problem was, it was mine."

One big problem for Belle was that he was a perfectionist. "It took my brother a long, long time to realize that he

HISTORY LESSON

Belle, who is knowledgeable about the old Negro League and its stars in the days before the major leagues allowed African Americans to play, was happy to play in Cleveland. "When I came to Cleveland, I found out they have a kind of Negro League tradition," Belle told the *Sporting News*. "It was fun to meet and get to talk to some of the old players. I appreciate what they did. I read about Jackie Robinson, but, you know, I kind of went through the same kind of thing he did. Playing in Mississippi and Alabama, standing there for three straight hours, hearing the people yell racial slurs." Belle has helped several former Negro League players financially.

wasn't going to hit .400 in the major leagues," Belle's twin brother, Terry, told the *Sporting News*. "As he has gotten older and gotten to know the pitchers, he has come to realize that he can't get a hit every at-bat. Even if he's a superstar, he's still going to fail 70 percent of the time—and still be considered a success. He didn't realize that at first."

CLEVELAND CRUSHER. Belle rejoined the Indians in 1991. As part of his treatment, he dropped the name he had been using since childhood—Joey Belle—in favor of the more formal Albert. Despite a brief return to the minor leagues, Belle put up great numbers. He batted .282, hit 28 home runs, and drove in 95 in just 123 games. Cleveland fans accepted Belle, as Bill Livingstone wrote in *Sport* magazine: "In Cleveland, where they have known failure for 38 straight seasons, a man [like Belle] who hates it [failure] and fights so hard against it, as Belle does, can become a fan favorite." The Indians lost 105 games in 1991, but Belle tried to not let the losing get him down. "Even though we were losing, I was excited to come to the ballpark every day because that might be the day we turn it around," Belle explained in the *Sporting News*.

ALL-STAR. Belle had a breakthrough season in 1992. He hit 34 home runs, drove in 112 runs (fourth in the American League), and batted .260. Belle repeated his performance in 1993, his second straight season to exceed 30 home runs and 100 runs batted in (RBI). He led the major leagues in RBI (129), was fourth in the American League in home runs (38), and raised his batting average to .290. American League manager Cito Gaston of the Toronto Blue Jays named Belle to his first All-Star Game. "Albert has improved so much," teammate Carlos Baerga stated in *Baseball Digest*. "He's become a complete hitter."

"Albert is the most popular player we have," Indians general manager John Hart revealed in the *New York Times*. "He is a folk hero. We brought him up. He struggled as a young player. They've [the fans have] seen him mature as a human being. Albert does more community things behind the scenes than anyone we have. The community just threw themselves behind him."

Superstar

STRUCK OUT. The last time the Indians won an American League pennant or appeared in the play-offs was 1954. That team set a major league record with 111 wins but lost four straight games to the New York Giants in the World Series. The 1994 Indians set out to end the slump. Cleveland had a powerful lineup, featuring Belle, future Hall-of-Fame candidate and first baseman Eddie Murray, second baseman Carlos Baerga, and center fielder Kenny Lofton. The Indians also had a new stadium, Jacobs Field, which the team sold out most every game. "I was tickled pink to be playing there," Belle explained in *Baseball Digest*. "We had sellout crowds and were winning."

The Indians were struggling with the Chicago White Sox for the lead in the newly formed American League Central Division. Unfortunately, the most exciting summer in Cleveland in 40 years ended when the players went on strike in August. A disagreement between the players and owners on issues such as free agency caused the strike. The strike shortened the season to only 113 games and caused the cancellation of the play-offs and the World Series.

Belle had his best season yet in 1994. He hit .357 (second in the American League), had 36 home runs (third in the American League), and drove in 101 runs (third in the American League). "When I started last season, I felt I could hit .290 to .300," Belle recalled in *Baseball Digest* after the season. "It turned out a lot better than I expected. I was in a zone pretty much all last year. I had very few slumps."

BEST RECORD. Nothing could stop the Indians in 1995. Cleveland finished with a 100-44 record and won the American League Central Division by a record 30-game margin. The Indians did so well because of an awesome offense and stingy pitching staff. The team's batting average was .291, the highest in 45 years. Former Cy Young Award winner Orel Hershiser and Dennis Martinez anchored the pitching staff, and reliever Jose Mesa led the American League in saves. The Indians led the American League in both batting average and earned run average.

The leader of the 1995 Indians, however, was Belle. His statistics were incredible. Belle became the first player in major league history to hit 50 home runs (led the major leagues) and more than 50 doubles (52). "Albert doesn't hit singles anymore," Indians manager Mike Hargrove declared in *Sports Illustrated.* "Albert only hits bombs." He accomplished this feat even though the players' strike shortened the 1995 season by 18 games. Belle hit 36 home runs in the second half of the season and 18 in his last 29 games. Belle tied the record set by Babe Ruth in 1927 by hitting 17 home runs in September. He batted .317 and tied for the American League lead in runs batted in (RBI) with 126.

Belle also took on more of a leadership role with the young Indians team. "When I first met Albert, it was kind of hard for him to open up to a lot of guys," teammate Wayne Kirby said in the *Sporting News.* "But now that we have a young team, a lot of players look up to him. At one time he used to walk to first base. Now I always see him running. He used to throw his helmet all the time. Not anymore." Despite his great numbers and his team's success, Belle finished second in the voting for the American League's Most Valuable Player, following **Mo Vaughn** (see entry) of the Boston Red Sox.

PLAY-OFF RUN. Belle took revenge on Vaughn by helping the Indians sweep the Red Sox in the first round of the play-offs. The Indians then faced the Seattle Mariners in the American League Championship Series. Cleveland fell behind the Mariners two games to one but came back to win Games Four and Five. In Game Six, the Indians faced the overpowering **Randy Johnson** (see entry), who had already won four times during the postseason in games where a loss would have eliminated the Mariners. Cleveland dealt Johnson his first postseason defeat, claiming a 4-0 victory that sent the Indians to the World Series.

WORLD SERIES. The Indians faced the Atlanta Braves in the World Series. The Braves featured one of the best pitching staffs of all time, including four-time Cy Young Award winner Greg Maddux and former Cy Young winner **Tom Glavine** (see entry). Pitching ruled in the first two games of the Series, both Atlanta victories. Maddux and Glavine held Cleveland to a total of eight hits, only one for extra bases. Belle and Carlos Baerga had only one hit in 14 at-bats in the defeats.

The Series then moved to Cleveland for the first time since 1954. The Indians won Game Three, 7-6, but dropped Game Four, 5-2. Cleveland stayed alive with a Game Five victory, forcing a return to Atlanta. Glavine took the mound for the Braves in Game Six, and the Indians could not figure him out. Cleveland had only one hit in the game and lost 1-0. The Indians batted only .179 in the Series. Twice the Braves held the Indians to fewer than three hits, the only time this happened to them all season.

The Braves pitched around Belle. He batted only seven times in the World Series with runners on base, and Atlanta walked him on four of those occasions. Belle batted .235 in the Series, and that was good enough to lead the Indians in hit-

SHORT FUSE

During his career Belle has had trouble with a bad temper. Coaches and league officials have suspended him several times during his college and professional careers for arguing with umpires and fighting with players and fans. In 1991 Belle threw a ball at a fan who was making fun of him and received a seven-day suspension. In 1994 the American League suspended Belle when the Chicago White Sox discovered he was using an illegal bat. Belle refuses to talk to the media following games, a policy that many experts believe cost him the American League Most Valuable Player award in 1995. (Reporters vote on the award.) Belle received at least one suspension in each of his first four seasons with the Indians.

Belle's personality has not prevented him from becoming popular. "The fans in Cleveland love him, his teammates like him and his employers think he's terrific," journalist Murray Chase explained in the *New York Times.* Belle refuses to apologize for any of his behavior, as he told the *Sporting News:* "If I had to do it again from day one of childhood, I wouldn't change a thing. I don't care. People can think whatever they want."

ting. The Braves could pitch around Belle because Eddie Murray, hitting behind Belle in the batting order, hit only .105 during the Series.

OFF THE FIELD. Belle lives in Euclid, Ohio. He is active in several charities, including the Black on Black Crime Commission, the United Way, and the Albert Belle Charity Golf Outing. Galilee Baptist Church in Shreveport named a baseball field after him. Belle likes to play basketball, chess, and golf. He is also the reigning Cleveland Indians Ping-Pong champion. Belle does crossword puzzles in his spare time.

Belle says his road to the top has been tough. "I had to work harder to get where I am," Belle revealed in the *Sporting News*. "I pretty much came out of nowhere and probably had to work three times as hard to get my name on the scene. Now I feel like I've earned the right to be out there every day, no matter what."

Sources

Baseball Digest, August 1995.
Cleveland Plain Dealer, August 29, 1993; July 30, 1994.
Houston Chronicle, June 20, 1993.
New York Times, July 29, 1994.
Pittsburgh Post-Gazette, July 31, 1994.
Seattle Times, May 14, 1991.
Sport, February 1992.
Sporting News, July 4, 1994; July 25, 1994; August 1, 1994.
Sports Illustrated, June 24, 1991; June 8, 1992; July 25, 1994; October 9, 1995;
    October 16, 1995; October 23, 1995; October 30, 1995; November 6, 1995.
USA Today, May 3, 1993; July 26, 1994.
Washington Post, May 20, 1993.

WHERE TO WRITE:
C/O CLEVELAND INDIANS, JACOBS FIELD,
2401 ONTARIO ST.,
CLEVELAND, OH 44115.

Drew Bledsoe

1972—

D rew Bledsoe has the perfect body to play quarterback in the National Football League (NFL). At six-feet-five-inches tall, he can see over his offensive linemen and find open receivers. Bledsoe has a rifle arm to thread the needle between defenders or to throw the long bomb. He also has the intelligence to read defenses and the leadership ability to make his team better. All these factors led the New England Patriots to make Bledsoe the first-pick overall in the 1993 NFL Draft. They also have made him the best young quarterback to come into the league in quite some time.

"He is Larry Bird in shoulder pads."
—Journalist Dan Shaughnessy

Growing Up

LIKE FATHER LIKE SON. Drew Bledsoe was born February 14, 1972, in Ellensburg, Washington. His parents, Mac and Barbara, were both English teachers, and his father was also a football coach. The family moved five times before Bledsoe

SCOREBOARD

FIRST PLAYER CHOSEN
IN 1993 NFL DRAFT.

SET NFL RECORD WITH 691
PASSING ATTEMPTS IN 1994.

LED NFL WITH 4,555 YARDS
PASSING IN 1994.

SIZE, STRENGTH, AND
INTELLIGENCE MAKE BLEDSOE
THE NFL'S BEST YOUNG
QUARTERBACK.

was in the sixth grade as his father looked for coaching jobs. From an early age Bledsoe loved football. "He always dressed for Halloween as a football player," his mom recalled in *Sport* magazine. "I always knew he'd be one of those people to make the world a better place, but I never dreamed it would be through professional football."

Bledsoe would go to football camp with his father and watch the professional players working out. This early education gave him a head start, and he learned his lessons well. Bledsoe also decided what he wanted to do. "Playing in the NFL is a childhood dream come true," he admitted in the *New York Times*. "My heroes would change whenever a new player would come to my father's camp." Football could not get him out of doing his chores, however. "Even if we won a big game in high school, I still had to come home and clean my room," Bledsoe confessed to *Sport* magazine.

CLOSE TO HOME. The Bledsoe family finally settled in Walla Walla, Washington, where Mr. Bledsoe coached the high school football team. Bledsoe starred for his father at Walla Walla High School, earning first-team all-state honors in football after his senior season. "He's a clinic in how to throw," his dad told *Sports Illustrated*. "Watch him throw an out [pattern]. I mean, it's coming. It whistles."

The *Seattle Times* named Bledsoe Washington State Player of the Year after his senior season. He also lettered in basketball. College football powerhouses like the University of Miami and the University of Washington recruited him. However, when it came time to choose a college, Bledsoe picked Washington State University, only a two-hour drive from home.

COUGAR SIGNAL CALLER. Bledsoe became the first freshman in 30 years to start at Washington State. "I was kind of like a hometown hero who went to Washington State and then got to start as a freshman," Bledsoe remembered in the *New York Times*. "I ran onto the field and looked around the Coliseum, and it was like a dream. And there was this big replay screen at one end that showed me running down the field, and when I looked up and saw it, I realized that I wasn't dreaming."

PEER PROBLEMS. The dream soon became a nightmare. Some members of the team did not think Bledsoe should be the starting quarterback. "There were three separate cliques [groups] on the team, and the ones that weren't for me wouldn't talk to me," Bledsoe recounted in *Sports Illustrated*. "Running backs and receivers I was throwing to would come back to the huddle and never say a word to me." Washington State finished the season 3-8, losing four of the five games with Bledsoe as the starter.

It would have been easy for Bledsoe to quit after his disappointing freshman season, but he kept working. He made the All-Pacific Ten (PAC-10) team as a junior and was ninth in the nation in total yardage. In 1992 the Cougars were ranked in the top 20 through most of the season. Bledsoe finished second on the school's all-time passing list with 7,818 yards and 46 touchdowns during his career. He finished his career at Washington State with a bang, throwing for a school-record 476 yards in a Copper Bowl victory over the University of Utah.

Superstar

TOP PICK. Bledsoe decided to leave Washington State after his junior year and entered the 1993 NFL Draft. Most teams had him listed as one of the two top-rated quarterbacks in the draft, along with Rick Mirer from Notre Dame. The New England Patriots held the top pick in the draft and chose Bledsoe. "I think about playing in the NFL, and it's still a dream to me," he confessed to the *New York Times*. "It's funny to think that someone would pay me to play."

TOMMY KNECHD

The last time Bledsoe did not play quarterback on the school team was in seventh grade at Pioneer Junior High School. A youngster named Tommy Knechd has the honor of being the last quarterback to start in front of Bledsoe at quarterback for an entire season.

The Patriots were a poor team during the 1992 season, finishing 2-14. New England fans expected much of the rookie quarterback, but Bledsoe tried to keep things in perspective. "If I'm playing well, I imagine I'll be out there on the field," he explained to the *New York Times*. "If I'm not and I'm not helping the team, then I won't be out there."

COACH AND PUPIL. Before the 1993 season New England signed coach Bill Parcells, who had led the New York Giants to two Super Bowl titles. Parcells was a tough coach, and he worked hard on making Bledsoe an NFL quarterback. He insisted that Bledsoe come to practice early and stay late to study the playbook and prepare for games. "I wasn't particularly critical of Bledsoe," Parcells recounted in the *Sporting News*. "He [Bledsoe] needs to understand that there's a sense of urgency." Bledsoe came to understand what his coach was trying to do. "You realize there's always a reason behind everything he says, whether he's trying to correct something or in one way or another trying to motivate," Bledsoe told the *Sporting News.*

ROOKIE ROCKET. The hard work paid off. Bledsoe became an instant sensation for the Patriots. Parcells, normally a coach who emphasizes the running game, named him the starting quarterback. Bledsoe rewrote the Patriots' rookie record book. He threw for 2,494 yards and 15 touchdowns during the season, despite missing three games with a knee injury. Bledsoe saved his best for last, throwing for 329 yards and four touchdowns in a 33-27 overtime victory over the Miami Dolphins in the season's final game. He learned a lot in his rookie season. "What I learned," he explained to the *Boston Globe,* "was that I love the football side—being able to play a game and get paid to do it. But I also learned I could live without the star status involved with being a quarterback in the NFL." He added in *Sports Illustrated:* "At first I thought seeing my face in the media was pretty cool. Now, I'm more interested in whether I sound like an idiot or not."

RECORD SETTER. The 1994 season was great for both Bledsoe and the Patriots. "There is a big difference for me from

last year to this year," Bledsoe told the *Sporting News* before his sophomore NFL season. "Last year, I was 3,000 miles from home, I was in completely new surroundings, with a new coaching staff, new players, new friends and a completely new offensive system. All kinds of things went on. This year, I know everybody. I know the coaches, I know the offense, I know where I'm going to have a house, all that. Everything is so much easier."

Bledsoe broke the NFL record by throwing 691 passes and led the league with 400 completions and 4,555 yards in 1994. He also finished fourth in the league with 25 touchdown passes and set eight team records. Bledsoe's most impressive performance came against the Minnesota Vikings on November 13 in a game New England had to win. The Patriots had

Bledsoe carries the ball nine yards against the Cleveland Browns.

Being an NFL quarterback has given Bledsoe a new outlook on the heroes he had when he was younger. "When I was a kid, I had the impression all those years that professional athletes were different from regular people," Bledsoe said in the *Boston Globe.* "[Dan] Marino, John Elway. You almost gave them god status. Now I'd been playing against them, not doing as well, but playing against them, and I was just me. That tends to bring everyone down a little closer to earth in your mind."

lost three straight games and trailed the Vikings 20-0 with only 58 seconds remaining in the first half. Bledsoe led the Patriots to a 26-20 overtime victory, setting NFL single-game records with 45 completions and 70 passing attempts. This victory led to a seven-game win streak to close the season.

New England clinched its first play-off berth in eight seasons with a 13-3 final-game victory over the Chicago Bears. The Patriots played the Cleveland Browns in the first round of the play-offs, losing 20-13. Bledsoe had an off game, completing only 21 of 50 passes and throwing three interceptions. After the season 22-year-old Bledsoe became the youngest quarterback ever to play in the Pro Bowl game. Football experts understand that Bledsoe is destined for greatness. "Drew is the Man," wrote Dan Shaughnessy in the *Boston Globe*. "He is among the best there ever was. He is big, young, strong and fearless. He can throw the long bomb or the soft-touch pass. He can take a hit. He's got the quick release. He is Larry Bird in shoulder pads."

LOST YEAR. New England fans expected a great season in 1995. Instead, the Patriots struggled, finishing the year 6-10. Bledsoe separated his left shoulder early in the season in a game against the San Francisco 49ers. He returned to the line-up before the injury completely healed and could not perform up to his ability. Later in the year Bledsoe slightly separated his right shoulder. The injuries slowed down Bledsoe and the Patriots offense. Bledsoe threw for 3,507 yards and 13 touchdowns, but he finished near the bottom in the NFL's complicated quarterback efficiency ratings. Bledsoe hopes to be completely healthy for the beginning of the 1996 season.

OFF THE FIELD. Bledsoe is single and lives in Walla Walla during the off-season with his girlfriend, Maura Healy. He majored in education at Washington State. Bledsoe honored his grandfather by establishing the Albert S. "Stu" Bledsoe Endowed Football Scholarship, a $150,000 program at Washington State. In his spare time, Bledsoe likes to read, scuba dive, snow ski, and listen to music. His favorite bands are Hootie and the Blowfish and U2.

Bledsoe has tried not to let success go to his head. "I know I don't have to play football to gain the acceptance of anyone or to prove I'm a good person," Bledsoe acknowledged in the *Boston Globe*. "Football has opened a lot of doors for me but because of the way I was brought up, if I didn't have all this stuff, it would have no bearing on what kind of person I am."

Sources

Boston Globe, September 11, 1994; September 20, 1994.
New York Times, October 28, 1992; April 15, 1993; July 7, 1993; October 13, 1994.
Sport, September 1995.
Sporting News, February 8, 1993; September 27, 1993; August 29, 1994; January 9, 1995.
Sports Illustrated, April 19, 1993; August 2, 1993; September 27, 1993; December 6, 1993; November 7, 1994; October 23, 1995.
Sports Illustrated for Kids, October 1995.
Additional information provided by New England Patriots.

 WHERE TO WRITE:
C/O NEW ENGLAND PATRIOTS, FOXBORO STADIUM,
60 WASHINGTON ST.,
FOXBORO, MA 02035.

Surya Bonaly

1973—

"[Surya Bonaly] can out-jump almost every woman to compete in the sport and many of the men."
—Journalist Randy Harvey

Surya Bonaly of France has held a spot near the top of the figure skating world for some time. In a sport dominated by white athletes, Bonaly has been a role model for black fans throughout the world. Trained as a gymnast, Bonaly can do athletic jumps that few other women skaters have ever attempted. A five-time winner at the European Figure Skating Championships, Bonaly has twice fallen just short of winning the world championship. She continues to be an international star and a favorite to win every competition she enters.

Growing Up

MYSTERY OF BIRTH. Surya Bonaly (BONE-a-lee) was born in 1973 in Nice, France. She is the adopted daughter of Georges, an architect and government worker, and Suzanne, a physical education teacher. Mystery surrounds Bonaly's birth. For years her mother told the press that the youngster was born on the island of Réunion, a French territory in the Indian Ocean just east of Madagascar. Some stories even said that Bonaly had been abandoned on a beach with coconuts all around her. When Bonaly turned 18, however, her adoptive parents admitted their daughter was born in Nice, but that her biological mother was from Réunion.

TUMBLING TODDLER. Bonaly's parents adopted her as an infant. The Bonalys, who are both white, asked for a nonwhite baby because "they are the babies no one takes." Named "Surya," a Hindu word for "sun," young Bonaly grew up in Nice and later Paris. "I think it is fate that brought us together," Bonaly stated in *Sports Illustrated,* referring to her and her adopted parents. "I fell on a good family." The Bonaly family took long trips, traveling to places like Finland, Norway, and India. Because they could not afford to fly, the family spent many days traveling in the car.

SCOREBOARD

WON FIVE CONSECUTIVE WOMEN'S SINGLES TITLES AT EUROPEAN FIGURE SKATING CHAMPIONSHIPS (1991-95).

FINISHED SECOND IN WOMEN'S SINGLES COMPETITION AT WORLD FIGURE SKATING CHAMPIONSHIPS (1994 AND 1995).

ROLE MODEL FOR BLACK FIGURE SKATING FANS THROUGHOUT THE WORLD.

POSSESSING A RARE COMBINATION OF STRENGTH AND GRACE, BONALY HAS BEEN A TOP-RANKED FIGURE SKATER FOR SEVERAL YEARS.

From an early age Bonaly showed a natural ability for gymnastics and sports of all kinds. Her mother taught tumbling and floor exercises both privately and in schools, so Bonaly began her own tumbling career as a toddler. Within just a few years she improved so much that she qualified to compete in junior meets throughout France. She won a national novice tumbling championship before age ten.

One day her mother took Bonaly and her tumbling class to the only skating rink in Nice. Bonaly took to skating right away, just as she had to other sports. The rink, however, was located outdoors and could only stay open four months a year. This fact made it difficult for Bonaly to take up skating seriously at an early age.

HARD WORKER. Despite the limitations of the rink in Nice, Bonaly soon attracted the attention of Didier Gailhaguet, a Paris-based skating coach who worked with top-caliber

Bonaly performs her silver medal-winning routine during the 1995 World Figure Skating Championships.

French athletes. Gailhaguet invited Bonaly to Paris for skating lessons, and the family soon moved to the French capital. "I was impressed with how hard she worked," he recalled in the *Chicago Tribune*. "It is very rare to find French athletes [who] work so hard."

For two years Bonaly combined tumbling and skating. By age 12 Bonaly could execute difficult triple jumps and decided to give up gymnastics completely and concentrate on skating. Her parents supported the decision, as they realized Bonaly could make more money on the ice. Once she took up skating full time her skills improved rapidly. Soon Bonaly completed a quadruple jump in practice—a move no other female skater had ever done. She also perfected an on-ice back flip, a crowd-pleasing maneuver that is illegal in amateur figure skating competitions. To save money, the Bonaly family traveled to competitions throughout Europe in a camper.

EUROPEAN CHAMP. In 1989 Bonaly competed in her first World Figure Skating Championships. She finished tenth in the competition but claimed a place for herself among the women's figure skating elite. Bonaly moved up to ninth in the world during 1990, and in 1991 she won the first of five consecutive European championships. She also finished a more-than-respectable fifth in the world championships later that year. *Los Angeles Times* reporter Randy Harvey described Bonaly as a skater who "can out-jump almost every woman to compete in the sport and many of the men. She is so powerful that she has difficulty finding skates strong enough to withstand the torque [force] of her takeoffs without wobbling."

PROBLEMS WITH MOM. As Bonaly moved up the ranks of the world's best female figure skaters, her mother took more control of her daughter's career. Mrs. Bonaly refused to let her daughter talk to reporters and earned the nickname "Dragon Lady" for the way she treated the media, coaches, and her daughter. Most skating experts thought the interference of her mother damaged Bonaly's career. Many coaches have refused to work with Bonaly because of her mother.

DEBBIE THOMAS

Debbie Thomas of the United States was the first black person to ever win a world figure skating championship. She won the 1986 women's singles title, defeating Katarina Witt in the process. Thomas is also the only black person to ever win an Olympic medal in figure skating. She took the silver medal at the 1988 Olympics, this time finishing second to Witt.

OLYMPIC PRESSURE. Her success in the world championships made Bonaly a favorite to win a medal at the 1992 Winter Olympics in Albertville, France. As a French citizen Bonaly would have the home ice advantage, and the French fans who already adored her promised to give her support. A first-place victory would make Bonaly the first black person ever to win an Olympic gold medal in figure skating.

Unfortunately, Bonaly ran into problems before the Olympics even began. Her mother got into an argument with Gailhaguet and took Bonaly to the United States for a month of private training. "Surya has a lot of pressure from her mother," Gailhaguet told the *Baltimore Sun*. "That does not help her. The mother feels the pressure, and puts the pressure on the kid."

The pressure affected Bonaly's Olympic performance. She won over the crowd with a long program that simulated a bullfight, but she missed several jumps. Bonaly ignored her coach and decided to attempt a quadruple jump, a maneuver no woman had ever successfully completed in competition. She fell. These mistakes dropped her to fifth, far behind gold medal winner Kristi Yamaguchi of the United States.

Superstar

CAREER DECISION. Bonaly hit a low point later in 1992 when she finished eleventh at the World Figure Skating Championships. Her performance disappointed the young skater, and she considered giving up figure skating. Bonaly also argued with her mother. Soon, however, mother and daughter made up and Bonaly returned to the ice working with a new coach, Alain Giletti.

Bonaly's performance in the 1992 Olympics and world championships made her decide to change her style. Before this she specialized in amazing jumps but lost points because of weak artistic performances, a vital part of judging in figure skating. Michelle Kaufman explained Bonaly's problems in the *Detroit Free Press*. "Bonaly was trained as a gymnast, not a skater," Kaufman wrote. "She can jump high, do a backflip on skates and land a quadruple toe-loop. But Bonaly's performances aren't as fluid as those of other top skaters. She races across the ice, slows down, jumps, races, slows down, jumps."

Bonaly and her mother decided to concentrate less on jumping and more on providing an artistic show. The skater began to spend summers at the Lake Arrowhead Ice Castle in California. There she studied with American coach Frank Carroll, who introduced a new gracefulness to her style. "The main thing I stressed to Surya and her mother was not to be so selfish about who they were trying to please," Carroll told the *Chicago Tribune*. "They thought quads and triple axels were the answer, but they were really doing them to please themselves and getting beat by people who couldn't do those jumps. I told them to start pleasing the people who hold up the scores."

TOP CONTENDER. Bonaly won the European Figure Skating Championships again in 1993, and then finished second in the 1993 world championships behind Oksana Baiul of the Ukraine. In 1994, just before the Winter Olympics, Bonaly beat Baiul in the European championships. Her win over Baiul made Bonaly a top contender for a gold medal at the Olympics in Lillehammer, Norway.

Many experts believed that the field of women figure skaters at the 1994 Olympics was the strongest ever. The competition included two-time gold medal winner Katarina Witt, **Nancy Kerrigan** (see entry) of the United States, Chen Lu of China, and Baiul. The competition received even more attention because of the attack on Kerrigan by friends of fellow American skater Tonya Harding.

OUT OF THE MEDALS. Bonaly gave a strong third-place performance in the short program at the 1994 Winter Olympics. (During the short program, a skater must complete required jumps and maneuvers.) She seemed assured of a medal in the

KEEPING SCORE

Keeping score in a figure skating competition is a complicated procedure. Each skater receives two scores, one for technical ability and the other for artistic merit. The technical portion of the score judges the skater's ability to successfully complete jumps and other maneuvers in a routine. The score for artistic merit deals with areas such as music, costumes, and choreography. (Choreography is the way a contestant skates to the music he or she has chosen.) Each score counts the same amount in the skater's final marks, so it is important to concentrate on both areas when designing a routine. Bonaly does not like the fact that artistic impression counts for so much. "In other sports they don't care how you run," Bonaly explained in *Sports Illustrated.* "You're faster, and that's it. It's not about your dress."

competition, but she fell during her long program trying to complete a difficult jump. The mistake dropped her to fourth place as Baiul won the gold medal and Kerrigan took the silver.

NO LUCK. Baiul and Kerrigan skipped the 1994 World Figure Skating Championships in Chuba, Japan, and Bonaly hoped to capture her first international championship. Again she fell short against Yuka Sato of Japan. Although Bonaly executed several difficult triple jumps in her long program—a maneuver Sato did not include in her program—the French skater finished the competition in second place, only a fraction of a point behind Sato. The difference in the competition turned out to be artistic presentation, again pointing out Bonaly's weakness in this important area.

The disappointment of the loss proved too great for the French skater. Bonaly cried during the medal ceremony. At first she refused to stand on the second-place podium, and then she took her silver medal off the moment officials placed it around her neck. Asked about her feelings by reporters moments later, Bonaly refused to say that the judges cheated her, but she did say: "I'm just not lucky." Then, with her mom at her side, she ran for her dressing room. "I was fed up," Bonaly said later. "I have done everything for the judges, but it is not enough. It is crazy."

THE FUTURE. In 1995 Bonaly won her fifth straight European Figure Skating Championships, one away from the record of six straight held by Sonja Henie and Katarina Witt. She again finished second in the world championships, this time behind Chen Lu of China. A broken toe on her right foot bothered Bonaly during the competition. Despite her disappointing losses, Bonaly still enjoys skating. She told the *Chicago Tribune* that she especially enjoys training with Carroll, who provided the choreography for her Olympic programs. "I love California," Bonaly said. "I am becoming half-French, half-American."

OFF THE ICE. Bonaly does not eat meat or cheese and milk products. She usually eats birdseed, whole grains, fruits, and vegetables. "I prefer to see the animals alive in the fields, not killed," Bonaly told the Knight-Ridder wire service. Bonaly likes traveling with ice shows and hopes to make a living on the ice for years to come. "You see skating on TV," she commented in the *Chicago Tribune*. "After competition, there are many times more professional opportunities."

Bonaly defends her mother and the private life they have chosen, so different from other skaters. "When somebody is different, people like to talk about them," Bonaly stated in *Sports Illustrated*. "But we are just simple people. Very shy, very private. Some like to go to the reception, and some like to go into the forest. But if we have a choice, we prefer to walk in the forest. Skating is not often a nice place. But this is life."

Sources

Baltimore Sun, February 18, 1992.
Chicago Tribune, August 5, 1990; February 21, 1992; March 12, 1993; January 23, 1994.
Detroit Free Press, February 21, 1992.
Essence, February 1992.
Jet, April 18, 1994.
Life, February 1994.
Los Angeles Times, February 23, 1994.
San Francisco Chronicle, February 11, 1994.
Sports Illustrated, March 7, 1994; March 6, 1995.
Time, February 21, 1994.
Washington Post, February 17, 1994.
Additional information taken from Knight-Ridder newspaper wire report, January 8, 1992, Reuters wire report, October 29, 1994, and an Associated Press wire report, March 27, 1994.

WHERE TO WRITE:
C/O INTERNATIONAL OLYMPIC COMMITTEE,
CHATEAU DE VIDY, CASE POSTALE 356, CH-1001,
LAUSANNE, SWITZERLAND.

Sergei Bubka

1963—

"I want to be an artist of the pole vault."
—Sergei Bubka

Setting a track-and-field world record is a great accomplishment. Imagine breaking a world record more than 30 times! The only person to ever do this is pole-vaulter Sergei Bubka of the Ukraine, a man experts call "the Czar of Vaulting." He set his first world record in 1984 and did not lose a pole-vaulting competition until 1990. In 1988 Bubka won a gold medal at the Summer Olympics in Seoul, South Korean, and in 1991 he became the first pole-vaulter to clear 20 feet. An amazing athlete, Bubka has dominated his sport like no one else in the history of sports and is a favorite to win his second gold medal at the 1996 Summer Olympics in Atlanta, Georgia.

Growing Up

BUBKA BORN. Sergei Bubka (SER-hee BOOB-ka) was born November 4, 1963, in Voroshilovgrad, a coal-mining city in what was then the Soviet Union. His father, Nazar, was a sergeant in the Soviet army, and his mother, Valentina, worked in a hospital. Bubka's father was very strict and often treated Bubka and his brother, Vasily, like they, too, were in the army.

STARTS VAULTING. Bubka first became interested in vaulting at age nine when a friend invited him to join a pole vault club. He was one of 1,000 children at the club, but experts recognized his ability right away. Soon Bubka began working with the coach Vitaly Petrov. Petrov, who pole-vaulted himself, taught his young pupil all the secrets he had learned. Several times Bubka's father tried to force his son to quit, but Bubka kept jumping.

SCOREBOARD

SET MORE THAN 30 SEPARATE WORLD RECORDS IN THE POLE VAULT, THE MOST BY ANY TRACK-AND-FIELD ATHLETE IN HISTORY.

FIRST PERSON TO CLEAR 20 FEET IN THE POLE VAULT.

WON GOLD MEDAL IN THE POLE VAULT AT 1988 SUMMER OLYMPICS.

BUBKA HAS DOMINATED HIS SPORT LIKE NO OTHER ATHLETE IN HISTORY.

When Bubka was 15, his parents divorced. He went to live with his older brother, Vasily, also a pole-vaulter, in nearby Donetsk, a manufacturing city also known for its rosebushes. There he continued to work out with Petrov and went to school at the same time. "There are many things good about Donetsk," Bubka recalled in *Sports Illustrated*. "And a few things not so good." Life was hard for the two brothers, who lived in a factory dormitory. Twice Bubka broke his foot, and doctors advised him to give up the sport. He refused and kept vaulting.

WORLD CHAMPION. Bubka took the world by storm in 1983 in his first meet outside of the Soviet Union. Almost a complete unknown in the West, Bubka won the pole vault at the World Track and Field Championships in Helsinki, Finland. He vaulted 18 feet 8 ¼ inches despite facing a stiff wind. Other vaulters worried about the wind, but Bubka, who had nothing to lose, was fearless. A crowd of fans greeted him at the airport when he returned to Donetsk.

BEGINS BREAKING RECORDS. On January 14, 1984, Bubka broke the world indoor record previously set by Billy Olson of the United States by vaulting 19 feet ¾ inch. On February

HANGING AROUND

As a child, Bubka loved to explore. "I was looking for heroic deeds, and I always seemed to find them," Bubka recounted in *Sports Illustrated.* When he was four, he climbed a tree in his backyard after his parents had left home. Just before reaching the top, Bubka fell. He could have seriously injured himself, but his coat caught on a branch just before he hit the ground. Bubka hung from the tree for several hours until his parents got home.

1, 1984, he broke his own record, jumping 19 feet 1 inch. Then, on February 10, Bubka again broke the indoor record at 19 feet, 1½ inches. The vault also tied the outdoor record held by Thierry Vigneron of France. "That guy [Bubka] gets so high in the air it's unbelievable," high jumper Debbie Brill exclaimed in *Sports Illustrated.*

MISSES OLYMPICS. Bubka had a frustrating year in 1984. In 1980 the United States did not compete in the Olympics, held that year in Moscow, because of the involvement of the Soviet Union in a war in Afghanistan. As a result of the United States' not participating in the 1980 Olympics, the Soviet Union and its allies decided not to compete in the 1984 Summer Olympics in Los Angeles, California. Bubka, being from the Soviet Union, was not allowed to compete in the 1984 Olympics by his government.

Bubka could have easily won a gold medal at the 1984 Olympics. Just two weeks before the Olympics began, he raised his world-record height to 19 feet 4½ inches. At the Olympics, the gold medal winner in the pole vault, Pierre Quinon of France, won with a jump six inches lower than Bubka's best. "I know I can vault higher than anyone in the world," Bubka later stated in *Sports Illustrated.* "That is more important than winning any medal."

GETS MEDAL. In 1985 Bubka broke another barrier when he vaulted more than 19 feet 8¼ inches. In the four years from 1984 to 1988, Bubka broke the world record nine times. In 1988, for the first time in 12 years, all the major countries of the world participated in the Summer Olympics, held in Seoul, South Korea. "The Olympic gold is the only medal I have not yet won," Bubka explained in *Life* magazine. "Winning it is my dream." Bubka easily won the gold medal in the pole vault, setting an Olympic record in the process.

Bubka vaults at the 1992 Olympics in Barcelona, Spain.

Superstar

CLEARS 20 FEET. Bubka continued to soar higher and higher. After suffering back problems in 1990, causing him to lose his first meet since 1984, he came back in 1991 to set yet another remarkable record. At a meet in San Sebastián, Spain, Bubka became the first person to pole-vault 20 feet. He thought he could do even better. "My jump was imperfect, my run-in was too short and my hands were too far back at take-off," Bubka explained in *Sports Illustrated.* "When I manage to iron out these faults, I am sure I can improve."

Bubka went on to clear the 20-foot barrier in both indoor and outdoor competition. His highest jump was 20 feet 1½ inches. Within an eight-day span, Bubka broke his own record three times. Incredibly, he vaulted seven inches higher than his nearest competitor. In most competitions, Bubka had only the world record to compete against. "On a bad day [Bubka] still outclasses the rest of the vaulters in the world," journalist Frank Costello wrote in the *Washington Post.* "He is perhaps the greatest athlete in all of track and field."

In June 1992 Bubka broke the world pole vault record for the thirtieth time at a meet in Dijon, France. With this record-breaking vault, he broke yet another record. In the 1920s and 1930s the great Finnish distance runner Paavo Nurmi broke 29 world records. Bubka had now broken more track-and-field world records than any other athlete.

SOVIET STAR. Because of his success, Bubka received privileges other Soviet citizens did not have. Soviet officials allowed him to accept a sponsorship deal with Nike, and he was allowed to keep all but 10 percent of the prize money he earned. Moreover, Bubka, unlike other Soviet athletes, celebrated and showed emotion at competitions. Because of the closed nature of the Soviet Communist society, however, he could not give interviews to reporters from the West, and he had to return to the Soviet Union after each competition. The Soviet government paid for Bubka's training and coaches.

Just before the 1992 Summer Olympics, great changes took place in the Soviet Union. "There are some big changes in Russia," Bubka told the *Boston Globe*. "Which flag I compete under, I don't know. So many things are happening in the Soviet Union, and I believe things will not be settled down quickly." The different republics that made up the Soviet Union, including the Ukraine, declared their independence. The republics decided to stay together for the 1992 Olympics, competing under the title of the Unified Team. Bubka, however, made clear he was competing for the Ukraine.

OLYMPIC SHOCKER. Experts believed Bubka would not only win the gold medal at the 1992 Summer Olympics in Barcelona, Spain, but would also set another world record. Unfortunately, the wind was very tricky in the Olympic stadium. Bubka missed his first two vaults and, amazingly, faced elimination from the competition. "Every meter the wind seemed to change back and forth," Bubka explained in *Sports Illustrated*. In a shock to all track-and-field experts, Bubka missed his third, and final, jump. The miss eliminated him from the competition without completing even one vault. "I'm not a machine," Bubka told the same magazine after the Olympics. "I'm human, and now we will see who's a friend and who is not."

STILL THE BEST. Bubka did not let his Olympic disappointment stop him. In September 1992 he set his thirty-first world record in the pole vault, only three weeks after the Olympics. In both 1993 and 1995 Bubka won the pole vault at the World Track and Field Championships. Even though he no longer vaults world-record heights, he still outjumps his opposition by a wide margin. After 13 years of international competition, Bubka remains the clear favorite to win the pole vault gold medal at the 1996 Summer Olympics in Atlanta, Georgia.

WHY SO GOOD? Bubka holds the pole closer to the end than most vaulters. "I think it's a little bit secret," reporter

THE AIRS MEET

Bubka met with Michael "Air" Jordan, a member of the U.S. basketball "Dream Team," just before the 1992 Olympics. Both athletes are spokespersons for Nike, and both are the best in their sport. Bubka admitted to Jordan that he could not play basketball and missed when he tried to dunk. Jordan, however, did not try to pole-vault. "No way I'd try that," Jordan admitted in *Sports Illustrated*. "You won't catch me killing myself."

Vladimir Gheskin told the *New York Times*. "I asked him. He doesn't answer. All sportsmen have little secrets." Bubka's style requires great strength, as does his pole, which is longer and stiffer than the average. The stiffness helps lift Bubka higher into the air.

Bubka is a great overall athlete. Once he ran the 100-meter dash in 10.3 seconds, a great time. Bubka's speed allows him to race down the runway faster than his opponents. He once also leapt 26 feet in the long jump. Experts think that if Bubka wanted to he could be an excellent decathlon athlete. (The decathlon requires an athlete to compete in ten different track-and-field events.)

Unlike other vaulters, Bubka uses gymnastics to improve his jumping ability. "Pole-vaulting is just a form of gymnastics," Bubka told *Life* magazine. Bubka also runs and lifts weights as part of his training program.

OFF THE TRACK. Bubka lives with his wife, Liliya, and two sons, Vitaly and Sergeivich. Bubka wants historians to remember him as the best in his sport. "I want to be an artist of the pole vault," Bubka stated in *Sports Illustrated*. "I want to create something new and unusual. I want to break barriers. I pole-vault from the bottom of my heart."

Sources

Life, October 1988.
Newsweek, September 19, 1988.
New York Times, February 21, 1984; August 12, 1995.
Sports Illustrated, February 20, 1984; September 14, 1988; March 25, 1991;
    June 22, 1992; July 22, 1992; August 17, 1992; September 7, 1992.
Sports Illustrated for Kids, July 1992.
Time, September 19, 1988; October 10, 1988.

WHERE TO WRITE:
C/O INTERNATIONAL OLYMPIC COMMITTEE,
CHATEAU DE VIDY, CASE POSTALE 356, CH-1001,
LAUSANNE, SWITZERLAND.

Colorado Silver Bullets

In 1954 major league commissioner Ford Frick issued an order that banned women from playing in organized professional baseball. The decision crushed the dreams of many young girls. Forty years later, the dreams of another generation have now come true. The National Association of Baseball Leagues, the governing body of professional baseball, recognized the Colorado Silver Bullets as an all-woman baseball team. In 1994 the team took on all-male teams from around the country. The Silver Bullets improved dramatically in 1995 and became a competitive force to be reckoned with. In time the Silver Bullets hope to achieve their goal: a spot for their team in minor league baseball and spots for women players in the major leagues.

Getting Started

DON'T LOSE HOPE. The idea for the Silver Bullets came from a man named Bob Hope (not the actor). Hope was the public

"The Silver Bullets provide thousands of young girls hope for a future in professional sports, and they speak to children and adolescents about following their dream." —U.S. Representative Patricia Schroeder

SCOREBOARD

FIRST ALL-FEMALE TEAM
RECOGNIZED BY ORGANIZED
PROFESSIONAL BASEBALL.

IMPROVED IN ALL AREAS IN 1995
OVER FIRST SEASON IN 1994.

THE SILVER BULLETS HOPE TO
INSPIRE GIRLS THROUGHOUT THE
WORLD TO GO FOR THEIR DREAMS.

relations and marketing director of the Atlanta Braves and Hawks. Hope won fame in Atlanta with his wacky promotions at games. Two of these were ostrich races and a UFO night. Hope's daughter, Claire, always asked him why she had to play softball, not baseball. This gave him the idea for the Silver Bullets. In 1984 he unsuccessfully tried to organize a team of men and women. "People in baseball just laughed," Hope recalled in the *Miami Herald.* "They said it was crazy."

The idea seemed dead until the release of the movie *A League of Their Own.* The film was the story of women's baseball teams that played during World War II. The movie changed the views of many people about the ability of women to play baseball. "The movie made it easier," Hope told the *Miami Herald.* "Easier for getting money and easier for acceptance. When I made the presentation to the National Association of Baseball Leagues, they said, 'Oh, like *A League of Their Own.*'"

RECOGNITION. The National Association of Professional Baseball Teams officially recognized the Colorado Silver Bullets on December 10, 1993. Women would now be allowed to play men's professional baseball teams in the United States for the first time since the commissioner of baseball banned women from the game in 1954. (Commissioner Kenesaw Mountain Landis had originally banned women from organized baseball in 1931, saying the game was "too strenuous" for them.) The Coors Light brand of the Coors Brewing Company sponsors the team, and the team's name comes from a Coors advertising campaign.

DREAM TEAM. The Silver Bullets team was a dream come true for many players. Alyson Habetz had gone to court fighting to play on her high school team in Louisiana. When she

Silver Bullets second base player Michele McAnany leaps for a ball. ▶

THE MISSION

"The Colorado Silver Bullets is a team founded with the purpose to provide a nurturing environment for top women athletes to learn and play professional baseball against existing men's teams within the ranks of minor league, semipro, college and amateur baseball. Its aspiration [goal] is to inspire female athletes to play the game of baseball at all levels, from Little League through professional leagues, and encourage all forms of organized baseball to accept women athletes as players." (From the 1995 Colorado Silver Bullets Souvenir Program)

lost, she went to her room and cried. "I was crying because I couldn't get into baseball," Habetz told the *Miami Herald.* Eventually Habetz won the right to play on her high school team.

Pitcher Lee Ann Ketcham thought her dream would never come true. "I dreamed of playing in the majors," Ketcham told the *Miami Herald.* "I guess I gave up on that dream about the time I got to high school. When I was 12 years old I stopped growing." Ketcham, who is now five feet four inches tall, helped win five of the Bullets' victories in their first season and struck out 14 players in one seven-inning game. "We are paving the way," Ketcham continued. "There will be a woman in the major leagues some day."

The Silver Bullets signed up professionals to help prepare them for their entry into professional baseball. Their manager is Phil Niekro, a probable future Hall of Famer who pitched for the Atlanta Braves and the New York Yankees and won 318 major league games. "Women should have every opportunity to play competitive professional ball," Niekro said. He hired his brother, Joe, and former major league outfielder Johnny Grubb as coaches. Niekro knew his job would be tough. "They [the Silver Bullets] had to learn baseball when they were 20, 21 years old," he told the *Syracuse Herald-American/Post Standard.* "I learned when I was six, seven years old."

TEAM PICKED. The selection of the Silver Bullets began with an invitation-only tryout of the top female players in the country. The invitees selected were recommended by college coaches and scouts. Most of the players were former softball stars. Later, open tryouts produced 1,150 women wanting to play on the team. The Silver Bullets invited 55 players to spring training to compete for the 20 to 25 spots on the team. The athletes worked out seven days a week, working on pitching, hitting, and catching. The Silver Bullets announced their first 24-player squad on April 3, 1994.

The work ethic of his players impressed Niekro. "They're very coachable," he told the *Gettysburg Times*. "They want to learn real quick. I don't think they realize it takes a little while to learn how to play this game. You've got to realize these players have only been playing this game for [a short time]. We're playing against guys that have been playing since high school." Only two players on the first Silver Bullets roster had come from baseball backgrounds. The others had played softball, a much different game played on a field only 50 percent as large as a baseball diamond and with bats that are much lighter. Most girls are forced to give up baseball and play softball when they enter high school.

It was not always easy to be a pioneer. In 1973 pitcher Gina Satriano was the first girl to play in Little League in California. "Since I broke into baseball when I was seven years old all the way up through the years, I've had to face adversities," Satriano told the *Syracuse Herald-American/Post Standard*. "Facing the opposition and the name-calling and the harassment from the other team members that we played against, all of that is something I've experienced along the way. We are pioneers because this is the first professional women's team to compete against men. So that automatically makes us some sort of pioneers. There's the stereotype that young girls don't dream of playing baseball. Only boys do. That's a stereotype that's being shattered by the creation of this team. Everybody kept telling me, 'No, no, no, you can't have those dreams, you're a girl.' I didn't know baseball was going to be an opportunity for me as a woman, to be a professional baseball player."

After one game in San Diego, a woman approached Satriano and told her that her fight to play Little League baseball had encouraged her to do the same thing. "That's what this is all about," Satriano told the *Miami Herald*. "It's about dreaming big." Satriano's father, Tom, played for the Boston Red Sox and the California Angels.

ALL-AMERICAN GIRLS BASEBALL LEAGUE

During World War II most of the best male baseball players in the United States were away fighting in Europe and Asia. The absence of these stars led to the formation of the All-American Girls Baseball League (AAGBL). The founder of the league was chewing gum manufacturer Philip K. Wrigley, owner of the Chicago Cubs. All-female teams played against each other on the field; off the field, league officials forced players to attend charm school. The league folded after major leaguers returned from the war. The AAGBL was the subject of the hit movie *A League of Their Own*.

Superstars

OPENING DAY. The 1994 season was the first for the Silver Bullets. Their first game was on Mother's Day, May 8, 1994. The Bullets played men's college, semiprofessional, amateur, and military all-star teams. The team finished the season with a 6-37 record, competitive for most new men's teams. The Silver Bullets had trouble hitting, batting only .141 as a team and scoring only 83 runs. They also had trouble stopping other teams from scoring. The earned run average (ERA) for the team was 7.09, and they gave up 268 runs. The team was shut out 16 times in 43 games. The Bullets were a popular attraction, drawing 33,000 fans in Denver, Colorado, and 42,000 in San Francisco, California. After the game in San Francisco, Barry Bonds of the San Francisco Giants asked Silver Bullets outfielder Kim Braatz for her autograph.

MOVING AHEAD. To try to improve for the 1995 season, the Silver Bullets went after the best baseball players in tryouts, not the best overall athletes. Seven players who were on the team in 1994 could not make the 1995 team. The Silver Bullets improved in almost every phase of the game. They raised their team batting average to .183, scored 183 runs, and lowered their team ERA to 5.08. The Silver Bullets failed to score in only three of 44 games. They almost doubled their win total to 11, against much tougher competition.

"We've come a long way, but we've got a long way to go," Niekro explained in the *Gettysburg Times*. "I don't think we're as intimidated as we were last year. As far as aggressiveness, attitude, heart and desire, we've got more of that than we ever had." Pitcher Missy Coombes and third baseman Stacey Sunny were named the 1995 Players of the Year. Coombes led the pitching staff with a 5-8 record, 3.90 ERA, 7 complete games, and 48 strikeouts. Sunny led the team in hitting with a .246 average and drove in a team-leading 17 runs.

Despite the improvement, the Silver Bullets know they have to win to sustain interest in their team. "If you don't win, people aren't going to watch you play," second baseman Michele McAnany admitted in the *Syracuse Herald-American/Post Standard*. "It starts to shut down. People like winners, and I don't care if you're on a female or male team, you need to win."

The Silver Bullets have no home field. They travel around the country and play local teams. In 1995 the team played in 50 cities throughout the United States The Bullets played in major league ballparks like Fenway Park in Boston, Massachusetts, and Candlestick Park in San Francisco, California. Pay for new players is $20,000, and $25,000 for returning players. The players say they are not in this for the money, however. In fact, many players have taken risks to make their dreams come true. Pitcher Gina Satriano left her job with the Los Angeles District Attorney's Office to play with the Silver Bullets. "I took a big risk of losing my job completely and losing advancement in the office, which I've done since I've come to play baseball," Satriano confessed in the *Syracuse Herald-American/Post Standard*. The team donates tickets to local programs for use in fund-raising to fight domestic violence. Players often stay hours after the game is over to sign autographs.

Not all baseball fans have been happy about the Silver Bullets. One night in Texas, an angry man gained control of the public address system. He directed a stream of insults to the players before being thrown out of the stadium. Other fans yell mean things, but the players just ignore them. "You hear things, but you just stay professional about it," Satriano told the *Miami Herald*. And most fans have cheered them on. "We were treated with respect everywhere we went because we earned it," pitcher Julie Croteau told the *Sporting News*. "We were 20 professional, focused women."

The Silver Bullets were honored in June 1995 by the National Baseball Hall of Fame and Museum. The team played at Doubleday Field in Cooperstown, New York, and was honored as part of the Hall of Fame's *Women in Baseball* exhibit. "The Silver Bullets are pioneers in baseball in addition to being excellent baseball players," Hall of Fame President Donald C. Marr Jr. said. "We are pleased not only to have a chance to display the Silver Bullets uniform as part of our *Women in Baseball* exhibit to honor their contribution to baseball, but also to personally pay tribute to the players in a ceremony at the Hall. This is a special occasion for all of us."

U.S. Representative Patricia Schroeder, of Colorado, honored the Silver Bullets in Congress, as noted in the *Congressional Record:* "The Silver Bullets provide thousands of young girls hope for a future in professional sports, and they speak to children and adolescents about following their dream."

The Silver Bullets have applied to play in a registered Single A professional minor league in 1997 or 1998. The players think that would be a good idea. "Nobody wants to travel all summer," Stacey Sunny admitted in the *Syracuse Post Standard*. "I think it's a tremendous move in the right direction. That's what this is all about."

If the team wants to join a minor league, they have to improve their hitting, especially their power. "We have two or three players who might be able to hold their own, but team-wise right now, no, we're not ready," Niekro told the *Post Standard*. "But give us two years. If they can learn as much in the next two years as they have in the last year, then they'll be real close." And, as team general manager Shereen Samonds told the *Sporting News:* "Maybe by the year 2000 you might see a woman playing major league baseball, if she's good enough to compete."

Sources

Daily Star (Oneonta, NY), June 10, 1995.
Gettysburg Times (Pennsylvania), June 10, 1995.
Knoxville News-Sentinel, July 23, 1995.
Miami Herald, May 7, 1995; May 8, 1995.
Sporting News, May 30, 1994; September 12, 1994.
Sports Illustrated for Kids, June 1995; August 1995.
Syracuse Herald-American/Post Standard, July 2, 1995; July 4, 1995.

Women's Sports and Fitness, April 1994.
Additional information provided by Colorado Silver Bullets.

 WHERE TO WRITE:
COLORADO SILVER BULLETS,
1575 SHERIDAN BLVD. NE,
ATLANTA, GA 30324.

Dominique Dawes

1976—

"I do want to excel no matter what I do."—Dominique Dawes

Dominique Dawes is the perfect example of what hard work can do. Training seven hours a day, seven days a week, she has made herself one of the best gymnasts in the United States and in the world. In 1994 Dawes became only the second woman—and the first African American—to win every competition at the U.S. Gymnastics Championships. She also helped the U.S. national team win a bronze medal at the 1992 Summer Olympics and a silver medal at the 1994 World Gymnastics Championships. And despite her training schedule, Dawes still finds time to make a difference in her community. She truly has earned her nickname, "Awesome Dawesome."

Growing Up

ROAD RUNNER. Dominique Dawes was born November 20, 1976, in Silver Spring, Maryland. She was the second of three children of Don Dawes, a health products salesman, and his wife, Loretta. Her parents separated in 1993, and now Dawes visits her father on Sundays. Even at a young age, Dawes was very active. "At four or five she was running around like the Road Runner," Don Dawes told *People*.

Because Dawes had so much energy, her parents enrolled her in gymnastics classes at age six. "I also took tap dancing and ballet, but gymnastics was more enjoyable," Dawes recalled in *Southern Living*. "Tumbling was my specialty when I started. Now I do most everything." She added in *Seventeen*, "I had no technique at first, but I was good because I could bounce really high."

The young gymnast has always been a competitor. When Dawes was nine, she wrote the word *determination* over and over again on her bedroom mirror. "I was amazed that she even knew how to spell it, but it worked," her father explained in *People*. Kelli Hill, the only coach Dawes has ever had, noticed something unique about the athlete. "There are other people with God-given ability, but it takes a very special person to pursue it day after day," Hill stated in *People*. Dawes was bowlegged and had to do special exercises to get her toes to point straight during her routines.

OLYMPIAN. Dawes started competing in national and international events at age 12. In 1990 she finished third in the junior all-around competition at the U.S. Gymnastics Championships. She first qualified for the U.S. national gymnastics team in 1991, winning the floor exercise competition at the U.S. Gymnastics Championships. To prepare for the 1992 Summer Olympics, Dawes moved in with Hill and transferred to a high school near his gym. In a competition in 1992 against Japan, Dawes scored a perfect 10 on her floor routine. Later that year she won on the uneven parallel bars at the U.S. Gymnastics Championships and finished fourth in the all-around competition.

SCOREBOARD

IN 1994 BECAME THE SECOND WOMAN—AND FIRST AFRICAN AMERICAN—TO WIN ALL FIVE EVENTS AT U.S. GYMNASTICS CHAMPIONSHIPS.

WON THREE SILVER MEDALS AT WORLD GYMNASTICS CHAMPIONSHIPS, THE MOST BY ANY BLACK GYMNAST.

FIRST AFRICAN AMERICAN GYMNAST TO COMPETE IN THE OLYMPICS (1992).

DAWES HAS BECOME ONE OF THE BEST THROUGH HARD WORK AND DETERMINATION.

Dawes was only 15 when she competed in the 1992 Olympics, the first African American gymnast to do so. "It's like a normal competition, but a much bigger deal because you have the pride in representing the United States," Dawes admitted in *Southern Living*. She won a bronze medal as part of the U.S. team, which finished behind the silver medal-winning Romanian team and gold medal-winning Unified Team (formerly the Soviet Union team). Dawes finished twenty-sixth in the all-around competition.

MOVING UP. Dawes had a breakthrough year in 1993. She won gold medals in the balance beam and vault, silver medals in the all-around competition and floor exercise, and a bronze medal in the uneven parallel bars at the U.S. Gymnastics Championships. Then, at the World Gymnastics Championships in Birmingham, England, Dawes won silver medals in the uneven parallel bars and the balance beam. Her success made her the first black gymnast to win two silver medals at the world championships.

Dawes could have won even more medals at the world championships. She led the all-around competition going into her last event, the vault. During the competition Dawes decided to change her usual routine and try a more difficult vault, but fell while attempting it. The fall cost Dawes the championship and dropped her to fourth place. Her teammate, Shannon Miller, won the title. "My performance at the worlds has been the biggest thrill for me so far," Dawes told *Sports Illustrated for Kids*. "I was upset about falling on a vault trick I knew was giving me trouble. It taught me that I have to train harder on the things I know I have problems with." USA Gymnastics, a national gymnastics organization, named Dawes the 1993 Athlete of the Year.

Superstar

THE BEST. In August 1994 Dawes made history. She became only the second gymnast and the first since 1969 to win each event at the U.S. Gymnastics Championships in Nashville, Tennessee. (Joyce Schroeder accomplished the feat in 1969.) Dawes won four individual gold medals—in the vault, the uneven parallel bars, the balance beam, and the floor exercise—and one more for the overall National Champion title. Her national championship victory made her the first African American to reach this goal. Dawes won the championship by defeating two-time world champion Shannon Miller, who finished second in every event. "I didn't go in trying to beat

Shannon," Dawes declared in the *Washington Post.* "I don't consider us to be competing against each other."

"It's kind of overwhelming," Dawes said in the *Washington Post* after the competition. "It seems kind of neat for me, that it's only been done one time before. It's neat for my self-esteem. It means I've accomplished something very unusual. I just went out there to hit my sets. I never imagined I'd win all the events."

Her accomplishment also impressed other gymnasts. "Dominique Dawes won everything," the famous American gymnast Mary Lou Retton exclaimed in the *Washington Post.* "That's amazing. Most gymnasts have some weak events and some strong events. She's strong in all of them. I truly, truly respect what she did. I never did that. She's been so close to number one these past few years. She's been in the shadow of Shannon Miller. Now, it's Dominique's turn." USA Gymnastics named Dawes 1994 Sportsperson of the Year.

TEAM LEADER. In December 1994 Dawes helped the U.S. team win the silver medal at the World Gymnastics Championships in Dortmund, Germany. "It feels great to be second in the world with the six people we had on this team," Dawes said after the competition. Once again, a fall in the vault cost Dawes a medal in the all-around competition, dropping her to fifth. In early 1995 Dawes was a finalist for the prestigious Sullivan Award, given annually to the best amateur athlete in the United States.

Dawes followed up her 1994 success with another strong performance at the 1995 U.S. Gymnastics Championships. She won the floor exercise and uneven parallel bars competitions, finished third in the balance beam, and came in fourth in the vault and all-around competition. Dawes finished fifth at the World Team Trials and missed out a second chance to compete in the World Gymnastics Championships. (Only the top four finishers qualify for the world championship team.)

PROM QUEEN. Dawes graduated from Gaithersburg High School in 1994. She received an athletic scholarship to attend

Stanford University but delayed enrolling at the school to continue practicing for the 1996 Summer Olympics in Atlanta, Georgia. Because she practices so hard, Dawes has not had much time for socializing. "At the end of school last year, it was really neat, because people were starting to get to know me because of publicity for gymnastics, and I was getting a little more popular," Dawes revealed in *Seventeen*. "Before that, I was really shy so I didn't talk a lot. I was even picked as queen at the prom. I wasn't that into going, but it turned out to be really fun. I wore a black dress with white lace on top and a black collar."

HER LUCKY CHARMS

Dawes is superstitious and has routines she likes to follow. "If I wear a pair of earrings the day before a meet, I can't wear the same earrings," Dawes explained in *Seventeen*. "I think it's better luck if I change them. I like switching between my sparkly crystal earrings and my little hoops. Some girls are afraid of wearing a leotard they got hurt in, but I still wear them."

HARD WORK. Despite practicing seven hours a day, Dawes maintained an A average throughout her senior year in high school and made the honor roll. She worked out at the Hill's Angels Gym two hours before school and five hours after. Included in her workouts were ballet and jazz dance classes. "You just get used to it after a while," Dawes told *Southern Living*. "I finish at 8:10 every night, eat dinner, and go to sleep. Ten years down the road, I think I'll know that this was all worthwhile. It was worth working the amount of hours I've put into it. Everything is paying off."

Workouts are not always easy, however. "During the summer, we train eight hours a day," Dawes recalled in *Seventeen*. "There's no air-conditioning in our gym, and by 3:00 p.m. it gets to be more than 90 degrees in there. Sometimes our hands bleed because of the humidity—they stick to the bars and rip—and our legs get scabby from climbing the rope and getting rope burn. One day it was so hot, our coach let us just watch gymnastics on TV and give each other back massages. That was pretty cool."

3-D DAWES. Dawes's specialty is her explosive floor routine, including one 11-move sequence. Without stopping, she does two handless back handsprings, two twists in the air, two flips, two back handsprings, one and a half more twists in the

GOOD SPORT

Dawes is very active with good causes in her community, something her family taught her. She visits children in hospitals and schools in the Washington, D.C., area and tells kids to stay off drugs. President Bill Clinton invited Dawes to speak at the White House as part of his No Drug Use campaign. Dawes made an exercise video for kids that is shown in schools throughout the country. "I don't think she has ever said no," Luan Peszek, an official of USA Gymnastics told *Sports Illustrated for Kids*. Dawes won the 1995 Henry P. Iba Citizen Athlete Award, given annually to athletes who help others in their community, state, and nation. In 1995 *Sports Illustrated for Kids* named Dawes one of their Good Sports. "I feel really good about reaching out to the community, especially to kids," Dawes revealed in *Sports Illustrated for Kids*. "If I can touch just one kid, it's worth it."

air, and another flip. "Very few gymnasts have as much strength," Hill told *Seventeen*. "Dominique's spirit shows in her performances." To help her concentrate at meets, Dawes developed a saying she repeats before performing. "To help me think positively at a meet, I think of 'D3'—determination, dedication, dynamic," Dawes said in *Seventeen*. "I made it up using my initials."

NO PRESSURE. Unlike many other young athletes, Dawes is not pressured by her parents. "My mom and dad are laid-back about my gymnastics, they don't pressure me," Dawes explained in *Seventeen*. "But I do get more nervous if they're in the audience, because I want to do better. Sometimes they're like, 'Oh wow, you know how to do that?' and that's pretty cool."

THE FUTURE. Dawes tried not to think too much about qualifying for the 1996 Summer Olympics. She admitted in *Southern Living*, "I have confidence that I will, if I train to my ability. But I have to do well in other meets first." Dawes added, "I'm trying to learn stronger routines because I see other competitors coming up."

OUT OF THE GYM. Dawes lives in Silver Spring, Maryland. She likes to read, play basketball and miniature golf, ride bikes, and high dive. Her favorite music is by Warren G and Boys II Men. Dawes likes to watch the television shows *Martin* and *Living Single* and to read Stephen King novels. She has a dream for after her gymnastic career ends. "I really want to be an actress," Dawes revealed in *Seventeen*. "I took theater in school and I really enjoyed it." She plans to major in theater at Stanford. Her favorite actor is Jean-Claude Van Damme.

Dawes tries to eat right. "Coaches aren't watching what we eat or anything," Dawes explained in *Seventeen*. "I know which foods are good for me and which ones aren't. If I eat French fries, I'll eat the frozen kind—they don't have very much fat at all. I eat a lot of carbohydrates for energy—pasta, rice, cereal. I don't like greasy foods that much, and candy makes me sick." Dawes loves vinegar and puts it on pizza and bread, and she does not eat meat.

Like many athletes, Dawes receives a lot of fan mail. She tries to answer all of it, but sometimes gets behind. "I write back and ask questions because I like knowing someone from somewhere else," Dawes told *Seventeen*. "I like to know what's going on where other people live."

Dawes has had a great deal of success in gymnastics. "Once I tried putting all my medals on at once, and my neck nearly broke they were so heavy," Dawes told *Seventeen*. Although Dawes has talked of retiring from gymnastics, she continues to train. "I'm in gymnastics to reach my goals and be satisfied with what I'm doing," Dawes explained in *Southern Living*. "If I don't, life goes on. There are other things I can excel at, but I do want to excel no matter what I do."

Sources

Ebony, May 1995.
Jet, May 17, 1993; September 12, 1994; December 12, 1994.
Los Angeles Times, March 4, 1995.
People, November 14, 1994.
Seventeen, February 1995.
Southern Living, September 1995.
Sports Illustrated for Kids, October 1993; January 1995; December 1995.
Washington Post, August 30, 1994.
Additional information provided by USA Gymnastics.

WHERE TO WRITE:
C/O USA GYMNASTICS FEDERATION,
PAN AMERICAN PLAZA, STE. 300, 201 S. CAPITOL AVE.,
INDIANAPOLIS, IN 46225.

Gail Devers

1966—

"I don't wish what I've been through on anyone, but I'm a stronger, more determined person because of it."
—Gail Devers

Gail Devers is one of the fastest women in the world. In 1992 she achieved fame by winning the 100-meter sprint in the Summer Olympics in Barcelona, Spain. Possessing a rare combination of skills, Devers is also a world-class hurdler. However, Devers faced the toughest race of her life when she fought Graves' disease, a dangerous illness that affects the thyroid gland. Devers overcame the disease to become one of the leading track and field performers in the world. Her life may be the greatest comeback story in the history of the sport.

Growing Up

LEAVE IT TO THE DEVERS. Yolanda Gail Devers was born November 19, 1966, in Seattle, Washington. Devers developed a strong religious faith as a child. Her father, the Reverend Larry Devers, is a Baptist pastor. Her mother, Alabe, is a teacher's aide. Devers grew up in San Diego, California. "We were a 'Leave It to Beaver' family," Devers recalled in *Sports Illustrated.* "We had picnics, rode bikes and played touch football together. We did Bible studies together."

DASHING DEVERS. Devers began winning gold medals as a teenager. While attending Sweetwater High School in National City, California, her outstanding performance on the women's track team helped the school win the San Diego sectional track and field team title. In 1984, at age 17, Devers won the 100-meter dash and the 100-meter hurdles at the state high school track and field championships. She also took second in the long jump.

SCOREBOARD

WON 1992 OLYMPIC GOLD MEDAL IN WOMEN'S 100-METER DASH.

SET WORLD RECORD FOR WOMEN IN 60-METER DASH (1993).

SET AMERICAN RECORDS FOR WOMEN IN 60- AND 100-METER DASHES AND 100-METER HURDLES.

DEVERS OVERCAME A LIFE-THREATENING ILLNESS TO BECOME THE WORLD'S FASTEST WOMAN.

MEETS COACH. Devers attended the University of California at Los Angeles (UCLA). It was at UCLA that she met her coach, Bob Kersee. Kersee is the husband and coach of famous track and field star Jackie Joyner-Kersee. He is also a tough coach who asks a lot of his students. Kersee prepared Valerie Brisco to win three Olympic gold medals in 1984, Florence Griffith Joyner to win three in 1988, and his wife to capture three more Olympic first place finishes between 1988 and 1992.

Kersee saw potential in Devers and put her on a grueling training program. He convinced Devers, who planned to give up hurdling in college because of her small size, to continue participating in both sprints and the hurdles. By 1988 Devers ranked as one of the top female hurdlers in the United States "I loved doing six or seven events in a meet because I was the first to start and the last to finish and there was no time in between to just sit around," Devers recounted in *Track and Field News.*

TOP OF THE WORLD. In 1988 Devers set a national record of 12.61 seconds in the 100-meter hurdles and won the National Collegiate Athletic Association (NCAA) championship in the 100-meter dash. Devers qualified to compete for the U.S.

OH, SIS!

Though her parents were strict, Devers never challenged their authority. Her brother, Parenthesis, did, however. "He was 14 months older and a rebel without a cause," Devers remembered in *Sports Illustrated*. "When it started to get dark we had to be in the house before the streetlight stopped flickering. My brother hated that rule. I would be a little mother, tugging him in, explaining to him that later he'd understand. My mom says I've always been old."

team in the 100-meter hurdles at the 1988 Olympics in Seoul, South Korea. She also graduated from UCLA and married her college sweetheart, Ron Roberts, the captain of the UCLA men's track team.

STRANGE PROBLEMS. Just as Devers approached her peak as an athlete, she started to suffer from several physical problems. She had muscle pulls and tired legs, making it difficult to complete simple workouts. Devers's problems affected her at the Olympics, where she produced her slowest time in the 100-meter hurdles since high school. She failed to qualify for the finals. "Mentally, I was up and ready to run," Devers recalled in *Sports Illustrated for Kids*. "But physically, my body was saying, 'Gail, I just can't do it.'"

After returning from the Olympics, Devers suffered from impaired hearing, memory loss, migraine headaches, and involuntary shakes and convulsions. Her hair began falling out, and by January 1989 Devers had lost nearly 23 pounds. Her weight loss forced her to wear children's clothing. Devers's husband became concerned, but she denied she had a problem. "My coach would tell me to do something, and I'd walk across the track and forget what he had said," Devers recounted in *Sports Illustrated for Kids*. "It was hard for me to remember my phone number and address."

Over the next two and a half years, Devers visited more than a dozen physicians. Several doctors told her that her training caused the problems, while others thought she had diabetes. Meanwhile, Devers's condition worsened. She had vision problems, and other symptoms appeared. At one point, Devers seriously considered ending her track career. "I felt like a washed-up athlete, and I began to doubt I could ever again compete at my former level," she explained in *Family Circle*.

NEVER QUIT. Kersee convinced Devers not to quit. "Gail, you've got too much God-given talent to give up on yourself,"

Devers clears the hurdles and qualifies for the 1992 Olympics.

her coach told her. After an almost two-year layoff, Devers tested her condition in a minor track meet in 1990. She did not do well. Then in the fall of 1990 a team physician at UCLA solved the mystery. The doctor noticed that Devers's eyes bulged and that she had a goiter (growth) on her throat. Both of these conditions reflect a thyroid condition. (The thyroid is a gland located in the throat that regulates the amount of energy one has.)

GRAVES' DISEASE. More tests revealed that Devers had Graves' disease, a condition resulting from an overactive thyroid gland.

"Hearing that was scary, but it was also a relief," Devers admitted in *Sports Illustrated for Kids.* "I finally realized I wasn't going crazy. There was a reason I was feeling bad." The Olympic governing body banned athletes from taking the medication used for fighting Graves' disease. Because of this rule, Devers underwent radiation treatment to battle the disease.

Several weeks of treatment improved her symptoms, making Devers think she was better. However, new problems emerged in early 1991, among them severely painful blood blisters on the soles of her feet and between her toes. "The pain was so excruciating [bad] that I sometimes crawled because it hurt too much to walk," Devers recalled in *Family Circle.* Devers went to a podiatrist (foot doctor) who wrongly told her she had a severe case of athlete's foot.

Eventually, the pain of walking became so great that her parents had to carry Devers around her apartment. Devers began to believe that she might never walk again, a nightmare that almost came true when one doctor told her that he might have to amputate her feet. After she got a second opinion, however, doctors learned that Devers's problems with her extremities and skin were side effects from the radiation. The radiation also destroyed her thyroid gland, forcing Devers to take medication daily for the rest of her life. One month after stopping her radiation treatments, Devers was healthy again. The only symptoms remaining are a sensitivity to the sun and occasional skin-related problems, side effects of her medication.

WALKS BEFORE SHE RUNS. Devers began practicing at UCLA almost as soon as she could walk again. The first workout of her comeback was a slow walk around the track. She walked wearing only socks because shoes still hurt her feet. Devers improved rapidly and soon began to jog and then sprint. She regained her strength in time for a meet in March 1991 at which she qualified for the prestigious TAC (The Athletics Congress) Meet in June. Devers hoped to run well enough at the TAC Meet to qualify for the U.S. team at the World Track and Field Championships.

Surprisingly, Devers won the 100-meter hurdles at the TAC Meet, running the fastest time by an American woman that year, 12.83 seconds. The following summer Devers took second place in the 100-meter hurdles at the World Track and Field Championships in Tokyo, Japan. Two weeks after that she set a new American record in the event at a track meet in Berlin, Germany.

Superstar

OLYMPIC CHAMP. Devers continued to train for the 1992 Summer Olympics in Barcelona, Spain. Kersee convinced Devers to put more effort into the 100-meter dash because he had always believed that was her best event. With her physical problems behind her, Devers trained harder than ever and made the 1992 Olympic team in both the 100-meter dash and the 100-meter hurdles.

"GO GET IT." Devers got a scare while at the Olympics. During the quarterfinals of the 100 meters, she temporarily lost all feeling in her feet in the starting blocks. She feared her illness might return, but she kept on racing. She reached the finals of the 100 meters. Before the big race, Jackie Joyner-Kersee gave encouragement to her friend. "You worked hard for this," she told Devers, according to *Family Circle*. "Go get it."

Settling into the starting blocks, Devers concentrated on what she needed to do to win. Shocking all the experts, she ran the race of her life and her best time ever over this distance. The race was too close to call, with five runners neck-and-neck. The photograph of the race showed that Devers broke the tape .01 second ahead of second-place finisher Julie Cuthbert of Jamaica. She earned the gold medal and the title as the world's fastest woman. "The race itself was a 11-second blur," Devers told *Family Circle*. "But later, standing proudly at the top of the medals platform in the enormous stadium, I realized a dream come true."

TRIP AND FALL. Devers now had the chance to achieve a rare double feat: Olympic gold medals in both the 100-meter sprint and 100-meter hurdles. Only one woman—Francina Blankers-Koen of the Netherlands in 1948—had ever won both Olympic races the same year. The finals of the 100-meter hurdles took place five days after her sprint victory. Devers took the lead in the race and seemed on the way to victory. She ran so hard, however, that she tripped over the last hurdle. Devers tried to break her fall and stumbled across the finish line. "As I went down, my only thought was to finish and I just kept scrambling until I got over the line," she recalled. The miscue allowed four runners to pass her, dropping Devers to fifth place in the event. "I guess it just isn't meant to be," she said after the race.

BEST IN THE WORLD. Confirming her position as the fastest woman in the world, Devers dominated the indoor track season in 1993. She focused almost exclusively on sprinting and lost just one indoor dash in eight performances, an outstanding achievement, since she had paid little attention to indoor running before that year. In February, she set an American record of 6.99 seconds in the 60-meter dash at the USA/Mobil Indoor Track and Field Championships in New Jersey. In March, Devers sped to a world-record time of 6.95 seconds while winning the event at the World Indoor Track and Field Championships held in Toronto, Canada.

Devers suffered a pulled leg muscle early in her outdoor training in the spring of 1993. She bounced back quickly, however, and was in peak condition for the World Track and Field Championships, held in Stuttgart, Germany, in August. Devers won titles in both the 100-meter hurdles and the 100-meter dash. Her victory over Merlene Ottey of Jamaica in the dash was so close that it took judges three minutes to study the photograph taken at the finish before they could confirm Devers as the winner. The judges upheld her victory despite protests from the Jamaican team. Devers earned three major titles in 1993 and finished the year with a phenomenal 21 victories in 23 races. She also ran the fastest times by a woman in both the 100-meter dash and 100-meter hurdles that year. Both the U.S. Olympic Committee and *Track and Field News* named Devers the U.S. Female Athlete of the Year.

THE FUTURE. Devers concentrated on exclusively on the hurdles in 1995 because her hamstring continued to bother her. She won the 100-meter hurdles at the 1995 World Track and Field

Championships, defeating Olga Shishigina of Kazakhstan. Devers hopes her hamstring problem will be healed in time for the 1996 Summer Olympics in Atlanta, Georgia. "Surgery will be next, if nothing else works," Devers explained.

OFF THE TRACK. Devers divorced her husband during her illness. She lives with her boyfriend, triple-jump competitor Kenny Harrison, in the Los Angeles, California, area. A big fan of *I Love Lucy,* Devers collects videotapes of the show. "My dream growing up was to spend the night with Lucy," Devers confessed in *Sports Illustrated.* She also likes puzzles, collecting stuffed monkey dolls, and taking care of her Rottweiler dogs. Devers earned her bachelor's degree from UCLA in 1988 and loves to read. Someday she would like to open her own day-care center and work with children.

Devers has shown a rare blend of power, speed, and intense concentration. "I never know where I am in a race," Devers admitted in the *New York Times.* "When I cross the finish line, I wait for someone to say, 'Gail Devers, you won' or 'Gail Devers, you lost.'"

FAITH

A deeply religious woman, Devers believes that God played a vital role in defeating her illness and helping her realize her potential as an athlete. "My family and friends gave me tremendous support, but faith in God and myself kept me going," she confessed in *Family Circle.* "I don't wish what I've been through on anyone, but I'm a stronger, more determined person because of it. After conquering Graves' disease, I know there's no hurdle I can't get over."

Sources

Essence, May 1993.
Family Circle, May 18, 1993.
Jet, August 17, 1992; January 31, 1994.
New York Times, August 2, 1992; February 24, 1993; February 27, 1993; March 13, 1993; August 17, 1993.
Sporting News, August 17, 1992.
Sports Illustrated, August 10, 1992; May 10, 1993.
Sports Illustrated for Kids, June 1992; October 1992.
Track and Field News, October 1992; November 1993; February 1994.

WHERE TO WRITE:
C/O U.S. TRACK AND FIELD,
P.O. BOX 120,
INDIANAPOLIS, IN 46206.

Tom Dolan

1975—

"He's the best. He's got the body, the desire, the competitive instinct. Put it all together, and you've got a champion."—Jon Urbanchek, University of Michigan swimming coach

Imagine jumping into a pool of water and worrying about being able to breathe. Swimmer Tom Dolan does this thousands of times every year. Since he was a child, Dolan has suffered from asthma, a disease that makes it difficult for him to breathe. Through hard work Dolan has overcome his asthma and the fear it causes to win back-to-back U.S. Swimmer of the Year awards. He is also a world-record holder in the 400-meter individual medley and may be the best male swimmer in the United States. These accomplishments make Dolan a gold medal threat at the 1996 Summer Olympics in Atlanta, Georgia.

Growing Up

HARD TO BREATHE. Dolan was born September 15, 1975. He grew up in Alexandria, Virginia. His father's name is William, and his mother's name is Jef. Dolan began swimming at a country club when he was five years old. He also liked playing other sports. His sister, Kathleen, a former swimmer, "dragged him out of bed" and took him to practice before he had his driver's license.

Dolan suffers from a special kind of asthma that gets worse the more he exercises. In addition to his asthma, Dolan's esophagus (windpipe) is also unusually narrow, allowing the swimmer to receive only 20 percent of the oxygen that a normal person receives. "It can really get bad in our workouts," Dolan explained in *Sports Illustrated.* "There will be a real tightness in my chest, and I won't be able to get a lot of air. But my coach says it actually helps me in meets because it increases my ability to withstand stress."

During the summer, when most swimming meets are held, allergies make Dolan's asthma even worse. Swimming authorities have banned many of the medications he could take to make his asthma better. Dolan can use an inhaler and wear an adhesive strip across his nose to help him breathe.

GOING FOR DISTANCE. Dolan attended Yorktown High School. Twice he earned All-American honors and the *Washington Post* named him to its All-Metropolitan team. In addition to his swimming success, Dolan was an honor roll student. Besides swimming in high school, Dolan worked with a private coach, Rick Curl, at the Curl-Burke Swim Club.

American men had not done well in distance swimming in recent years, a fact Dolan wanted to try to change. "Since I first started swimming, I've always known the U.S. has really weak distance swimmers," Dolan explained in the *Washington Post.* "I would say that growing up, I didn't have one swimmer who I wanted to be like. There weren't many distance role models to look at, but there were enough great U.S. swimmers that you could take certain qualities from each one."

CHOOSES MICHIGAN. In 1993 Dolan won his first medal in international competition, a silver in the 400-meter individual

SCOREBOARD

WORLD-RECORD HOLDER IN 400-METER INDIVIDUAL MEDLEY (4:12.30).

TWICE NAMED U.S. SWIMMER OF THE YEAR (1994 AND 1995).

SET THREE AMERICAN RECORDS AT 1995 NCAA SWIMMING CHAMPIONSHIPS.

DOLAN IS THE BEST AMERICAN HOPE FOR A GOLD MEDAL IN SWIMMING AT THE 1996 SUMMER OLYMPICS IN ATLANTA, GEORGIA.

medley (IM) at the Pan-Pacific Games. (The individual medley consists of 100 meters each in the backstroke, breaststroke, butterfly, and freestyle.) He also finished second in the 400-meter IM at the U.S. Summer Nationals and third in the 800-meter freestyle at the U.S. Spring Nationals. His strong performances earned him an athletic scholarship to attend the University of Michigan.

WOLVERINE WAVES. Dolan enrolled at Michigan in the fall of 1993. Curl had earlier worked with Michigan coach Jon Urbanchek to make Mike Barrowman of the United States into a world-record holder and Olympic gold medal winner in 1992. "I respect Jon as a coach," Curl stated in the *Washington Post*. Michigan was already a swimming powerhouse, with 1992 Olympian Eric Namesnik and 1993 NCAA champion Marcel Wouda. The two champions pushed Dolan to do his best.

Superstar

FAB FOUR. At the 1994 U.S. Spring Nationals, Dolan won four events, the first man to do so since the legendary Mark Spitz accomplished the feat in 1972. (Spitz won a record seven gold medals at the 1972 Summer Olympics.) He won the 400-, 800-, and 1,500-meter freestyle races and the 400-meter IM. Dolan broke the American record in the 400-meter IM, held previously by Michigan teammate Namesnik. His performance won Dolan the Kiphuth Award as the high-point scorer in the meet. Dolan qualified for the World Swimming Championships in Rome, Italy, by winning the 800-meter freestyle at the U.S. Summer Nationals. In September 1994 Dolan, at age 18, was the youngest member of the U.S. national swimming team.

WORLD RECORD. Dolan intended to just do his best and enjoy the trip to the world championships. Instead, he broke the 400-meter IM record set in 1991 by Tamas Darnyi of Hungary with a time of 4 minutes 12.30 seconds—.6 of a second better than the record. "I knew going into the last 50 [meters] I had the lead, but I didn't know I was that close to the record," Dolan told the *New York Times*. Darnyi had dominated the

event from 1985 until he retired in 1995, winning every Olympic and world championship race. "I came out with so much confidence," Dolan stated in *Sports Illustrated.* "I thought, Well, maybe I can compete with these guys."

AWARD WINNER. At the 1994 National Collegiate Athletic Association (NCAA) meet, Dolan won his first collegiate national championship as part of Michigan's victorious 800-meter freestyle relay team. He also finished second in the 500-meter freestyle and the 400-IM and third in the 1,650-meter freestyle. Dolan won many awards as a freshman. The Big Ten named him Freshman of the Year and Swimmer of the Year. U.S. Swimming, the national governing body for swimming in the United States, named Dolan the U.S. Swimmer of the Year and the U.S. Olympic Committee listed him as a finalist for the Athlete of the Year award.

REPEAT. In 1995 Dolan became only the third swimmer to win U.S. Swimming's Swimmer of the Year award in back-to-

Dolan competes in the 400-meter medley during the 1994 U.S. Swimming Championships.

NO FEAR

Dolan trains very hard, swimming 13 miles a day in a program that often makes his asthma almost unbearable. One time he climbed out of the pool after his workout and passed out. "He began to feel lightheaded, then his face got numb," Dolan's father recounted in *USA Today.* "Finally, he got out of the pool, and went to the coach's office and passed out." The incident scared his coach. "I thought, Oh, my god, he's going to die on me," Urbanchek admitted in *Sports Illustrated.* "But he had just hyperventilated because of all the coughing. The next day he was back in the pool."

Dolan underwent medical tests to make sure he was fine. "The concern for awhile was that maybe I'd put so much stress on my heart, it would fail," Dolan confessed in *USA Today.* "But the doctors don't think that's possible, so I don't think about it much anymore. The biggest problem for me is not to get too frustrated when I can't do what I want, because that only makes it worse."

"He probably has the best-documented case of asthma in the world," his father told *USA Today.* "We've asked over and over and over, and he's tested specifically. There comes a point when you know you have the best advice available when you just have to trust those people."

"There are times when I stop and say, Is this really worth it?" Dolan confessed in *Sports Illustrated.* "Like last summer [1994]. It was one of the worst summers I ever had. I had all kinds of trouble breathing. Then I go to the world championships and break the record. So you never know. I just try to relax and not worry. I can't widen my esophagus, so why worry?"

back years. (Janet Evans and Mike Barrowman are the others.) He won four medals at the Pan-Pacific Championships, including gold medals in the 200- and 400-meter IM races. At the Summer Nationals, Dolan won two gold medals (400- and 800-meter freestyle relays), two silvers (200-meter backstroke and 400-meter IM), and two bronze medals (400- and 1,500-meter freestyle).

MORE RECORDS. Dolan made another big splash at the 1995 NCAA Swimming Championships in Indianapolis, Indiana, in March 1995. He set three American records and led Michigan

MR. VERSATILITY

Dolan has the ability to qualify for the 1996 U.S. Olympic swimming team in five different events. "In 20-plus years of coaching, I've never seen a man with as much versatility," Curl told in *USA Today*. Dolan plans to concentrate on two or three events at the 1996 Summer Olympics in Atlanta, Georgia. "I'd much rather do well in the Olympics in two or three events than just make it in five," he stated in *USA Today*. He added in the *Chicago Tribune:* "I see myself as a 400-IM swimmer and distance freestyler, and I will take success wherever I can get it." Dolan ranked second in the world in the 400-meter IM and third in both the 200-meter IM and 400-meter freestyle at the end of 1995.

to its first NCAA swimming championship in 34 years. Dolan set records in the 500-meter freestyle, 400-meter IM, and the 1,650-meter freestyle. In each event Dolan shattered the U.S. record by more than two seconds. "Usually you see records broken by tenths of a second," Urbanchek explained in *Sports Illustrated*. "He broke them by two or three seconds." Dolan also helped Michigan win the 800-meter freestyle relay.

Dolan became the first swimmer since 1987 to set three American records at one meet. "I was in a zone," Dolan described in *Sports Illustrated*. "It might not be like basketball, where you go on a hot shooting streak, but you definitely get your confidence up, and you feel like no one can stop you." Dolan finished as a finalist for the 1995 Sullivan Award, given annually to the best amateur athlete in the United States.

THE FUTURE. Dolan stands six feet six inches tall and has only 3 percent body fat. His long body and reach make him perfect for distance swimming. Dolan is ahead of his coach's schedule. "My aim with Tom was to get him ready for 1996," Urbanchek told the *Washington Post*. "The Atlanta Olympics were my goal, and I thought he could be the number one IMer by then. He beat me by almost two years. I thought the road would be longer, but it took a lot less time."

OUT OF THE POOL. Dolan is a rap disc jockey with the nickname MC Mass Confusion. "That's our great disappointment," Mr. Dolan told *USA Today.* "His mother and I have at least gotten him to the point that only half of the tapes are rap. Maybe one day he'll come to realize that rock 'n' roll is the only way to go." Dolan wears an earring and a goatee beard that is bleached from brown to red by the chlorine in the pool. Many swimmers shave all the hair on their body to help them swim faster, but not Dolan. "He'll shave some, but that silly-looking goatee will stay," Curl explained in *USA Today.* Dolan majors in economics at Michigan.

Urbanchek appreciates his prize pupil, as he told *Sports Illustrated:* "He's the best. He's got the body, the desire, the competitive instinct. Put it all together, and you've got a champion."

Sources

Chicago Tribune, September 7, 1994.
New York Times, September 7, 1994.
Sports Illustrated, April 3, 1995.
USA Today, July 31, 1995.
Washington Post, April 7, 1994.
Additional information provided by the University of Michigan.

WHERE TO WRITE:
C/O THE UNIVERSITY OF MICHIGAN,
ATHLETIC PUBLIC RELATIONS, 1000 S. STATE ST.,
ANN ARBOR, MI 48109.

Dale Earnhardt

1952—

O n a racetrack, no one is tougher than Dale Earnhardt, "the Man in Black." No one is better, either. In 1994 he won his seventh National Association for Stock Car Auto Racing (NASCAR) season points championship, tying him for the all-time record with the legendary Richard Petty. Earnhardt has also won more money than any other stock car racer and is a big reason the sport is growing in popularity. Not bad for someone who started racing at 15 on the dirt tracks of North Carolina made famous by his race car-driving father.

"I drive like somebody's chasing me."
—Dale Earnhardt

Growing Up

BORN TO RACE. Ralph Dale Earnhardt was born April 29, 1952. He grew up in Kannapolis, North Carolina, in an area called "Car Town" because the city named the streets after automobiles and engines. His father, Ralph Earnhardt, was a race car driver who won the 1958 Late Model Sportsmen

SCOREBOARD

WON SEVEN NASCAR
SEASON POINTS CHAMPIONSHIPS
(1980, 1986, 1987, 1990, 1991, 1993,
AND 1994).

TIED WITH RICHARD PETTY FOR
MOST NASCAR SEASON POINTS
CHAMPIONSHIPS (SEVEN).

1979 NASCAR
ROOKIE OF THE YEAR.

EARNHARDT IS THE HARDEST-
DRIVING AND MOST POPULAR
STOCK CAR DRIVER IN THE WORLD.

championship. Ralph Earnhardt earned the name Ironheart because he never backed down from other drivers. He was a legend at the local dirt track, the Metrolina, in Charlotte, North Carolina. Earnhardt's mother, Martha, worked as a waitress at the Dinette, a local restaurant.

Earnhardt inherited his love for racing from his father. "That's why I'm racing today," he explained in *Car and Driver.* "Grew up around my dad, so it just seemed natural that's what I did. He taught me good common-sense things. He didn't have a high-school education, but as far as I'm concerned he was pretty sharp. He knew race cars, knew what the ins and outs were and how to win, how to make the money count, how to take care of his equipment. He won so many races they hardly could count 'em all. Probably up in the hundreds."

STARTS RACING. Earnhardt won his first race at the same local track where his father had won so many races. His neighbor David Oliver gave him his first chance to race, at age 15. "First time I saw him race, he drove a car for us," Oliver recalled in *Car and Driver.* "What they called 'Semi-Modified,' little six-cylinder cars, wasn't much to them. But you could see there was a lot of ability there. There's people drove for years and Dale run with them."

Soon Earnhardt established a 20-race winning streak. He also proved to be an excellent mechanic. One night he built his father an engine in the family's living room. Many times father and son raced on the same day, but never in the same races.

DROPS OUT. To race full-time, Earnhardt dropped out of school in the ninth grade. "It was the only thing I ever let my daddy down over," Earnhardt admitted in *Sports Illustrated.* "He wanted me to finish; it was the only thing he ever pleaded with me to do. But I was so hardheaded. For about a year and a half after that, we didn't have a close relationship."

Displaying his trophy,
Earnhardt flashes a smile.

Earnhardt's parents tried to get him to go back to school by offering him a new car. He turned them down and kept racing. Earnhardt made another mistake when he entered into a teenage marriage at 17 and had a child. He confessed in *Sports Illustrated* that his family "probably should have been on welfare. We didn't have money to buy groceries." By the time Earnhardt was 24, his first marriage had ended, he had remarried, and he had two more children with his second wife.

DAD DIES. Ralph Earnhardt died at the racetrack in 1973 from a heart attack during a practice drive. "It was very emotional when he died," Earnhardt admitted in the *New York Times*. "But I didn't really start missing him till I started into asphalt racing and I didn't have his experience to help me. He never did encourage me to race, but once he knew that was what I was gonna do he gave me everything he could." Earnhardt took over the family workshop in the back of the house after his father's death.

Earnhardt spent all the money he had buying racing cars and equipment. Often he borrowed money on Friday and hoped to win it back during a race over the weekend. His devotion to racing cost him his second marriage. "For our family cars, we drove old junk Chevelles—anything you could get for $200," Earnhardt recounted in *Sports Illustrated*. Soon Earnhardt was $11,000 in debt. "After he [his father] died, I raced in debt a lot," Earnhardt recalled in the *New York Times*. "Daddy never did that. He'd have felt bad at me about it. But it's like going in debt for a house. You pay and you pay, and suddenly it's paid off. You got a home. Now, all of a sudden, I got racing."

Superstar

TOP ROOKIE. When things seemed their worst, Earnhardt caught the eye of Rod Osterlund, a California-based racing sponsor. In 1978 Osterlund gave the young driver a one-race tryout in Atlanta, Georgia. Earnhardt did well enough in that race to earn a one-year contract to be Osterlund's sole driver during 1979. He became only one of four rookies at the time to win a Grand National Event on the NASCAR circuit, the Southeastern 500. He was also the first rookie to win more than $200,000. Earnhardt won Rookie-of-the-Year honors and finished seventh in the overall NASCAR point standings. He accomplished all this despite breaking both collarbones in a race.

"That first year everything seemed like it happened so fast, I couldn't get ahold of it," Earnhardt told the *New York*

Times. "I couldn't take it all in. It was like I was missing something. I didn't really have the time to savor it and enjoy it like I thought I would." Martha Earnhardt was happy for her son. "This was all he ever wanted to do," she told the same newspaper. "I didn't know if he could take care of himself. But he's proved he can."

NASCAR CHAMP. His rookie success earned Earnhardt a five-year contract with Osterlund. Proving that Osterlund made a good decision, Earnhardt went out in 1980 and won his first NASCAR season points championship, edging the legendary Cale Yarborough in the last race of the season. He won the championship despite having a problem all year getting his engine to generate enough horsepower. "I'll tell you what makes that car run," David Ifft, crew chief for Earnhardt's fellow driver Benny Parsons, explained to *Sports Illustrated.* "Dale Earnhardt makes that car run. He's been driving like a wild man to make up for lack of horsepower all year." Earnhardt won five races and finished in the top five 19 times in 31 races. He became the first second-year driver to win the NASCAR championship.

Earnhardt won consistently his next five years but could not capture another championship for Osterlund. In 1985 he moved to the Richard Childress Chevrolet team and his career took off. In 1986 he won five races and finished in the top five 16 times, earning his second NASCAR championship. In 1987 Earnhardt had his best season ever, winning an amazing 11 races and finishing in the top five 21 times in only 29 races, results good enough to make him the runaway NASCAR season points champion.

CRASH LANDING. Despite his success, Earnhardt earned a reputation for being reckless and willing to cause an accident to gain an advantage. At least three times in 1986 Earnhardt won a race after bumping the leader out of the way. "With Earnhardt, every lap is a controlled crash," archrival Darrell Waltrip told *Sports Illustrated.* On the small tracks where he learned to race, it was an accepted tactic to knock another driver out of a race by bumping him. "They [other drivers] ain't ever seen the kind of rough racing I've had to do in my life just to survive," Earnhardt explained in *Sports Illustrated*. "They don't want to mess with this ol' boy."

In NASCAR, however, where cars cost millions of dollars and travel at close to 200 miles an hour, the same tactics are not acceptable. In 1987 NASCAR president Bill France Jr. warned Earnhardt to clean up his act. Earnhardt listened and has had fewer problems with other drivers since then. "I care about winning races, not if they like me," Earnhardt explained to *Sports Illustrated*. "All I can do is drive the best I can and stand my ground. I got to do what I got to do."

KEEPS WINNING. Despite backing off a little bit, Earnhardt kept winning. In 1989 Rusty Wallace edged Earnhardt by 12 points for the NASCAR crown. In 1990 Earnhardt battled rookie Mark Martin for the championship. Earnhardt won nine races and Martin three, but Earnhardt led the points race by only six points—4,260 to 4,254—heading into the last race in Atlanta, Georgia. In that race, Earnhardt finished third and Martin sixth, so the Man in Black had his fourth NASCAR points championship. Earnhardt also won the three-race International Race of Champions series, which includes drivers from different forms of racing. "Dale Earnhardt's opinion in the garage area is like God's to us," fellow driver Ernie Irvan stated in *Sports Illustrated*. "Right now he's the ultimate driver."

Earnhardt won nine races in 1990 and his fifth NASCAR season points title in 1991. Alan Kulwicki broke Earnhardt's string of championships in 1992, keeping him from winning a record-tying third consecutive title. (Kulwicki died in a plane crash in 1993.) Earnhardt suffered a series of mechanical breakdowns and did not show his usual flash in 1992. He finished twelfth in the points standings.

Earnhardt came back strong in 1993, however, and won his sixth NASCAR points championship. He won six races and became the all-time leader in earnings, with $17 million in his career. Rusty Wallace won ten races in 1993 but could not earn enough points in races he did not win to catch Earnhardt. Though not flashy, Earnhardt, "the Intimidator," showed consistency, finishing in the top ten 21 times in 30 races.

RECORD BREAKER. Wallace challenged Earnhardt again in 1994—winning eight races to Earnhardt's four—but again fell short in the overall points standings. When Earnhardt won the AC Delco 500 in Rockingham, North Carolina, he clinched his seventh NASCAR points championship. The victory tied him with the legendary Richard Petty for the all-time lead in season championships. "I never thought I'd win one [title]," Earnhardt admitted in the *Greensboro News and Record*. Earnhardt was honored to be tied with Petty. "Richard Petty is still the king," Earnhardt explained in the same newspaper. "I'm a seven-time champion." Earnhardt dedicated his championship to his good friend Neil Bonnett, who had died in a crash earlier in the year at Daytona.

"WONDER BOY." Earnhardt was the undisputed king of stock car racing entering the 1995 season. Experts were confident he would win his record-breaking eighth championship. **Jeff Gordon** (see entry), whom Earnhardt called "Wonder Boy," jumped out to an early lead in the Winston Cup points race. Slowly, however, the Intimidator charged, and Gordon stumbled. Earnhardt won the second ever Brickyard 400, held at the legendary Indianapolis Motor Speedway. "Do you think people have really forgotten about me?" Earnhardt asked in the *New York Times* after his victory. Despite Earnhardt's strong finish, during which he almost made up a 305-point deficit, Gordon had too big an early lead for Earnhardt to catch up. His record-breaking eighth championship would have to wait.

OFF THE TRACK. Earnhardt lives on Lake Norman in North Carolina, and he maintains a farm nearby. He has two daugh-

---

THE KING

Richard "The King" Petty won more stock car races in his career than any other racer—200—and leads the second-place driver, David Pearson, by 95 wins. He raced from 1958 through 1992 and won seven NASCAR points championships. Petty won the Daytona 500 a record seven times (1964, 1966, 1971, 1973, 1974, 1979, and 1981) and was the first stock car driver to win more than $1 million. His red, white, and blue number 43 car was always a fan favorite and Petty was the most popular champion in the history of stock car racing. "I never claimed to be a great driver," Petty admitted in *Sports Illustrated*. "All I wanted to be known as was a winner." Petty now owns a racing team that includes his son, Kyle.

DAYTONA DREAMING

The only stock car race Earnhardt has not been able to win is the biggest of them all—the Daytona 500 in Daytona, Florida. "I've never won it," Earnhardt told *Sports Illustrated.* "I've won 24 races at the Daytona Speedway. More races there than anybody else, ever. But I've never won the Daytona 500. It bothers y'all [the media]. It don't bother me. I'm still confident that I've got several shots to win it."

Earnhardt has finished second in the Dayton 500 three times. In 1990 Earnhardt dominated the race for 199 of 200 laps. Then disaster struck. A cut on his tire knocked him out of the lead and the race on the very last lap. In 1991 Ernie Irvan, a driver Earnhardt helped get into NASCAR racing, passed him with only five laps to go to win. In 1995 Earnhardt pulled off a tremendous comeback that fell just short. He stood in fourteenth place with only 11 laps to go but moved through traffic to advance to second with only three laps remaining. Earnhardt finished only .61 of a second behind Sterling Marlin, who won the race for the second straight year. He took the loss in stride. "This is the Daytona 500," Earnhardt told *Sports Illustrated.* "I ain't supposed to win."

ters, Kelly and Taylor, and two sons, Kerry and Dale Jr. Dale Jr. is following in his father's racing tracks, and Kelly once took a test drive around a track. Earnhardt picks up Elvis Presley mementos for his mother, a big fan of "the King." He likes to hunt and fish. Earnhardt also owns a Chevrolet dealership. He supports young racers, giving them advice and financial support to help them succeed.

Earnhardt married for the third time in 1982. He proposed to his wife, Teresa, from a hospital bed after crashing in a race at Pocono Motor Speedway. "She's always been a good friend, but when we got married she became instrumental in helping me," Earnhardt told *Car and Driver.* "And [she] keeps Dale Earnhardt straight."

Earnhardt has worked to build up his image as the bad boy of NASCAR racing. Besides the nicknames "the Man in Black" and "the Intimidator," others also call him "Ironhead." Earnhardt sells souvenirs of all kinds at a record pace. Fans love him even though he refuses to sign autographs. "We've got what we think is the hottest property in motor sports in the world," his agent, Don Hawk, explained to *Sports Illustrated.* With his souvenirs sales and his earnings on the track, Earnhardt has made more money than any other race car driver in history. "Racing comes just like breathing to me," Earnhardt told the same magazine. "It's always going to be there, like my heartbeat."

Though he spends a lot of time making public appearances for fans and for his sponsor, Mr. Goodwrench, racing is still what makes Earnhardt happy. "The fun time is when I sit down in that car and crank her up and she rolls off the line— and there's not anybody around but me," he explained to *Car and Driver.* "And we go out there and do our business." Earnhardt told the same magazine why he always runs flat out: "I drive like somebody's chasing me."

Sources

Atlanta Journal and Constitution, January 19, 1995.
Car and Driver, November 1990; January 1991.
Forbes, July 3, 1995.
Greensboro News and Record, October 24, 1994.
Los Angeles Times, February 20, 1995.
New York Times, August 4, 1980; August 6, 1995; August 7, 1995.
Sport, February 1994.
Sporting News, February 27, 1995.
Sports Illustrated, November 24, 1980; September 7, 1987; November 2, 1990; February 6, 1995; February 27, 1995.
Additional information provided by NASCAR.

WHERE TO WRITE:
C/O NATIONAL ASSOCIATION FOR STOCK CAR AUTO RACING (NASCAR),
P.O. BOX 2875, 1801 VOLUSIA AVE.,
DAYTONA BEACH, FL 32114.

Teresa Edwards

1964—

> *"She may not beat you with her shooting or her passing. But somehow, she will find a way to beat you."—University of Georgia basketball coach Andy Landers*

Teresa Edwards, or "T" as her teammates call her, sets a new record every time she plays a game for the U.S. women's Olympic basketball team. She represented her country in 1984, 1988, and 1992, becoming the first American—man or woman—to play on three Olympic basketball teams. In the 1996 Summer Olympics in Atlanta, Georgia, Edwards will extend her record to four as she once again represents the United States. She hopes she also sets another record—winning her third Olympic basketball gold medal.

Growing Up

RAISED BY MOM. Teresa Edwards was born July 19, 1964, in Cairo, Georgia. Edwards was the oldest of five children and the only girl. Her mother, Mildred, dropped out of school at 16 when Teresa was born and went to work in the vegetable fields near Cairo. "At the time, I felt like my life was all over," Mildred Edwards recalled in *Sports Illustrated*. "I knew I wouldn't and couldn't go back to school. I had wanted to become a nurse, but I decided to take care of my responsibility." Edwards's father, Leroy Copeland, never married or lived with her mother, but did provide financial support.

ONE OF THE BOYS. Edwards and the boys in the neighborhood created their own sports arena in an empty lot near her home. The children played football, practiced karate, and ran races against each other. To play basketball, the young athletes used a plastic ball and a trash can. Later, Edwards knocked the spokes out of a bicycle tire and nailed the rim to a tree as a basket. She began playing basketball to keep up with her brothers. "It was the only game growing up where I could go up against the boys and beat them," Edwards explained.

MAKES TEAM. In the seventh grade Edwards asked her mother for permission to play on her school's basketball team. Her mother, who worked all day at a factory, said no because she needed Edwards to watch her four younger brothers. Ms. Edwards also doubted that her daughter could play the game. Without her mother's knowledge, Edwards tried out for the team anyway and made the squad. "She kept coming home late from school and laying it off on some teacher: 'I'm helping Miss So-and-so,'" Mildred Edwards recalled in *Sports Illustrated*. "Then one day she said, 'I need a new pair of sneakers because I made the team.' I said, 'Girl, you can't play basketball.' And Teresa said, 'Mama, I made the team.'" All doubts about her daughter's ability disappeared once she saw Edwards play. "I was quickly convinced," Ms. Edwards explained in *Sports Illustrated for Kids*. "I never missed a game after that."

TWO-SPORT STAR. In 1982 Edwards earned high school All-American honors in basketball at Cairo High. She also starred

SCOREBOARD

PLAYED ON THREE U.S. OLYMPIC BASKETBALL TEAMS (1984, 1988, AND 1992), MORE THAN ANY AMERICAN PLAYER, MAN OR WOMAN.

WON TWO GOLD AND ONE BRONZE OLYMPIC BASKETBALL MEDALS, THE MOST WON BY ANY AMERICAN PLAYER.

AVERAGED 28 POINTS PER GAME FOR MITSUBISHI ELECTRIC CORPORATION PROFESSIONAL TEAM IN JAPAN.

EDWARDS IS THE MOST DECORATED INTERNATIONAL BASKETBALL PLAYER IN HISTORY.

Edwards takes the ball from a Czechoslovakian player during the 1992 Olympics.

on the school's track team. In 1980 Edwards led Cairo High to a second-place finish in the Georgia state track meet. She won the high jump and finished third in the 440-yard dash.

LADY BULLDOG. When it came time to choose a college, Edwards decided to stay close to home and accepted an athletic scholarship to attend the University of Georgia. She made an instant contribution, scoring 13 points per game her first season on a team that won the Southeastern Conference

Championship (SEC) and advanced to the National Collegiate Athletic Association (NCAA) Final Four. Edwards lifted her scoring average to 14.1 points and 5.7 assists per game in her sophomore season. "Teresa is the greatest competitor ever to lace up a pair of basketball shoes," Georgia coach Andy Landers exclaimed in *Sports Illustrated for Kids*. "She may not beat you with her shooting or her passing. But somehow, she will find a way to beat you."

OLYMPICS I. Edwards got her first taste of international competition in 1983 on the gold medal-winning U.S. Junior Pan-American team. She also earned Most Valuable Player honors at the 1983 National Sports Festival, averaging 15.3 points and 4.3 rebounds per game.

The U.S. Olympic Committee invited Edwards to try out for the 1984 U.S. women's Olympic basketball team. She made the team and was the youngest player on the squad. The U.S. team won the 1984 gold medal at the Summer Olympics in Los Angeles, California. A boycott of the games by the Soviet Union and its allies made the competition much easier.

Playing on the Olympic team was revealing for Edwards. During her career she had always been the best player on the court, but there were many great players on the U.S. team. Edwards played limited minutes as a reserve during the Olympics and scored only 2.5 points per game. "That was a very valuable and humbling experience," Edwards admitted in *Sports Illustrated for Kids*. "Now I appreciate just getting to play."

BACK TO THE BULLDOGS. Edwards returned to Georgia in 1985 and continued to shine. She averaged 15.5 points and 5.7 assists and led the Lady Bulldogs to an SEC title and back to the NCAA Final Four. Her senior season, 1986, was her best yet. Edwards scored just under 20 points per game (19.7). For her career, Edwards averaged 15.5 points per game and set school records in assists (653) and steals (312). She earned All-American honors in 1985 and 1986. The Lady Bulldogs compiled a 116-17 record in Edwards's four years. She became one of only three women basketball players to have her number (number 5) retired by Georgia.

Beyond her college playing, Edwards continued to play well for the United States in international competition. In 1986 she helped the U.S. team to gold medals at both the Goodwill Games (14 points per game) and the World Basketball Championships (15.3 points per game). Edwards followed up those performances by helping the United States win a gold medal at the 1987 Pan-American Games. There she averaged 16.8 points per game (second best on the team) and a team-leading 5.8 assists a contest.

TURNS PRO. In 1986 Edwards left home for the first time to play professional basketball in Italy. She quickly became homesick, missing her family and friends. "I was fresh out of college, and I just couldn't handle it," Edwards confessed to *Sports Illustrated for Kids*. Edwards played for two seasons in Italy, earning $50,000 each year.

OLYMPICS II. Edwards again made the U.S. team for the 1988 Summer Olympics in Seoul, South Korea. No longer fighting for playing time, Edwards started for the American squad. She led the team in assists (17) and steals (23) and was second in scoring with a 16.6 average. The U.S. team rolled to another gold medal, this time against the best competition in the world.

Superstar

JAPANESE JUMPER. After the 1988 Olympics, Edwards again left the United States to play professional basketball, this time in Japan. She played guard and forward for the Mitsubishi Electric Corporation team. "Teresa plays like she has eyes in the back of her head," Naomi Nakamura, captain of the Mitsubishi team, said in *Sports Illustrated for Kids*. Edwards averaged 28.5 points and five assists per game in the pros and made $200,000 per season.

Playing professional basketball helped Edwards improve her game. "Playing overseas has made me mentally tough," she explained in *Sports Illustrated*. "[If it] hadn't been for the professional leagues, my best years as a player would have been wasted. I got so much better after college. I'm at my prime."

Edwards played on the winning U.S. 1990 world championship and Goodwill Games teams. In 1991 she led the U.S. team in scoring (18 points per game) at the Pan-American Games. Unfortunately, Cuba upset the Americans, 86-81, and the U.S. team finished with a bronze medal. "I've never been surrounded by this much talent, experience and maturity," Edwards admitted in *Sports Illustrated* after the loss. "Since our loss in the Pan Am, we couldn't wait to get back together to prove we're the best."

OLYMPICS III. Edwards made history in 1992 at the Summer Olympics in Barcelona, Spain, becoming the first player—male or female—to play on three U.S. Olympic basketball teams. The U.S. team expected to roll to another gold medal but lost to the Unified Team (formerly the Soviet Union) in the semifinals, 79-73. The Americans then defeated the Cuban team to win the bronze medal. "It was one of the best teams I've played on," a disappointed Edwards, co-captain of the U.S. team, told *Sports Illustrated for Kids*. "Just because we lost doesn't make it a bad summer. A bronze medal is good too." Edwards contributed 12.6 points (third on the team) and a team-leading 5.4 assists to the U.S. squad. Her third Olympic basketball medal set a new American record.

OLYMPICS IV. In 1994 Edwards again played professionally, this time in Spain and France, but returned to the United States to begin practicing with the U.S. national team. She helped the American women win a bronze medal at the 1994 world championships and earned All-Tournament honors. She averaged 12.7 points and three assists per game. Edwards will

CULTURE SHOCK

Because Edwards plays so far away, her family and friends rarely get to see her perform. But she does not feel as homesick in Japan as she did in Italy. "The movies are in English and the grocery store food is more like ours, believe it or not," Edwards told *Sports Illustrated for Kids*. There are some Japanese customs that Edwards does not like, such as eating raw fish and sitting on the floor to eat at low tables. "My legs are much longer than everyone else's," Edwards explained to the same magazine. "Eating on the floor hurts." Edwards spent so much time practicing that she could not learn Japanese. She had to use an interpreter to talk with her teammates.

FAMILY FIRST

Edwards received her bachelor's degree in recreation in 1989. "I was the first in my family to graduate from college," Edwards stated in *Sports Illustrated*. "That's the biggest example I could make for my brothers. It means more than any shot I could ever take."

Edwards is extremely close to her mother. In fact, the two of them shared a bedroom when Edwards was growing up. Basketball has helped Edwards give back something to her mother. "My family is bigger to me than basketball," Edwards told *Sports Illustrated*. "I earned money so I could give back to my mom. It's my turn to accept responsibility of supporting her. What are you living for if you can't provide somebody with a better way of life? There's no mom like my mom. They don't make them like her anymore. She's not my best friend. She's my best mom."

again make history in 1996 by playing on her fourth U.S. Olympic basketball team at the Summer Olympics in Atlanta, Georgia. Edwards, who lives in Atlanta, will be right at home.

WHY SO GOOD? Edwards has an accurate shot, is a very good passer, and has explosive speed. An all-around player, she excels at both the offensive and defensive ends of the court. What sets Edwards apart, however, is her intensity. She plays every game as if it was her last and has tremendous drive, perseverance, and motivation. "Someone of her stature, who is as good as she is, you'd expect to be more involved with herself," Theresa Grentz, 1992 U.S. Olympic women's basketball coach explained in *Sports Illustrated*. "Teresa's down-to-earth. She can't be bought. Values are important to her. Her humility and her simplicity of life make her very special to be around."

OFF THE COURT. Edwards lives in Atlanta, Georgia. She bought a house for her mother and four brothers. Other sports Edwards enjoys are football, softball, track and field, and volleyball. She says she believes that if she had not played basketball, she would have been a good tennis player. "It's a very intense sport with great motivating value and you can only fail yourself."

Edwards's basketball idols are Ann Meyers and Lynnette Woodard, both great former college players. She likes Denzel Washington movies and the television shows *All My Children* and *Living Single*. Edwards also enjoys "Garfield" cartoons, *Ebony* magazine, and chocolate ice cream. She is a fan of Michael Jackson and Whitney Houston. Edwards plans to coach basketball once her playing days are through.

After Edwards played on the 1988 Olympic team, the city of Cairo renamed the street she grew up on Teresa Edwards Street. Her mother gave Edwards the best advice she has ever received, as she told *Sports Illustrated for Kids:* "If you are going to do anything, do it right or don't do it at all."

Sources

Jet, June 29, 1992.
Sports Illustrated, July 22, 1992.
Sports Illustrated for Kids, December 1992.
Additional information provided by USA Basketball.

WHERE TO WRITE:
C/O USA BASKETBALL,
5465 MARK DABLING BLVD.,
COLORADO SPRINGS, CO 80918.

Marshall Faulk

1973—

"At his best, he is a blur."—Journalist Paul Attner

Marshall Faulk has always had to move fast. He grew up in an area where if you got caught, you might not survive. Football kept Faulk on the move, from New Orleans, Louisiana, to San Diego State University. There he set numerous National Collegiate Athletic Association (NCAA) records and became the best collegiate running back in the nation. Now Faulk moves up and down the field for the Indianapolis Colts fast enough to make him one of the best running backs in the National Football League (NFL). He does not plan to stop until he is among the all-time greats.

Growing Up

TOUGH TOWN. Marshall William Faulk was born February 26, 1973, in New Orleans, Louisiana. He grew up in the Desire Housing Project, one of the roughest projects in the United States. Faulk's speed helped him survive. "You grow up in the ghetto, you hear gunshots, you run. It was instinct,"

Faulk revealed in *Boys' Life*. His father, Roosevelt, ran a bar and restaurant and worked part-time for a trucking company. His mother, Cecile, did odd jobs and raised six children. "My mom didn't have a profession," Faulk recalled in *Sports Illustrated*. "Her profession was her kids." His mom was also Faulk's role model. "My mom never quit at anything," he bragged to *Boys' Life*.

Faulk could have wound up a victim of the streets, but his family helped pull him through. "It's because I have older brothers, and growing up in my situation, you have to grow up quick or die young," he explained in the *Sporting News*. "The environment I grew up in still helps me make critical decisions in my life, not only who to hang with but to know what is right or wrong, what I want to do, where I want to go, what road I want to take." Faulk's brother, Raymond, is in jail for robbery. "On the streets, you learn things your mother can't teach you, school can't teach you, your uncle can't teach you," Faulk related in *Sport* magazine. "I think about some of my friends who are still there, and some of my friends who were killed there. I say to myself: 'I made it. I was one of the lucky ones to make it out.'"

FATHER FIGURE. Faulk and his dad did not have a good relationship. His father never saw his son play football, and Faulk still does not like talking about his dad, who died in 1991 of throat cancer. Faulk's substitute father was Wayne Reese, the football coach at George Washington Carver High School. Reese first noticed Faulk when the youngster was in junior high. "[Faulk] was like any other kid from the area," Reese recounted in *Sports Illustrated*. "That is, he was leaning more to being bad than to being good. What separated him from the others was his intelligence. Being from the street, a really tough kid, Marshall was strong enough to meet a whole lot head-on that others his age would run from."

SCOREBOARD

TWICE LED COLLEGE RUNNING BACKS IN RUSHING (1991 AND 1993).

1994 NFL OFFENSIVE ROOKIE OF THE YEAR.

MOST VALUABLE PLAYER AT 1995 PRO BOWL GAME.

FAULK ESCAPED THE PROJECTS TO BECOME OF ONE THE BRIGHT YOUNG STARS IN THE NFL.

Faulk played running back, quarterback, tight end, wide receiver, and cornerback at George Washington Carver. He also lettered in track, running the 100-meters in 10.3 seconds. At one point Faulk was considering quitting the team and getting a job to help the family. Reese talked him out of it, convincing Faulk that he had a future in football. The coach also got his star player a job at school, helping the custodial staff. Faulk also sold popcorn at the Superdome, home of the New Orleans Saints.

Despite being on the football team, Faulk and many of his high school teammates were still affected by the violence on the streets. Many of Faulk's teammates fell in with bad crowds and were claimed by the streets. "My senior year," Faulk recalled in *Sports Illustrated,* "we lost a cornerback. He was arrested on a manslaughter charge. Believe me, it hurt us." Even with these distractions, Faulk ran for 1,800 yards and scored 32 touchdowns his last two seasons at George Washington Carver.

RUNNING BACK OR BUST. Football powers like Nebraska and the University of Miami heavily recruited Faulk. Unfortunately for those schools, they could not promise him that he would play running back. Because Faulk played so many positions on offense, many schools did not know how good a running back he actually was. Most schools figured he would play defensive back.

Faulk decided to hold out for what he wanted. "I didn't know if I was going to be real good playing football, but I knew if I was going to play football, coming from where I came from, that I was going to play the position where I was happy, running back," Faulk told *Sport* magazine. "I was going to play running back because I was going to school to get my education, and if I didn't make it in football, I just didn't make it."

FRESHMAN FLASH. Faulk finally chose San Diego State because the school offered him the chance to play running back. "If another school had come through the door that day promising to let me run the ball, I'd have gone there," Faulk confessed to *Sports Illustrated*. "You get your mind set, and you stick with it. I'm a firm believer that whatever I want to do, I'm going to do it." Faulk went on to be a star. He replaced an injured teammate in the second game of the season and gained an NCAA single-game record 386 yards rushing. Faulk also scored seven touchdowns in that game. He gained 1,429 yards rushing and scored 23 touchdowns as a freshman in 1991, becoming the first freshman ever to lead the nation in both rushing (158.8 yards per game) and scoring (15.6 points per game). United Press International (UPI) named Faulk Freshman of the Year, and the Associated Press voted him a first-team All-American.

Faulk repeated his rushing championship in his sophomore year, gaining 1,630 yards in 1992. He finished second in balloting for the prestigious Heisman Trophy. Faulk continued to star as a junior, rushing for 1,530 yards and 24 touchdowns, despite having defenses gang up to stop him. Football experts voted him to All-American teams every year of his college career.

RECORD BREAKER. Faulk played three seasons at San Diego State and broke the school record for rushing yards (4,589 yards) and scored 62 touchdowns. He gained over 100 yards in 23 of 32 games during his college career, gaining over 200 yards seven times and 300 yards twice. Faulk owned or shared 19 NCAA records.

Superstar

YOUNG COLT. After consulting with his high school coaches and teachers, Faulk decided to leave San Diego State early and enter the NFL Draft after his junior season. He was the second pick in the 1994 NFL Draft, chosen by the Indianapolis Colts. The Colts had been a poor team for many years, finishing 4-12 in 1993 and last making the play-offs in 1987. Their offense in 1993 was weak, finishing near the bottom in all categories. "The Colts were the ideal team, been last in rushing, and I was probably the best running back in my class, so it was the perfect match," Faulk explained in *Sport* magazine.

Faulk (number 28) slips through the Tampa Bay Buccaneers defense.

ROOKIE OF THE YEAR. Faulk helped change the Colts' attack. He earned NFL Offensive Rookie-of-the-Year honors after gaining 1,282 yards rushing (fifth in the NFL) and 522 yards receiving. Faulk also scored 12 touchdowns (fourth in the NFL). "He's everything we hoped for and more," Colts coach Ted Marchibroda told the *Sporting News*. "Marshall is the home-run hitter that our offense lacked. With him back there, we know we can break the big play at any time."

Faulk began his rookie season with a bang, rushing for 143 yards and three touchdowns against the Houston Oilers, his best game of the season. "This game reminded me of David and Goliath," Oilers linebacker Michael Barrow confessed in the *Sporting News*. "We were Goliath. They were David. This time, Marshall Faulk was the slingshot."

Faulk gained over 100 yards rushing three other times and gained over 100 yards receiving once. "I expected to have a good year, but some of the numbers even surprised me a little," Faulk admitted in the *Sporting News*. "I would have traded a good chunk of the yardage and all the individual accolades, though, if we had just made it to the play-offs. That's really the only thing that matters to me. I try not to get too caught up in the hype. I know it sounds corny, but I just try to go out and do my best and find ways to help us win."

The Colts did improve, finishing a respectable 8-8. Faulk earned the respect of his teammates. "He takes ordinary plays and turns them into unordinary results," Colts quarterback Jim Harbaugh told the *Sporting News*. When the Colts needed a big play, they looked to Faulk. "In the huddle, my line would look at me like, 'Marshall, let's go, we need you right here, nothing can stop us,'" Faulk explained in *Sport* magazine. "My teammates never had to wonder if I was going to get there because they knew I was going to show up ready to play."

MVP. Faulk's fellow players named him a starter in the 1995 Pro Bowl, the only rookie named to the team. He made the most of his opportunity. Faulk set four Pro-Bowl records, including 180 yards rushing. He also scored a touchdown, running 49 yards on a fake punt. Journalists covering the game voted to give Faulk the game's Most Valuable Player trophy. "I'm not going to tell you I thought I could walk into this league and do this well right away," Faulk confessed in the *Sporting News*. "You don't have strong doubts, but you always wonder, watching these guys on TV. They look so big and strong. Can you keep up?"

FAULK STACKS UP

Faulk reminded many experts of the premier running backs in the NFL, Barry Sanders of the Detroit Lions, Emmitt Smith of the Dallas Cowboys, and Thurman Thomas of the Buffalo Bills. "Faulk is a great player already," Redskins General Manager Charley Casserly told the *Sporting News.* "An elite player. Is he better than Sanders or Thomas or Smith? You can't say he isn't, but he is going to have to prove it. But he has that kind of ability." Faulk does not like the comparisons. "I'm just Marshall Faulk," he explained in *Boys' Life.* "I don't plan to be anybody but myself." The following stats show how Faulk's rookie year stacked up with those of the NFL's best:

	Rushing	Receiving	Total
M. Faulk	1,282	522	1,804
B. Sanders	1,470	282	1,752
E. Smith	937	228	1,165
T. Thomas	881	208	1,089

SUPER CLOSE. Faulk had another great year in 1995. He accounted for nearly 32 percent of the Colts offense with 1,078 yards rushing (sixth in the AFC) and 475 yards receiving. Voters elected Faulk to the Pro Bowl for the second straight season. Quarterback Jim Harbaugh helped make Faulk's job easier by playing at an All-Pro level. Indianapolis finished the year 9-7 and qualified for the play-offs for the first time since 1987.

INJURED. Indianapolis played the defending AFC champion San Diego Chargers in the first round of the play-offs. Faulk carried the ball for 16 yards early in the game, but reinjured his left knee. He originally hurt the knee in a game on December 10 against the Jacksonville Jaguars. The injury forced Faulk to miss the rest of the game, but the Colts defeated the Chargers 35-20 without their superstar. Zack Crockett filled in for Faulk and gained 147 yards against a weak San Diego run defense.

Doctors told Faulk soon after the game that he would need surgery to remove loose cartilage from his injured knee.

HOMETOWN HERO

Faulk is the biggest star to survive his old neighborhood. When he returns to George Washington Carver High School, kids skip class to go see him. "Marshall is the salvation of his community," Reese told *Sports Illustrated.* "He could move back here tomorrow and be a city councilman if he wanted. Everything shuts down when he comes home. The principal says, 'Where're all the kids?' And I say, 'Marshall's back.' A student was telling me the other day, 'I've got to meet Marshall. If I meet Marshall, my life is fulfilled.'" Faulk bought new football uniforms for the Carver football team and realizes he is lucky to have achieved the success he has. "The reason I use the word luck in talking about getting out of Desire [his housing project] is that I've been around people who work here, who train real hard, did everything possible to get where they needed to be, and they still ain't there," Faulk said in *Sport* magazine. "I was privileged enough to finish school and make it to college. So there's a lot of luck in this, luck in everything we do."

He missed the Colts' next game, a 10-7 upset over the Kansas City Chiefs, the team with the NFL's best record during the regular season. "We won this for Marshall," Lamont Warren, Faulk's replacement, told the *Chicago Tribune.*

Unfortunately for Faulk and the Colts, the injury also kept the rushing star on the sidelines for the AFC Championship Game against the Pittsburgh Steelers. "I wish I could say he'll be able to go, but he will not be ready on Sunday," Marchibroda admitted to the Associated Press. "Hopefully, if we defeat Pittsburgh, he'll be available for the Super Bowl."

SO CLOSE. Indianapolis and Pittsburgh played a close, hard-fought game. The Colts led 16-13 with only minutes remaining in the game. Steelers quarterback Neil O'Donnell, however, led his team down the field. Pittsburgh running back Bam Morris took the ball into the end zone with just over one minute left in the game, putting the Steelers in the lead, 20-16.

The Colts had one last chance to win the game. Harbaugh threw up a desperation pass. Both Indianapolis and

Pittsburgh players batted the ball in the air. Wide receiver Aaron Bailey had his hands on the ball several times, but could not pull it in. When the referee waved his arms, signaling an incomplete pass, the Colts were eliminated. Pittsburgh lost the Super Bowl, 27-17, to the Dallas Cowboys.

OFF THE FIELD. Faulk is single and lives in New Orleans during the off-season. He also owns houses in Texas, California, and Indiana. Faulk has a son, Marshall William Faulk Jr. Faulk sends each touchdown scoring football to his mom. She has received 63 footballs from his college career and 12 from the NFL. He likes rap music, and his favorite athletes are Barry Sanders of the Detroit Lions and Michael Jordan of the Chicago Bulls. Faulk now owns 11 cars. Faulk is a good cook, as are his brothers, who work professionally as chefs.

Faulk contributes $2,000 for each touchdown he scores to the Marshall Plan, founded to support inner city youth in Indianapolis, New Orleans, and San Diego. "You can't forget where you come from," Faulk told the *Sporting News.* Faulk continues to work on a degree in public administration at San Diego State. "I applaud guys for going back and getting their degrees, it's important," Faulk said in *Sport* magazine.

Paul Attner described Faulk best when he wrote in the *Sporting News,* "At his best, he is a blur."

Sources

Boys' Life, October 1995.
Chicago Tribune, January 6, 1996; January 8, 1996.
Sport, July 1995.
Sporting News, December 6, 1993; January 30, 1994; September 12, 1994; September 26, 1994; January 8, 1996; January 15, 1996; January 22, 1996.
Sports Illustrated, July 24, 1995.
Additional information provided by Indianapolis Colts and the Associated Press, January 6, 1996, and January 12, 1996.

WHERE TO WRITE:
C/O INDIANAPOLIS COLTS,
P.O. BOX 53500,
INDIANAPOLIS, IN 46253.

Brett Favre

1969—

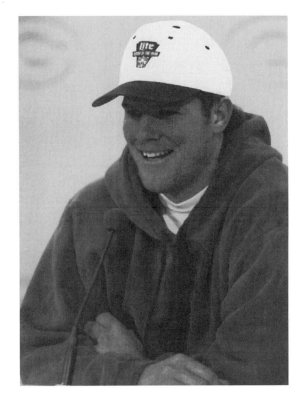

Quarterback Brett Favre of the Green Bay Packers has worked hard to earn respect. After high school, he attended the University of Southern Mississippi because national college football powerhouses did not think he was good enough to play for them. Then, after leading the Southern Mississippi Golden Eagles to upset wins over Florida State and Alabama, Favre again had to prove he could play, this time in the National Football League (NFL). Now, after winning the 1995 NFL Most Valuable Player award, Favre has nothing left to prove and is considered by many to be the best young quarterback in professional football.

"I'm willing to do whatever it takes to win."—Brett Favre

Growing Up

DOWN ON THE BAYOU. Brett Lorenzo Favre (pronounced Fahrv) was born October 10, 1969, in Pass Christian, Mississippi. Favre grew up in Kiln (pronounced Kill), Mississippi, a town of 7,500 residents. His family lived on Irvin Favre Road,

SCOREBOARD

1995 NFL MOST VALUABLE PLAYER.

LED THE NFL IN PASSING YARDS
(4,413) AND TOUCHDOWN PASSES
(38) IN 1995.

THREE-TIME SELECTION TO
PRO BOWL GAME
(1992, 1994, AND 1995).

FAVRE HAS RISEN FROM A SMALL
MISSISSIPPI TOWN TO BE ONE OF
THE BEST PLAYERS IN THE NFL.

a dirt street that dead-ended at a body of water called Rotten Bayou. The city named the street after Favre's father, the local high school baseball and football coach. Favre's mother, Bonita, is a special education teacher at Hancock County High School. Favre is one of three boys and shared a room with his brothers. He also has a sister, Brandi, a former Miss Teen Mississippi.

FINDS HIS POSITION. Favre began playing football at an early age. Coached by his father on his fifth grade team, Favre got his first taste of playing quarterback after starting a game at wide receiver. "I caught a pass, fell on the football and had the wind knocked out of me," Favre recalled in *Sport* magazine. "I'm laying there on the field, crying, and my dad comes out and says, 'Get up you baby.' I told him I didn't want to play wide receiver no more. So he put me at quarterback and that day I threw for two touchdowns and ran for two. I knew this was the position for me. The cheerleaders were cheering and the fans were yelling, and afterwards I felt like man, I'm really good."

PLAYS FOR DAD. Favre was a two-sport star at Hancock North Central High School. In baseball he lettered for four seasons and led the team in hitting each year. Favre played quarterback and safety in football, and also did the placekicking and punting. The Mississippi high school all-star football game invited him to play following his senior season. Hancock retired Favre's number 10 football jersey.

GOLDEN EAGLE. Major college football powerhouses ignored Favre after his senior high school season. He finally got an offer from the University of Southern Mississippi in Hattiesburg, Mississippi. "I've always had to struggle for what I've got," Favre explained in *Sports Illustrated*. "I was never recruited for college. No one really wanted me. Coming from down here, nobody knows who you are. Three days before the signing date, I was going to either Pear River Junior College or Delta State. Southern Miss took me as a defensive back. When I went there as a freshman, I worked out both ways at first. I was the seventh quarterback on the depth chart."

Soon Favre was the Golden Eagles' quarterback. He came into the second game of the season against Tulane and led Southern Mississippi to a victory with two touchdown passes. Favre was now the team's starting quarterback. Over the next four seasons (1987-90) he led the Golden Eagles to 29 victories and two bowl triumphs. Favre set school records for passing yards (8,193), passing attempts (1,234), completions (656), passing percentage (53%), and touchdowns (55). Five times he threw for more than 200 yards in a game, and five times he threw three touchdown passes in one contest.

Favre liked playing for Southern Mississippi because the Golden Eagles were always underdogs. "Southern Miss was a place where everyone had been rejected by the big schools for some reason," Favre said in *Sports Illustrated*. "We were the Island of Misfits. We thrived on that. We'd play Alabama, Auburn, and there'd be stories in the papers about how we'd been rejected by them. We'd come out and win the game, and guys would be yelling on the field, 'What's wrong with us now?' It was a great way to play."

BAD ACCIDENT. Favre's football career almost ended during the summer before his senior season at Southern Mississippi. As he was driving home from the beach, the headlights of another car blinded him and he swerved off the road. Favre's Nissan Maxima flipped over and hit a tree. His brother Scott was following in another car and rescued Favre by breaking the windshield with a golf club and pulling him out. Favre suffered a cracked bone in his back and underwent surgery to

GOOD ARM

Favre has one of the strongest arms in the NFL. He claims he inherited his strength from one of his parents. "Reporters would ask me where I got my arm," Favre revealed in *Sports Illustrated*. "I always thought it was from my father, but now I think I got it from my mother. She got mad at me last summer and threw a pastrami sandwich and hit me in the head. Hard. She really had something on that sandwich. I didn't even know what pastrami was. Except that it hurt." Mrs. Favre explained her actions in the same magazine: "I was really mad. I had the pastrami sandwich in my hand, and I just let it go, mustard and bread flying all over the place."

Favre goes back for a pass during a 1995 play-off game.

remove a 30-inch section of his intestine. "I was out of the hospital, and I thought I was O.K.," Favre recounted in *Sports Illustrated*. "I wasn't eating much, though, and when I did I was throwing up. I kept having these abdominal pains, and they started to get worse. I went back to the hospital, and they found that a lot of my intestines had died." Favre still suffers back and side pains from the accident.

Favre returned to the Golden Eagles lineup in time to start the season. He led Southern Miss to a 27-24 upset victory over Alabama. "You can call it a miracle or a legend or whatever you want to," Alabama coach Gene Stallings told reporters afterward. "I just know that on that day, Brett Favre was larger than life." Southern Mississippi finished Favre's senior year at 8-4. He earned the Most Valuable Player award at the East-West Shrine Game and participated in the Senior Bowl. Southern Mississippi retired Favre's number 4 jersey.

FAVRE AND FALCONS. Despite having a solid senior season at Southern Mississippi, NFL scouts wondered how the injuries suffered in his accident affected Favre. The Atlanta Falcons picked him in the second round of the 1991 NFL Draft, making him the thiry-third player chosen. Favre threw only five passes all season as the third-string quarterback with the Falcons. Not playing was hard on the young quarterback. Favre took out his frustration by partying, staying out late, and not showing up on time for team meetings. He quickly got a bad reputation throughout the league, and many experts thought he would never make it as an NFL quarterback.

PACKER PASSER. Two professionals who still thought highly of Favre were Mike Holmgren, then offensive coordinator of the San Francisco 49ers, and Ron Wolf, an executive with the New York Jets. After the 1991 season the Green Bay Packers hired Holmgren as head coach and Wolf as general manager. The Packers, one of the most successful franchises in NFL history, had won their last championship in 1967, in Super Bowl II.

The first move the new Green Bay leadership team made was to trade a first-round draft pick to the Falcons for Favre. The Packers needed a quarterback because starter Dan Majkowski had missed 14 games and parts of five others with injuries in 1990 and 1991. Experts questioned the trade. "'Have you lost your mind?' was what most people said," Wolf admitted in *Sports Illustrated*. "I just really liked him. He has that unexplainable something about him."

Favre got his chance to start in the third game of the 1992 season when Majkowski injured his ankle. He led the Packers to a 24-23 victory over the Cincinnati Bengals in his first start. Green Bay's last touchdown came on a 92-yard drive that began with only 1:07 to play. Favre hit wide receiver Kitrick Taylor with a 35-yard touchdown pass to win the game with only 13 seconds left.

Favre finished the season as the Packers' starting quarterback. He completed 302 passes for 3,227 yards and 18 touchdowns. Favre threw for 200 yards in each of 11 straight games and the Packers just missed the play-offs with a 9-7 record. His fellow NFL players voted him to the Pro Bowl game. Favre claimed his bad boy reputation helped him with the Packers. "My first year [in Green Bay] I just took everybody by storm, nobody blitzed me, teams just sat back and said, 'This kid will make his own mistakes,'" Favre said in *Sport* magazine.

STARTING QB. Favre's performance in his first season in Green Bay convinced the Packers to drop Majkowski. "If Brett can stay healthy, he will be the cornerstone of our football team for many years to come," Holmgren said. The Packers also won the battle to sign Reggie White, the dominating defensive end, formerly of the Philadelphia Eagles. The season before, White had injured Favre in the seventh game of the season by driving his left shoulder into the turf. The shoulder injury limited Favre's play the rest of the season. "Now Reggie's with us," Favre explained to *Sports Illustrated*. "I talked with him at minicamp. He said he thought for sure he had put me out. I told him I just about thought he had too. Then he put his arm around me. He told me not to worry, that this year we were on the same side. I liked that."

Favre had an up-and-down season in 1993. He threw for 3,303 yards and 19 touchdowns but also led the NFL with 24 interceptions. He forced many passes, always looking for the big play instead of the safe play. "I [tell] myself, 'There's gotta be something better,'" Favre revealed in *Sports Illustrated,* explaining why he often made mistakes. "That's my problem. Sometimes there's not something better." Favre added in *Sport* magazine: "Over the years, I've just got to where I love the big play. I love to hear the roar of the crowd. I like to roll left and throw right, throw underhand and dive, some of the things that give [Coach] Holmgren gray hair. That's what makes me tick." After two seasons as a starter, Favre had 37 touchdown passes and 37 interceptions.

PACKER PLAY-OFFS. The Packers had a chance to win the National Football Conference (NFC) Central Division title in their last regular season game against the Detroit Lions.

Favre, however, threw four interceptions, and Green Bay lost 30-20. The team still qualified for the play-offs for the first time since 1982. The Packers traveled to Detroit to face the Lions in their first play-off game. Favre threw an interception in the third quarter, which Lions cornerback Melvin Jenkins returned for a touchdown.

The Lions led 24-21 with only one minute remaining in the game. Green Bay had the ball near midfield, and Favre rolled out to pass. Amazingly, All-Pro receiver Sterling Sharpe was wide open in the corner of the end zone. Favre threw the ball, Sharpe caught it, and the Packers won the game 28-24. The winning touchdown pass traveled 60 yards in the air. "I lost my helmet, my earpads," an excited Favre told *Sports Illustrated* after the victory. "I started hyperventilating. I was looking for someone to kiss."

Next the Packers faced the defending Super Bowl champion Dallas Cowboys. Green Bay fell behind 17-3 at halftime and could not recover. Dallas won the game 27-17. Favre played well, throwing for 331 yards and two touchdowns. The Cowboys went on to win their second straight Super Bowl.

Superstar

ONE OF THE BEST. Before the 1994 season Favre signed a lucrative (well-paying) contract with the Packers. He earned his money in 1994 and took his place among the best quarterbacks in the NFL. He threw for 3,882 yards (second in the NFL) and 33 touchdowns (also second in the NFL). Favre also finished second to Steve Young of the San Francisco 49ers in the NFL's complicated passing efficiency system. "He's the best young quarterback I've seen in years," Denver Broncos lineman Gary Zimmerman told *Sport* magazine.

The Packers qualified for the NFL play-offs for the second straight season. They entered the play-offs without Sharpe, one of their major offensive weapons. Sharpe, who had caught 18 of Favre's touchdown passes during the season, suffered a career-threatening neck injury in the last game of the regular season. The Packers' defense came up big against the Lions in the first round of the play-offs, holding Barry Sanders to minus one yard rushing. Green Bay defeated Detroit, 16-12. Dallas crushed the Packers the next week, 35-9. Favre played well in the play-offs, but the offense missed Sharpe and had trouble moving the ball.

BEST SEASON. Before the 1995 season Sharpe announced his retirement because of his neck injury. The injury was serious enough that another hit could paralyze him. Experts believed the loss of the All-Pro receiver would hurt Favre. The Packer quarterback disagreed. "I know he was a great player, but we're a better team this year without Sterling," Favre said in *Sports Illustrated.* "Last year we'd put so many plays into the game plan designed for Sterling that I'd go back to pass thinking, I've got to get it to Sterling. Now I just go back and read. If the first guy's not free, I go to the next guy. We're spreading the ball among all our receivers."

MVP. Favre and the Packers had outstanding seasons in 1995. Robert Brooks more than adequately replaced Sharpe, catching 102 passes for 1,497 yards and 13 touchdowns, and tight end Mark Chmura turned in an All-Pro season. Having so many targets helped Favre lead the NFL in passing yards with 4,413 and in touchdowns with 38 scoring tosses, the most ever by an NFC quarterback and the third most in NFL history. (Only Dan Marino has thrown for more touchdowns in a season.) "In every phase, I still can get better," Favre admitted in the *Sporting News,* "but for me, better decision-making has been the difference—my ability to go to the third and fourth receiver a lot."

For the second straight season Favre finished second in passing efficiency in the NFL, this time trailing Jim Harbaugh of the Indianapolis Colts. More important, Favre showed improved maturity in leading the Packers to an 11-5 record and the NFC Central Division championship. His season earned Favre the 1995 NFL Most Valuable Player award.

SO CLOSE. Green Bay suffered another setback just before the play-offs began. Reggie White pulled a muscle in his leg, and doctors said the injury required surgery. Miraculously, White continued to play, although not at full speed. The Packers defeated the Atlanta Falcons in the first round of the play-offs, 37-20, before an enthusiastic crowd at Lambeau Field in Green Bay.

Most experts believed that was as far as the Packers would go because their next opponent was the defending Super Bowl champion San Francisco 49ers. In a stunning upset, Green Bay defeated the 49ers, 27-17. Favre played an almost perfect game. He completed 21 of 28 passes for two touchdowns and did not throw an interception.

BART STARR

The last time the Packers made the play-offs for three straight years was 1967. The quarterback of that team was Bart Starr. Starr played from 1956 to 1971 and threw for 24,718 yards and 152 touchdowns. He led the Packers to five NFL championships and two Super Bowl victories. The Professional Football Hall of Fame inducted Starr in 1977.

DALLAS DEAD-END. The Packers were in the NFC Championship Game, but for the third straight year they lost to the Cowboys, 38-27. Favre had an inconsistent game. He completed 21 of 39 passes for 307 yards and three touchdowns, but he also threw two important interceptions, his first of the play-offs. Both interceptions, including one by defensive lineman Leon Lett on the Packers' 13-yard line, led to Dallas touchdowns.

The loss disappointed Favre. "I'm just upset," he admitted in the *Sporting News*. "I know 28 teams have to go home before the Super Bowl, but we felt we could take the next step and go all the way this year. But I'd like to think that next year will be our Super Bowl year."

OFF THE FIELD. Favre built his family a new house on Irvin Favre Road in Kiln. He lives there in the off-season with his girlfriend, Deanna Tynes, and daughter, Brittany. "People say, 'You're the quarterback of the Green Bay Packers and you still live at home?'" Favre related in *Sports Illustrated*. "Well, I could be other places, but I can't think of one I'd rather be. Where else could I have so much fun? That's what this is all about. Having fun."

Favre likes to play basketball and golf and enjoys hunting. His nickname is "Country." In September 1994 the NFL named Favre's fourth grade teacher, Billy Ray Dedeaux, its

Teacher of the Month. Favre donates his time to work with the Special Olympics. He majored in special education at Southern Mississippi.

Favre is very intense on the field. "I'm willing to do whatever it takes to win," Favre explained to *Sport* magazine. "I love blocking and I love throwing the bomb. If I would've been [300] pounds, I could've been a nose tackle. I have that mentality, and I think that's great for a quarterback." He is also tough, starting 61 consecutive games, the longest current streak for NFL quarterbacks. Favre sets his goals high, as he related in *Sport* magazine: "I think I'll be in the Hall of Fame one day. Whether it happens or not, at least I think that way. And so far it's worked for me."

Sources

Sport, February 1994; November 1995.

Sporting News, January 17, 1994; January 24, 1994; January 9, 1995; January 16, 1995; January 8, 1996; January 15, 1996; January 22, 1996.

Sports Illustrated, October 5, 1992; August 23, 1993; January 17, 1994; January 16, 1995; October 30, 1995.

Additional information provided by Green Bay Packers and the University of Southern Mississippi.

WHERE TO WRITE:
C/O GREEN BAY PACKERS,
P.O. BOX 10628,
GREEN BAY, WI 54307.

Sergei Fedorov

1969—

O ver the course of the 1993-94 season, his fourth in the National Hockey League (NHL), Detroit Red Wings center Sergei Fedorov made a strong case for being the most complete player in hockey. Having established himself in his first three seasons as one of the game's finest two-way players—equally capable of scoring goals and stopping his opponent—Fedorov went from being an outstanding player to being one of the dominant stars in the league. Fedorov is the first non-Canadian-trained player to win the Hart Trophy, awarded annually to the NHL's Most Valuable Player (MVP).

> *"As far as I'm concerned, when the team [wins everyone] has fun."*
> *—Sergei Fedorov*

Fedorov followed his MVP season with another great year in 1995. He led the Red Wings to the Stanley Cup Finals, but unfortunately the New Jersey Devils were too tough. Not as tough, however, as what Fedorov had to overcome just to join the NHL.

SCOREBOARD

1993-94 HART MEMORIAL TROPHY WINNER AS THE NHL'S MOST VALUABLE PLAYER.

FIRST NON-CANADIAN-TRAINED PLAYER TO BE NHL MOST VALUABLE PLAYER.

ONE OF THE BEST TWO-WAY PLAYERS IN THE NHL, WHOSE GREATEST ESCAPE WAS FROM HIS NATIVE COUNTRY.

Growing Up

LEARNS FROM DAD. Sergei Fedorov (pronounced SAIR-gay FED-uh-rov) was born December 13, 1969, in Pskov, USSR (now Russia). His father, Viktor, was a hockey coach and former soccer player. His mother's name is Natalia. Fedorov's father had a big influence on him. "He knows a lot about hockey, about how to get from one level to another," Fedorov told *Inside Line*. "Even when I was playing at the highest levels in Russia he still would talk to me about it, how to prevent injuries and stuff, what I should do and shouldn't do. And he knew." Fedorov also played tennis in high school.

ARMY ATTACK. The USSR required all young men to serve in the military. Because of his talent, the powerful Central Red Army hockey team recruited Fedorov. His linemates were Pavel Bure and Alexander Mogilny, both of the Vancouver Canucks. "We were like kids playing together who had played together all our lives," Fedorov remembered in the *Sporting News*. "We had that great feeling you get when you understand a teammate so well. I don't know if we realized how good we all were individually, but we knew how well we worked together. It was fun. Nobody was thinking about anything like the NHL back then." The Red Army team was famous for its brilliant and creative play and played or practiced 11 months of the year. Fedorov helped his Central Red Army team win gold medals in the 1989 and 1990 world championships.

FLIES TO WINGS. Experts throughout the world knew Fedorov as one of the bright young stars of the Red Army team. In 1989 executives of the Detroit Red Wings used their fourth pick in the NHL Draft, the seventy-fourth pick overall, to choose Fedorov. The team sent a representative to Norway, where Fedorov was playing in a tournament, to inform him that the Red Wings were interested in signing him. Fedorov and the Red Army team

Fedorov plans his strategy.

toured the United States in January 1990. A Red Wings executive met with Fedorov in a Chicago, Illinois, hotel.

Six months later, while the Russian national team was in the United States to participate in the Goodwill Games, Fedorov slipped away from his teammates. He boarded the plane of Red Wings owner Mike Illitch in Portland, Oregon, leaving his home, family, friends, and teammates behind. He was now a Red Wing. "I felt like I had to do something," Fedorov told the *Sporting News,* "because I had no future as a hockey player in my country. By then, I knew I had a contract in the U.S., a place to live, a sports car."

DIFFERENT GAME. The move to the NHL was a big adjustment for Fedorov. Learning a new language was the biggest problem early on. "I try," he told *Inside Hockey*. "Sometimes I just get stuck. I forget some words and I get so frustrated my head just aches." The North American game itself was different from the faster, more graceful Soviet game. Getting used to the aggressive body-checking of the pro game was a challenge. "Hockey in the NHL is much more physical and quite different from European hockey," Fedorov explained in the *Sporting News*. "It's not very physical in Europe because of the big ice surface. I like the physical hockey. And I enjoy the speed and puckhandling. It was hard to learn at first, but I have grown to like this game better because it's such a challenge each night."

The other parts of Fedorov's game—his skating, stickhandling, passing, and shooting skills—were more than ready for the NHL. In Fedorov's first season, he led all rookies in the league in goals, assists, points, shots, and game-winning goals. He was selected for the 1990-91 All-Rookie team and finished second in the voting for the Calder Trophy, awarded to the league's best rookie.

A visit by his family to the United States between his first and second seasons helped lessen Fedorov's homesickness. His teammates, especially linemate Shawn Burr, tried to make him feel at home. Fedorov began to loosen up. He bought a Chevy Blazer and became a fan of heavy metal music, including Guns N' Roses, Mötley Crüe, and Ozzy Osbourne. He also took up in-line skating, fishing, and golf, and became more at ease with fans. "I think he's come a long way both on and off the ice here, especially maybe in understanding what the role of an NHL player is, understanding his role as a role model," his first Red Wing coach, Brian Murray, told *Inside Line*. "He was sometimes not very obliging at first about things like signing autographs, but only because he didn't understand what a big deal he, as an NHL player, was."

ALL-STAR. Fedorov continued to dominate the league in his second and third seasons. He made the NHL All-Star team each season. Fedorov also began to gain a reputation as a great all-around player. In 1991-92 he finished second in the voting for the Selke Trophy, awarded to the NHL's best defensive forward. "I like to play both ways," Fedorov told *Inside Hockey*. "It's more interesting. I would like to score more but I have many good changes. And I have great partners. I play to them. If I shoot, maybe it's a 60 percent, 80 percent goal. But if I pass to them, it's an open net and a goal 100 percent of the time."

Superstar

MVP. Fedorov brought his family to the United States during the 1993-94 season. The Red Wings also had a new coach, the legendary Scotty Bowman. When Captain Steve Yzerman injured his neck early in the season, Fedorov had his chance to grab the limelight. He made the most of his opportunity, improving every part of his game. Fedorov scored 56 goals (third in the NHL), 22 more than he had scored before in one season. He also had a career high 64 assists. Fedorov's 120 points placed him second in the NHL, next to Wayne Gretzky of the Los Angeles Kings. He was rewarded for his great season when he was presented with both the Selke and Hart Trophies. He became the first non-Canadian-trained player to be named the NHL's Most Valuable Player. Red Wings teammate Mark Howe, whose father, the great Gordie Howe, was the last Red Wing to win the Hart Trophy, described Fedorov in *Sports Illustrated* as "the strongest skater I've seen in 21 years. He's got unbelievable balance, strength, and speed. The guy just doesn't get knocked down."

The major disappointment of 1993-94, as it had been in each of Fedorov's other seasons in the NHL, was the Red Wings' early exit in the play-offs. The San Jose Sharks defeated the heavily favored Red Wings in seven games in the first round. "Last season was a little bit frustrating," Fedorov told *Inside Line* after the play-offs. "Maybe we put our noses in the air a little, you know, being the best scoring team in the

FAN HIMSELF

Fedorov quickly realized that being a fan in the United States is much different from being a fan in the USSR. "The first time I saw the band Guns N' Roses I wanted a signed CD for myself," Fedorov recalled in the *Sporting News*. "It was cool to have, it was fun. So I can understand someone maybe wanting an autograph with me and Paul Coffey and Steve Yzerman or something. You wouldn't see that with people in Russia because they're thinking about what they have to do to survive."

NHL. In the play-offs there can be many surprises. It's tough to think about because we lost. You can blame anything and anybody, but that's the way it is. The most important thing is to get together and work as hard as we can."

GOING HOME. A disagreement between the NHL players and owners threatened to cancel the 1994-95 season. The disagreement involved player salaries and free agency, the ability of a player to move from one team to another. Because of the disagreement, Fedorov returned to his homeland as part of a touring team of Russian NHL stars. The NHL team defeated the Central Red Army team 6-5. Fedorov also found time to get to know the great Wayne Gretzky, with whom he had become friends at the All-Star game. "He is a first class individual," Gretzky told the *Detroit News*. "He cares a lot about the game and he loves the game. When we have young people around like that, the league can only go up."

LEADERSHIP. It took until January 1995 to settle the disagreement between NHL owners and players. The NHL shortened the season to 48 games and decided that teams would only play opponents from their own conference. Before the season, Bowman called his team leaders, Fedorov, Yzerman, and defenseman Paul Coffey, together. He told them that he wanted to change the Red Wings' style. Bowman said he wanted the high-scoring team to concentrate more on defense, a key ingredient in play-off games. The team leaders agreed with their coach and pledged to set an example.

The new strategy worked. The Red Wings finished the season with more points than any other team in the NHL. They also finished second in the NHL in fewest goals given up. Fedorov, always a great defensive player, further sacrificed his offense. He finished fourteenth in the league in scoring with 20 goals and 30 assists, but his defense and leadership were outstanding. "Sergei's young, he's good defensively and he's a nightmare to stop on a breakaway," teammate Chris Osgood told *Sporting News*.

FINALS FLOP. The Red Wings flew through the play-offs and entered the Stanley Cup Finals as the overwhelming favorite to defeat the New Jersey Devils. Unfortunately, the Devils had different ideas. Using a tight defensive game-plan, the Devils shut down the Red Wings' offense. When it was over, the Red Wings had lost four straight games. Fedorov suffered an injured shoulder in the conference finals against the Chicago Blackhawks, an injury that slowed him down during the finals. Still, he led all NHL players in goals scored and points made during the play-offs.

Fellow NHL players recognize Fedorov as one of the league's best players. "I think he could be [as good as] Gretzky, he just doesn't realize it yet," Fedorov's teammate Paul Coffey, who played with both Gretzky and Mario Lemieux, told the *Sporting News*. "With a guy like Sergei, the sky's the limit. He could be the best player on the ice every night. He's got the ability, because of his skating, to pick the puck up and say, 'OK, I'm going to get a goal' or 'I'm going to set up a goal.'"

OFF THE ICE. Fedorov is single and lives in suburban Detroit. He enjoys playing golf. Being one of the top players in the league carries responsibility. "Hockey's such a great and exciting sport," Fedorov told the *Detroit News*. "I would like to do as much as I can for the league." Despite his personal success, Fedorov knows that the team comes first. "As far as I'm concerned," Fedorov told *Inside Line,* "when the team wins, everybody has fun."

Sources

Detroit News, June 17, 1994.
Inside Hockey, March/April 1992.
Inside Line, December 1993; October 1994.
New York Newsday, November 15, 1994.
Sporting News, January 4, 1993; December 27, 1993; January 24, 1994; February 21, 1994; May 9, 1994; May 30, 1994; April 17, 1995.
Sports Illustrated, January 24, 1994; May 9, 1994; July 3, 1995.
Vogue, November 1994.
Additional information provided by Detroit Red Wings.

WHERE TO WRITE:
C/O DETROIT RED WINGS, JOE LOUIS ARENA,
600 CIVIC CENTER DR.,
DETROIT, MI 48226.

Tom Glavine

1966—

"He's the type of pitcher who wins when he doesn't have his best stuff."
—Leo Mazzone, Atlanta Braves pitching coach

In October 1995 Tom Glavine stood on the mound facing the most powerful team he had ever pitched against. A win would give his team, the Atlanta Braves, the World Series championship. The road to this point had taken many turns for Glavine. He had given up a promising hockey career to play professional baseball, he had developed his trademark circle change-up pitch (by accident), and he had taken an unpopular stand for what he believed in during the players' strike that forced an early ending the 1994 season. Glavine's 1995 World Series-clinching victory against the Cleveland Indians made all the twists and turns of his career worth the trouble and further established him as one of the best pitchers in the major leagues.

Growing Up

LOVED SPORTS. Thomas Michael Glavine was born March 25, 1966, in Concord, Massachusetts. His father, Fred, owns a small construction business in their hometown of Billerica, Massachusetts, a suburb of Boston. Glavine's dad encouraged his son to play sports, but only if he wanted to. "He never pushed me to become an athlete," Glavine recalled in *Sports Illustrated for Kids*. "I became an athlete because I loved sports, especially baseball and hockey."

HOCKEY FAVORITE GAME. Glavine first began to skate when he was only four years old. He later played in local hockey leagues. He first played Little League baseball when he was seven, but hockey was still his favorite sport. "I was always playing football, baseball, or street hockey with the kids in my neighborhood," Glavine remembered in *Sports Illustrated for Kids*. "My dream was to become a professional athlete, but I knew that millions of kids had the same dream."

Glavine never told anyone about his dream. "Sometimes my teachers asked the class to write about what we wanted to be when we grew up," Glavine confessed in *Sports Illustrated for Kids*. "I always wrote about something other than becoming a pro athlete. I was never sure I would make it as a pro, and I was afraid they would think my dream was silly."

ALWAYS THE YOUNGEST. Most of the teams Glavine played on as a youngster were made up of older kids. "He had to be mature," his father told *Sports Illustrated*. "He's one of those kids who was always playing each level of sports at the earliest age. He was just an athlete, good enough so the older kids would let him play. He was always the youngest."

TWO-SPORT STAR. Glavine was an outstanding baseball and hockey player at Billerica Memorial High School. In hockey he played against future Pittsburgh Penguins stars Tom Barrasso and Kevin Stevens and New York Rangers Brian Leetch. Glavine was named the outstanding Boston area high school hockey player as a senior. A National Hockey League

SCOREBOARD

1991 NATIONAL LEAGUE CY YOUNG AWARD WINNER.

1995 WORLD SERIES MOST VALUABLE PLAYER.

WON 20 OR MORE GAMES FOR THREE STRAIGHT SEASONS (1991-93).

GLAVINE GAVE UP A PROMISING HOCKEY CAREER TO BECOME ONE OF THE BEST PITCHERS IN THE NATIONAL LEAGUE.

Firing a pitch, Glavine leads the Braves to a victory.

(NHL) scout evaluated Glavine and rated him fifty-sixth out of 240 draft-age players.

The Los Angeles Kings chose Glavine in the fourth round of the NHL Draft, ahead of such future stars as Brett Hull and Luc Robitaille. "I never was too keen about Tommy playing pro hockey," Mr. Glavine admitted in *Sports Illustrated*. "Hockey, it's a long haul. He probably could have made it, but to really succeed? It seems to me there are a number of players who are expendable every year. There's tremendous turnover."

Of course, Glavine was also a standout on the Billerica baseball team. His finest moment came in the state championship game against Brockton High. Glavine pitched the first nine innings and left the mound with the score tied 1-1. He moved to center field and threw a runner out at the plate in the eleventh inning. "Of all the things he did in high school, the one that's probably remembered best is that throw from center," Mr. Glavine stated in *Sports Illustrated*. "He got the kid by about 15 feet." In the thirteenth, Glavine singled and eventually scored the winning run. He earned the *Boston Globe* All-Scholastic and Player of the Year honors in both baseball and hockey.

BIG DECISION. The Atlanta Braves drafted Glavine in the second round of the 1984 major league baseball draft. "The decision never was whether to play hockey," Glavine explained in *Sports Illustrated*. "The decision was whether to go to college. I had a full hockey scholarship to the University of Lowell. That was a big thing. Four years of college for free." Glavine turned down the scholarship offer and signed with the Braves. "I thought my chances of a long career would be better as a pitcher," Glavine said in *Sports Illustrated for Kids*.

BIG LEAGUER. Glavine started out playing in a rookie league in Bradenton, Florida, where he struck out 34 batters in 32 innings. He then moved to the Braves Sumter, South Carolina, team in the South Atlantic League in 1985 and the Greenville, South Carolina, team in 1986. Glavine's rapid rise through the Braves' minor league system resulted in his call up to the big league team in August 1987. He won his first major league game August 22 against the Pittsburgh Pirates.

NEW PITCH. Glavine stayed with the Braves for the 1988 season. Atlanta was a bad team, finishing 54-106. Glavine pitched well, but wound up with a 7-17 record and 4.56 earned run average (ERA). Glavine realized he needed another pitch, something to keep hitters from teeing off on his aver-

FROM THE RINK TO THE MOUND

Has his hockey background helped Glavine become an outstanding major league pitcher? He says his competitiveness and mental toughness might come from the rink. "The question I'm always asked again and again is what I learned from hockey to bring to baseball," Glavine told *Sports Illustrated*. "I've thought about it a lot. The games are so different, requiring such different skills. What's the same? I suppose I could say mental toughness or aggressiveness, something like that might come from hockey."

age fastball. During spring training of 1989 Glavine stumbled on the answer. He picked up a ball during batting practice, gripped it in an unusual way, and threw it back into the infield. The unusual grip felt natural and was the key to Glavine's amazing change-up. "Throwing that way just seemed natural to me," Glavine recalled in *Sports Illustrated*. "I don't know why, but from that first throw the pitch was natural. I started throwing it that day."

The new pitch helped Glavine improve. He finished 14-8 in 1989 with a 3.68 ERA and seemed to be on his way. Glavine slumped, however, to 10-12 in 1990 with a 4.28 ERA. He admits now that the slump was caused by not using his change-up enough. "After the 1989 season, I thought I was going to take off," Glavine admitted in *Sports Illustrated*. "It didn't work out."

Superstar

CY YOUNG. John Schuerholz became the Braves' general manager in 1990, and former general manager Bobby Cox became the team's manager. Schuerholz slowly began putting together the pieces of a championship team. Glavine's breakthrough year was 1991. He started 6-0, and the National League named him the starting pitcher in the All-Star Game. Glavine pitched two innings in the mid-summer classic, holding the American League scoreless. He finished the season 20-11 with a 2.55 ERA (third in the National League). Reporters covering the National League rewarded Glavine for his great season by voting him winner of the Cy Young Award, symbolic of the best pitcher in the National League. He also won the Silver Slugger Award as the league's best-hitting pitcher.

WORST TO FIRST. Atlanta made a remarkable turnaround in 1991. The Braves, who had finished last in their division in 1990, won the National League West Division title. Atlanta defeated the Pittsburgh Pirates in a tough seven-game National League Championship Series. Glavine lost two games in the series, one of them a hard-luck 1-0 defeat. The Braves went on to face the American League champion, the Minnesota Twins, in the World Series. Minnesota had also gone "from worst to first" in the 1991 season.

WORLD SERIES I. The 1991 World Series was one of the most dramatic and hard-fought ever. Five of the seven games were decided by one run. Glavine lost Game Two, 3-2, but came back with a 14-5 victory in Game Five. Atlanta led the Series 3-2, but the last two games were in Minnesota. The Braves lost Game Six, 4-3, on an eleventh-inning home run by Kirby Puckett. Atlanta pitcher John Smoltz and Minnesota pitcher Jack Morris dueled in Game Seven. The game was tied 0-0 going into the bottom of the tenth inning. Dan Gladden of the Twins slid home with the Series-winning run in that inning, giving Minnesota the championship. The home team won every game in the Series.

WORLD SERIES II. Glavine followed up his Cy Young season with another great year in 1992. He went 20-8 with a 2.76 ERA. In one span, from May 27 to August 19, Glavine won 13 games in a row. He became the first National League pitcher to start back-to-back All-Star Games since Robin Roberts of the Philadelphia Phillies was given the honor in 1954 and 1955. Glavine finished second in the voting for the Cy Young Award, which went to Greg Maddux of the Chicago Cubs.

The Braves won the National League West Division title for the second straight season. They once again faced the Pirates in a seven-game National League Championship Series. Atlanta won the first two games at home, but Glavine lost Game Three in Pittsburgh, 3-2. Glavine had a chance to close out the series in Game Six, but lasted only one inning in a 13-4 loss. Atlanta trailed in the ninth inning of Game Seven, 2-0, but scored three runs in their final at-bats to win the game and the series.

Glavine won Game One of the World Series, defeating the Toronto Blue Jays, the American League champion, 3-1. Atlanta then dropped the next three, including a 2-1 complete-game (a pitcher is credited with a complete game when he pitches the entire game for his team) loss by Glavine in Game Four. The Braves won Game Five, 7-2, to keep their hopes alive, but lost Game Six, 4-3, in 11 innings. The Blue Jays became the first team from Canada to win the World Series.

FOUR ACES. The Braves improved themselves during the off-season when they signed Greg Maddux as a free agent. They now had the last two Cy Young Award winners on their staff, in addition to solid starters in John Smoltz and Steve Avery. "We all want each other to do well," Glavine told *Sports Illustrated*. "And we all want to do better than the last guy. No question, we all want to outdo each other."

The Braves dueled the San Francisco Giants and each other during the 1993 season. Glavine was outstanding again, winning more than 20 games—he finished 22-6—for the third straight season. This was the first time a National League pitcher had accomplished this feat since Ferguson Jenkins won 20 games each season from 1967 through 1972.

The Braves battled the Giants down the stretch. Glavine was almost perfect in the clutch. He won eight of his last nine games and 11 of his last 13 decisions when Atlanta had to win. The Braves came down to the last game of the season needing a win to capture their third straight National League West crown. Manager Bobby Cox gave the ball to Glavine, who did not let his manager down. He helped beat the Colorado Rockies to give the Braves the title. The Braves would not return to the World Series, however, losing in the National League Championship Series to the Philadelphia Phillies.

STRUCK OUT. The 1994 season was frustrating for Glavine. He finished the season with a 13-9 record, but his ERA rose to 3.96. The Braves were in contention for the lead in the newly formed National League East Division, fighting the Montreal Expos. Then, on August 12, the players went on strike, ending the season early. The players and owners could not agree on issues like players' salaries and free agency.

Glavine, as one of the leaders of the players' union, received a lot of criticism during the strike. Fans called local talk radio shows in Atlanta and said that he was greedy. "Normally, you're under scrutiny for what you do on the field," Glavine explained in the *Sporting News*. "It's difficult for me to be looked at in a positive or negative way for the situation we're in now. I'd rather people say he pitched good or he stinks, rather than form opinions on the labor situation. It's not what we all signed up to do."

COMEBACK. Glavine knew he would have to pitch well in 1995 to win back the fans, but the team's winning was most important, he said. "I certainly will try to get off to a good start, but I'll try to do it to help my team," Glavine told the *Sporting News*. "Obviously the more success I have the quicker people will forget." Atlanta fans booed Glavine on opening day, a tough experience for the Braves' player who had been with the team the longest.

The Braves and Glavine dominated the National League East in 1995. Atlanta ran away with the National League East Division title, far outdistancing the Phillies and the Expos. Glavine finished the season 16-7 with a 3.08 ERA. He wound up third in the voting for the National League's Cy Young Award, which was won for a record-setting fourth straight season by Maddux.

PENNANT CHASE. The Braves entered the 1995 play-offs as the favorite, but they were still nervous. They had been the best team in baseball during the 1990s but had not won a World Series. Atlanta had lost eight World Series games, six of them in the opposing team's last at-bat. Glavine was only 1-4 in the play-offs and 2-2 in the World Series. The Braves beat the Colorado Rockies in the Division Series, 3-1, and then swept the Cincinnati Reds in four straight games to win the National League pennant.

CHAMPIONS. The Braves faced the American League champion Cleveland Indians in the World Series. Cleveland had won an amazing 100 of 148 games during the regular season. The Indians' team batting average was .291, the best mark in 45 years. The Indians featured such hitters as **Albert Belle** (see entry), Carlos Baerga, and Eddie Murray. Glavine explained in *Sports Illustrated* that "everyone is talking about the key being their hitting against our pitching."

The Braves won the first two games in Atlanta. Maddux shut down the Indians in the first game, giving up only two hits in a 3-2 victory. Glavine pitched six strong innings in Game Two. The game was tied 2-2 when Atlanta catcher Javier Lopez hit a clutch two-run home run in the bottom of the sixth. The Braves' bull pen pitched the last three innings in a 4-3 Atlanta win.

The Indians came back to win two of the next three games, all in Cleveland. The Braves returned to Atlanta in a familiar position—one win away from the championship. Three times in five years Atlanta had failed to win the final game, each time losing by one run. Glavine would pitch Game Six, his first chance at winning a World Series clinching victory.

A CLASSIC. Glavine's performance was one of the greatest in World Series history. He pitched eight innings, gave up only one hit, and shut out the powerful Cleveland attack. Glavine fooled the Indians with his change-up, painting the outside corner with his best pitch. He left the game after the eighth inning with a 1-0 lead provided by a home run by outfielder Dave Justice. Closer Mark Wohlers blew away the Indians in the ninth inning, preserving the win for Glavine. Atlanta had finally won the World Series, the first team in the South to win baseball's biggest prize.

Glavine won the World Series Most Valuable Player Award. "Number one, you've got to trust yourself," Glavine told *Sports Illustrated* after the game. "I've got so much confidence in my change-up that I can stand on the mound and tell you it's coming and, if it's a good one, you're not going to hit it." Cleveland batted only .179 during the Series, and Glavine lowered his postseason ERA to 1.83 in 86 innings.

WHY SO GOOD? Glavine does not have an overpowering fastball to blow hitters away. He relies on fooling hitters, using his best pitch, the change-up. "He's got command of four pitches:

the fastball, curveball, slider, and change," Mazzone told *Sports Illustrated*. "He has great control, and he can change speeds as well as anyone in this game." Glavine's main strength, however, is his mental toughness. "Tommy's never let anything bother him," his mother revealed in *Sports Illustrated*. "Not even as a kid. I think our whole family's like that. We just don't let things bother us." Mazzone added in the *Sporting News:* "He takes care of business in a very professional manner. Whatever is working for him on a particular night, he'll use. He's the type of pitcher who wins when he doesn't have his best stuff."

OFF THE FIELD. Glavine lives in Alpharetta, Georgia, with his wife, Carri, and their daughter, Amber. He still plays hockey, and one time skated in practice with the Boston Bruins. Glavine also plays golf. He likes rock music, and his favorite movie is *Caddyshack.*

WHITEY FORD

The player Glavine is most often compared with is Whitey Ford, the great New York Yankees left-handed pitcher of the 1950s and 1960s. Ford started in 22 World Series games and won ten. This is more than any other pitcher in major league history. Ford never had an overpowering fastball but relied on changing speeds and control, much like Glavine. Braves pitching coach Leo Mazzone first noticed the similarities between the two pitchers. "I was telling him the other day that when I was growing up, my idol as a pitcher was Whitey Ford," Mazzone recalled in *Sports Illustrated.* "Tommy is the Whitey Ford of today."

Glavine's parents taught their son a very valuable lesson: "They taught me that sports are not a life-or-death situation," Glavine revealed in *Sports Illustrated for Kids.* "The main thing is to have fun."

Sources

Baseball Digest, September 1994.
Men's Health, September 1994.
Sporting News, October 18, 1993; May 1, 1995.
Sports Illustrated, June 10, 1991; July 13, 1992; April 5, 1993; October 16, 1995; October 23, 1995; October 30, 1995; November 6, 1995.
Sports Illustrated for Kids, December 1992.
Additional information provided by Atlanta Braves.

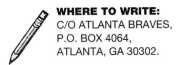

WHERE TO WRITE:
C/O ATLANTA BRAVES,
P.O. BOX 4064,
ATLANTA, GA 30302.

Jeff Gordon

1971—

"Nobody had to teach Michael Jordan how to play basketball, and nobody taught Jeff Gordon how to drive."
—Ray Evernham, Jeff Gordon's crew chief

Jeff Gordon was born to race. He first got behind the wheel at the age of four and has been there ever since. Gordon has won championships at every level and in 1995 became the second-youngest driver to win the prestigious National Association for Stock Car Automobile Racing (NASCAR) Winston Cup Series championship. The championship established Gordon as the hottest young driver in stock car racing. He is also among the most popular drivers in the fast growing world of motor sports.

Growing Up

BORN TO RACE. Jeff Gordon was born August 4, 1971, in Vallejo, California. Gordon's stepfather, John Bickford, got his son involved in racing at an early age. Gordon started in bicycle motocross at age four. His mother, Carol, put a stop to that, telling *Sports Illustrated* years later, "At BMX races they were hauling kids away in ambulances all the time."

Racing became Gordon's life, even when he played with his friends. "Man, I had lots and lots of Hot Wheels," the *Charlotte News and Observer* reported Gordon as saying. "Me and a buddy used to set up a track with my Lincoln Logs in the front room of our house and make a race track and race cars around. We used to make sprint cars out of Legos and we'd race those things around. We would go to sprint car races, make race tracks and cars and play in the dirt."

Bickford bought Gordon a quarter-midget, six-foot-long race car when his son was still a child. By the time Gordon was eight years old, Bickford had him racing 52 weekends a year, traveling over much of the country. In 1979 Gordon won the national quarter-midget championship.

SCOREBOARD

1995 WINSTON CUP SERIES CHAMPION.

SECOND-YOUNGEST DRIVER TO WIN WINSTON CUP SERIES CHAMPIONSHIP.

WON FIRST STOCK CAR RACE EVER HELD AT LEGENDARY INDIANAPOLIS MOTOR SPEEDWAY, THE 1994 BRICKYARD 400.

AT AGE 24, GORDON HAS WORKED HIS WAY TO THE VERY TOP OF HIS PROFESSION.

"GET OUTA HERE!" The following year Gordon moved up to go-carts with 10-horsepower engines. "All the other parents were saying Jeff was probably lying about his age, that he was probably 20 and just real little," Bickford recalled in *Sports Illustrated*. "Nobody wanted to race us. That was fine. We moved up to the junior class (with more horsepower), and he still [won]. These kids were 13 to 17, and he was killing them. We then moved up to superstock light. Now we were running against guys 17 and older—unlimited age. We were still winning. And those guys were going, 'There's no nine-year-old kid gonna run with us! Get outa here!'"

Gordon went back to quarter-midgets in 1981 and won his second national championship. He realized he needed to move up. "You get to be 12 years old, and you realize you've been in quarter-midgets for eight years," Gordon explained to *Sports Illustrated*. "What's next? I was getting older, not knowing what I wanted to do next."

BIG MOVE. To find tougher competition Gordon and his family moved to Pittsboro, Indiana, in 1986. Many tracks in the

Gordon and his crew chief talk strategy before the 1995 AC-Delco 400 in North Carolina.

Midwest did not have an age requirement, so Gordon could race larger sprint cars. He and his father built a 1,300-pound, 650-horsepower car for $25,000, and Gordon raced it in Ohio, Illinois, and Indiana. The young driver won three sprint races in Indiana before he was legally old enough to drive.

In 1990, at the age of 18, Gordon began racing on the United States Automobile Club (USAC) sprint car circuit. He drove both 815-horsepower open-wheel sprint cars and 320-horsepower full midgets. Gordon won the season's championship in the midget cars. The following year he made a major career move. Gordon raced both the USAC season and the NASCAR Busch Grand National season, the second most prestigious stock car racing circuit in the country after the NASCAR Winston Cup Series.

It turned out to be a good decision. Gordon won the Silver Crown championship in the sprint cars and Rookie of the Year honors on the Busch tour. Gordon fell in love with stock cars the first time he drove one, at Buck Baker's race care training school in Rockingham, North Carolina. "The car was different from anything I was used to," Gordon related in *Sports Illustrated*. "It was so big and heavy. It felt very fast but very smooth. I loved it." Gordon added in the *Atlanta Journal and Constitution,* "I knew right away, stock car racing was the way I wanted to go."

GETS NOTICED. In 1992 Gordon won 11 poles (the first spot in a race's starting lineup reserved for the car with the fastest qualifying time), setting a record for the Busch circuit. He won three races that season, including one that March in Atlanta, Georgia, which attracted the attention of successful Winston Cup car owner Rick Hendrick. "I caught this white car out of the corner of my eye," Hendrick remembered in *Sports Illustrated*. "As it went into the corner I could see that it was extremely loose (which makes a car faster but harder to control). I said, 'Man, that guy's gonna wreck!' Dale Earnhardt and Harry Gant were leading, and this white car was right up on them. I told the people with me, 'You just can't drive a car that loose.' But the car went on to win the race. I asked who the driver was. Somebody said, 'That's that kid Gordon.'"

Hendrick signed Gordon in May. "I already had two full-time teams, but I knew I had to make room for Jeff," Hendrick said. Gordon participated in one Winston Cup race in 1992, in Atlanta, where he failed to finish. The legendary Richard Petty raced for the last time in this event.

ROOKIE OF THE YEAR. Gordon raced the whole 1993 season with Hendrick. He had success as a rookie, finishing in the top five seven times. He became the first rookie in 30 years, and the youngest driver ever, to win one of the two 125-mile qualifying races for the Daytona 500, the most prestigious stock car race in the world. Gordon also won the pole for a 500-mile race in Charlotte, North Carolina. Racing experts named Gordon the Winston Cup Rookie of the Year.

FIRST PRIZE

In the winner's circle after his first Winston Cup victory, Gordon had another important first. It was there that he first met Brooke Sealey, one of that season's Miss Winston models and a former beauty contest winner. Normally the drivers and models do not date, but Gordon and Sealey fell in love. In order not to get caught, the two had to duck in and out of restaurants if other NASCAR participants came by. Gordon and Sealey did not tell anyone about their relationship until after the season.

"Brooke is my best friend," Gordon said, "the one I can share everything with. She knows everything that's going on in my life and she's a major part of that. There isn't anyone who has brought morals, God, into my life like she has. Before I met her I wasn't the nicest person I could be, the caringest person I could be. She has brought a tremendous amount of that into my life and helped me deal with a lot of the pressures, whether things are going good or bad."

The couple were engaged at Daytona in February 1994, a year after they first met, and were married that November.

Gordon's success on the track continued in 1994. He won two minor events early in the season, then made headlines by winning the Coca-Cola 600 at Charlotte Motor Speedway in North Carolina, one of the NASCAR circuit's major races. It was his first career win in a Winston Cup event that earned points toward the series championship.

MAKES HISTORY. Gordon's biggest moment of the year, however, came at the legendary Indianapolis Motor Speedway, home of the Indianapolis 500. For the first time ever stock cars raced at Indianapolis in a race called the Brickyard 400. No one thought Gordon would win the race, but the hometown press loved him. Pittsboro is just 20 minutes from the speedway, and Gordon had always dreamed of racing there. He qualified third in the 43-car field.

Gordon, Rusty Wallace, and Ernie Irvan battled for the lead throughout most of the race. Irvan led with five laps to go, but then got a flat tire. Gordon, in second place at the time, held off Brett Bodine to clinch the victory. "That's a tough break for Ernie," Gordon recalled in the *Daily Press,* "but you have to have everything going for you."

"This is the greatest thing in the world, far past our expectations," Gordon said during a teary victory lane celebration. "I'm a kid in a candy store with a big smile. Man, I never thought this would happen." Gordon led the race for 93 of the 160 laps and won a NASCAR record $613,000 from the record purse of $3.2 million. "It's pretty neat to be [the] first winner at Indy," Gordon exclaimed in the *Daily Press* after the race.

"WONDER BOY." The NASCAR circuit had been the private kingdom of **Dale Earnhardt** (see entry). Earnhardt won the Winston Cup Series for a record-tying seventh time in 1994, a record matched only by Petty. Earnhardt, poking fun at Gordon, gave him the nickname "Wonder Boy." Gordon finished eighth in the 1994 point standings.

Superstar

FLASH GORDON. The 1995 season began with a bang for Gordon. He won five poles and three races early in the year and finished out of the top four only three times. Gordon took over the lead in the Winston Cup point standings after he won the Slick 50 300 at Loudon, New Hampshire, on July 9. "This has turned into so much more than I ever anticipated," Gordon admitted to the *Atlanta Journal and Constitution*, discussing his fast lane to success. "I have to admit, at 23, you're not expected to do all this. It's amazing to me I've gotten this far."

Gordon outsmarted two rivals to win the Winston Select at the Charlotte Motor Speedway. Darrell Waltrip and Earnhardt tried to sandwich him, but Gordon let up on the gas and forced the two other drivers to bump. Both Earnhardt and Waltrip were forced out of the race, and Gordon won. "Dale got under me so I thought I'd go ahead and let them fight it out," said Gordon. "We were three abreast going into Turn 3. I looked ahead and said there's no way they're going to make it through Turn 4. Sure enough, they didn't. They were trying to take it away from us, and ended up taking it away from themselves."

TEAM LEADER. The biggest disappointment of the year for Gordon came at the Daytona 500. He led 61 of the first 91 laps. A mistake in his pits caused one of Gordon's tires to tear. This error cost him time and knocked his car out of the race when the tire went flat. "I think we had one of the best three cars today, but it doesn't help if you have a good car when you give away the race," Gordon told the *Orlando Sentinel*. "I guess it just wasn't meant to be today." Sterling Marlin edged out Earnhardt to take the checkered flag.

Gordon handled the mistake like a professional. "The Daytona deal … could have shattered this team," his crew chief, Ray Evernham, said after the race. "He, at 23 years old, was leading the Daytona 500 and we have the best or second-best car, he comes in leading and, boom, goes out 20-something because we drop it off the jack. He comes on the radio and says: 'Hey guys, it's just not our day. We can still have a good finish. Don't worry about it.' He could have yelled and screamed and that could have been the end of this team."

CUP CROWN. Gordon won seven races and $2.4 million during 1995 and led at least one lap in 29 of 31 events. He slumped at the end of the season, however, finishing thirtieth, twentieth, fifth, and thirty-second in his last four races. Earnhardt almost came back from a 305 point deficit in the final five races to overtake Gordon and win the championship. Gordon needed to finish forty-first or better in the season-ending NAPA 500 in Hampton, Georgia, to clinch the Winston Cup championship. He finished thirty-second and the championship was his.

"I'm just elated," Gordon exclaimed in the *Chicago Tribune*. "For me to be the Winston Cup champion is more than I even know how to comprehend." Gordon became the second youngest Winston Cup champion. (Bill Rexford was 23 when he won the title in 1950.)

OFF THE TRACK. Gordon and Brooke live on Lake Norman near Davidson, North Carolina. He likes to play basketball and golf and ride on jet skis. Gordon and Brooke like going to movies for a special reason. "The movies have been a great place for Brooke and I to go," Gordon explained in the *Atlanta Journal and Constitution*. "Not many race fans go to the movies during the week." Gordon once flew with the Blue Angels military stunt flying team, but got sick in the process.

NASCAR fans love Gordon. His fan club numbers more than 30,000, and his souvenir sales rank second on the circuit. Gordon gets many requests for interviews and personal appearances. He has become a teen idol, luring tens of thousands of new fans to the fastest-growing form of motor sports.

YOUGEST EVER

Youngest drivers to win the Winston Cup championship

Driver	Year	Age
Bill Rexford	1950	23 years, 229 days
Jeff Gordon	1995	24 years, 100 days
Richard Petty	1964	27 years, 129 days
Terry Labonte	1984	27 years, 360 days
Herb Thomas	1951	28 years, 233 days

Gordon, according to *GQ,* is one of 50 prominent athletes whom the magazine expects to make a significant impact on their professions during the next ten years. "Nobody had to teach Michael Jordan how to play basketball, and nobody taught Jeff Gordon how to drive," Ray Evernham said. "Both may have been taught the fundamentals, but you don't do what they do unless you're a natural."

Gordon appreciates what he has. "I think maybe some people see me and say, 'Here's a guy who's got the world in his hand. He's got everything, and he's just riding along.' It's not like that at all. It hasn't all been easy," Gordon related in *Stock Car Racing.* "It's been difficult at times, frustrating at times, stressful at times. But I have no complaints. I have great parents who gave me the opportunity to be a race car driver. To see the way it's all worked out, it makes my parents heroes in my mind. In Brooke, I met a person who has been wonderful for me. All of that stuff, on top of the racing, has been wonderful. I'm so happy with my life right now. I'd be crazy to say I wasn't."

Sources

Atlanta Journal and Constitution, May 28, 1995.
Beckett Racing, February 1995.
Charlotte Observer, May 21, 1995.

Chicago Tribune, November 13, 1995.
Cincinnati Enquirer, April 19, 1995.
Daily Press, August 6, 1994.
Detroit News, November 11, 1995.
Indianapolis Star, August 7, 1994.
News and Observer, May 13, 1995.
New York Times, July 16, 1995.
Orlando Sentinel, February 20, 1995.
Sport, February 1995.
Sports Illustrated, August 16, 1994; April 24, 1995.
St. Petersburg Times, February 11, 1995.
Stock Car Racing, April 1995.

WHERE TO WRITE:
C/O SPORTS MARKETING ENTERPRISES,
13 PLAZA, 401 NORTH MAIN STREET,
WINSTON-SALEM, NC 27102.

Tony Gwynn

1960—

H itting a baseball is probably the hardest thing to do in sports. A good major league hitter is successful if he gets a hit only three times out of every ten at bats. This fact makes what Tony Gwynn of the San Diego Padres has accomplished even more remarkable. Six times Gwynn has won the National League (NL) batting title, and he has hit over .300 for 13 consecutive seasons. In 1994 he batted .394, the highest average in the major leagues since 1941. A true student of the game, Gwynn is one of the best hitters of his generation.

Growing Up

BROUGHT UP RIGHT. Anthony Keith Gwynn was born May 9, 1960, in Los Angeles, California. His mother's name is Vandella, and his father's name was Charles. The second oldest of three boys, Gwynn grew up in nearby Long Beach, California. He had a close and warm relationship with his parents,

"What drives me is trying to be perfect."—Tony Gwynn

133

SCOREBOARD

HAS HIGHEST LIFETIME AVERAGE
OF ANY ACTIVE MAJOR LEAGUER
(.336).

WON SIX NATIONAL LEAGUE
BATTING TITLES (1984, 1987, 1988,
1989, 1994, AND 1995).

ELEVEN-TIME NATIONAL LEAGUE
ALL-STAR (1984-87, 1989-95).

GWYNN HAS BEEN ONE OF THE
BEST AND MOST CONSISTENT
HITTERS OF HIS ERA.

who he claims are responsible for his success. "They just instilled in me a will to treat people right," Gwynn recalled in the *Los Angeles Times*. "No big thing. Just treat them in the manner in which you were treated."

SOCKS THE BALL. Gwynn grew up in a home where his parents encouraged athletics. He spent every spare moment in the backyard of his home, playing baseball with his father and two brothers. "We'd just cut up socks on the line, put rubber bands around them and call them baseballs, even though they were the size of golf balls," Gwynn recalled in *Sports Illustrated*. "The pitcher would only be 15 feet away. I figure if you could hit one of those things, you could hit a baseball."

AZTEC ATTACK. Gwynn excelled in many sports in high school, playing on the baseball, basketball, and football teams. He earned an athletic scholarship to attend San Diego State University in 1978. As a freshman, Gwynn did not even play baseball. Instead, he made a name for himself as the point guard on the Aztec basketball team. (He still holds the all-time assist record at the school.) Gwynn first played baseball during his sophomore year and hit .423. The next year he batted .416 and caught the attention of pro baseball scouts.

PADRES PICK. Two hometown professional sports teams drafted Gwynn on the same day in June 1981. The San Diego Clippers (now the Los Angeles Clippers) of the National Basketball Association picked him, and the San Diego Padres baseball team selected him in the third round of major league baseball's free-agent draft. Gwynn did not have a hard time making his decision—baseball was his sport.

After the draft, Gwynn reported to the Padres' minor league team in Walla Walla, Washington. He was an instant success, batting .331 his first professional season and winning the Rookie Northwest League batting title and the Most Valuable Player award. Gwynn advanced rapidly through the San Diego farm system, spending time with teams in Texas, Hawaii, and Nevada.

BIG LEAGUER. On July 19, 1982, the Padres brought Gwynn to the major leagues. He went two-for-four in his first game and had his picture taken with the legendary Pete Rose. Gwynn played 54 games and batted .289 that first year, the last time he has finished a major league season with a batting average under .300. A broken wrist knocked him out of the lineup until just before mid-season in 1983. Gwynn picked up right where he left off with the Padres that year, batting .309 in 86 games and finishing the year with a 25-game hitting streak.

WORLD SERIES. Gwynn and the Padres had a magic season in 1984. The Padres won the National League West Division title for the first and only time in their history. Gwynn ran away with the National League batting title, leading the majors with a .351 average, 213 hits, and 69 multiple-hit games. "I hit the ball well all year long," Gwynn told the *Los Angeles Times*. "That will be the year that years from now, I'll be comparing things with. Everything I hit, I hit in the hole. It was an unbelievable year." Gwynn finished third in the balloting for National League Most Valuable Player.

San Diego faced the Chicago Cubs in the National League Championship Series. The Padres lost the first two games of the series in Chicago. San Diego came back to win Game Three, however. The two teams were tied 5-5 in the ninth inning of Game Four when first baseman Steve Garvey hit a home run to win the game and tie the series. In Game Five, Cubs first baseman Leon Durham let a ground ball by Tim Flannery go between his legs in the seventh inning to allow the tying run to score. Two batters later, Gwynn hit a ground ball to second base. The ball took a bad hop and went for a double. The Padres won the game, 6-3, and with it the National League pennant.

The Padres faced the Detroit Tigers in the World Series. The Tigers had an amazing campaign in 1984, starting the season 35-5 and never looking back. San Diego could not stop the

Gwynn makes a game winning run.

Tigers; they lost in five games. Gwynn hit .263 in the Series but did not drive in a run. He has not been in the play-offs since.

MR. CONSISTENCY. Gwynn went on to prove that 1984 was no fluke. In the next five years he won three more batting titles. In 1987 Gwynn won the NL title with a .370 average. He repeated as champion in 1988 with a .313 average, and led the league for a third straight year in 1989 by batting .335. Gwynn also led the league in hits three seasons—211 in 1986, 218 in 1987, and 203 in 1989. "Tony always seems to get good wood on the ball," former Cy Young Award-winning pitcher Orel Hershiser explained in *Boys' Life*. "And he usually hits it with authority. I don't even dream of trying to strike him out." A terrific fielder, he also won five Gold Glove Awards—in 1987, 1988, 1989, 1990, and 1991.

TOUGH TIMES. In 1988 Gwynn hurt his wrist and had to have surgery. The injury continued to bother him through the early 1990s. Injuries to his left knee also forced Gwynn to have surgery. The injuries kept him off the field. Gwynn played only 141 games in 1990, 134 in 1991, and 128 in 1992. He continued to hit well, but not at the level of his first six major league seasons. Gwynn hit .358 in 1993 but played in only 122 games because of injuries.

Despite Gwynn's great production, the Padres struggled as a team. Between 1985 and 1992, San Diego finished second once (1989) and third four times. Losing so often was hard on Gwynn, and some teammates even blamed him for the team's problems. Critics said that he worried too much about hitting for a high average and that he should try to hit more home runs.

Gwynn defended himself in *Sports Illustrated:* "One thing I've found is that we're [singles hitters are] called selfish more than anybody else. It's happened to me. It's happened to every contact hitter who's played the game. It's just a by-product of what we do. Anytime you're trying to do something perfect, so focused on what you do—well, it's not always pretty." He added in the same magazine: "I got a job to do. I can only do it the best way I know how. People put labels on you: 'He's only a singles hitter, he doesn't drive in runs, he doesn't hit homers.' I'm playing the style of play I play best. Even though a lot of people might not like that, I'm sorry, that's just the way it is."

STAYS IN SAN DIEGO. In 1993 the Padres began a long rebuilding process. To save money, the team traded away most of its good players. Gwynn's father tried to get his son to leave the Padres and become a free agent. "This team isn't going anywhere," Charles Gwynn told his son, according to *Sports Illustrated.* "Get out of Dodge!" Gwynn decided to stay. He told the same magazine: "The thing is, I'm happy here. One of the reasons I've been successful is that I'm not bigger than big. There's not that much pressure, not that much hype here. You've got to have time and room to work at your craft. They aren't that demanding in San Diego."

DAD DIES. On November 27, 1993, Gwynn suffered a tragedy. His father, Charles, died of a heart attack. "It's the first [season] I've gone into without my dad," Gwynn explained in *Sport* magazine during the 1994 campaign. "It's been tough, especially when I'm by myself and have time to reflect. I can focus on baseball like I always have, but during the course of the day, there's always a time when I'm thinking about not being able to talk to, or not being able to see, my dad." Gwynn had always called his father when he felt down or needed support.

STRUCK OUT. The baseball strike of 1994 disappointed everyone connected with baseball, but no one more than Gwynn. He was batting .394 when the strike ended the season and felt he could have reached the magic .400 average. The last major league player to hit .400 or better in a season was Ted Williams of the Boston Red Sox when he hit .406 in 1941. Williams was one of Gwynn's idols as a child, and the San Diego star memorized the great hitter's book, *The Science of Hitting*.

Not getting a chance to reach .400 disappointed Gwynn, even though he supported the strike. "I've wondered my whole life if I could be consistent enough across a whole season to get to four bills [.400] and then stay there," Gwynn admitted in *Esquire*. "I wondered if I could make my run." Gwynn may never get another chance. "Will I ever have a chance to hit .400 again?" Gwynn asked in *Baseball Digest*. "I doubt it. I felt like I was sharp enough to give it a run."

Superstar

SIXTH TITLE. Gwynn had another remarkable year in 1995. Despite a knee injury, he edged out **Mike Piazza** (see entry) of the Los Angeles Dodgers for the National League batting title. Gwynn hit .368, had 197 hits (tied for first in the NL), and drove in a career-high 90 runs. He became the first player since 1937 to hit over .350 for three straight seasons. (Joe Medwick hit .353 in 1935, .351 in 1936, and .374 in 1937.)

WHY SO GOOD? Gwynn is one of the most difficult players in baseball history to strike out, fanning only once in every 30 plate appearances. "I usually put the ball in play," Gwynn stated in *Baseball Digest*. "I don't strike out a lot." He keeps detailed records on every pitcher he faces and knows what they are going to throw. "I look at how the guy has pitched me in the past," Gwynn explained in *Boys' Life*. "Maybe he will try it again, maybe not. But it will be in my mind knowing what he might do, and that is an advantage to me as a hitter."

Gwynn videotapes his at bats and watches the tapes to look for flaws in his swing. He began doing this in 1983 with video equipment he bought to record his newborn son. Even though he is the best hitter in the National League, Gwynn still takes batting practice daily. "Tony's a tremendous student of the game and a flat-out great hitter," his manager, Jim Riggleman, told *USA Today*. "Tony's the first one out here every day working on his hitting." Gwynn also works hard on his fielding, practicing his throwing before games.

Gwynn is an institution in San Diego. The fans love him, and he has been loyal to the Padres, signing smaller-paying contracts because he likes living in San Diego. "[Gwynn is] probably the most popular and successful player in San Diego sports history," wrote Tim Kurkjian in *Sports Illustrated*. Gwynn intends to make the Padres winners. "I know it might be easier to win somewhere else," Gwynn told the *Los Angeles Times*. "I'll be here as long as it takes. I just want to be here when we're back on top."

At the end of the 1995 season, Gwynn had the highest lifetime average of any active major league player—.336. He has batted over .300 for 13 straight seasons (every year except his first season). Four times Gwynn has hit over .350 and has

BATTING KINGS

The following chart lists the eight players in major league history who have won five or more league batting championships. Gwynn is tied for sixth on the list, with six titles.

Player	Batting Titles
Ty Cobb	12
Honus Wagner	8
Rod Carew	7
Rogers Hornsby	7
Stan Musial	7
Tony Gwynn	6
Ted Williams	6
Wade Boggs	5

had more than 200 hits four times. He holds the San Diego records for hits (2,401), runs (1,073), triples (80), doubles (384), stolen bases (285), and batting average.

OFF THE FIELD. Gwynn lives with his wife, Alicia (his school sweetheart) and his children, Anthony II and Anisha Nicole, in Poway, California. His brother Chris also played at San Diego State and now plays in the major leagues. Gwynn participates in many charitable activities in the San Diego area. He is part owner of the San Diego School of Baseball.

Since going to the World Series in 1984, the Padres have not been in contention. Gwynn wants to win a championship more than anything before he retires. "I could care less about batting titles," Gwynn said in the *Los Angeles Times.* "I really don't care if I ever win another one. What I want, more than anything else, is that [World Series] ring. Maybe I'm old-fashioned, because all I think about is winning. Really, you can make all the money you want, but there's nothing like winning."

Sources

Baseball Digest, February 1995.
Boys' Life, September 1992.
Chicago Tribune, June 16, 1991.
Esquire, August 1995.
Los Angeles Times, July 7, 1985; February 28, 1988; March 16, 1990; July 11, 1991; March 1, 1992.
New York Times, August 24, 1994.
Sport, September 1994.
Sporting News, May 23, 1994; August 22, 1994.
Sports Illustrated, May 14, 1984; April 14, 1986; March 11, 1991; March 29, 1993; September 18, 1995.
Sports Illustrated for Kids, November 1995.
USA Today, July 25, 1994.
Additional information provided by San Diego Padres.

WHERE TO WRITE:
C/O SAN DIEGO PADRES, JACK MURPHY STADIUM,
9449 FRIARS RD.,
SAN DIEGO, CA 92108.

Mia Hamm

1972—

Mia Hamm has always been around people who can fly. Her father is a U.S. Air Force pilot, and she is married to a Marine Corps flyer. On the soccer field Hamm has always been a supersonic jet. She was the youngest player ever on the U.S. Women's National Soccer Team and starred in the first ever World Women's Soccer Championship in 1991. Hamm also flew past her opponents at the University of North Carolina. In four years her teams lost only one game, and the University of North Carolina Tar Heels won four straight National Collegiate Athletic Association (NCAA) championships. Hamm's next goal is to pilot the U.S. team to victory in the first ever women's soccer championship at the 1996 Summer Olympics in Atlanta, Georgia.

"When Mia is playing her best, there's no one better in the world."—Tony Diccico, U.S. Women's National Soccer Team coach

Growing Up

BALL OF FIRE. Mariel Margaret Hamm was born March 17, 1972, in Selma, Alabama. Her dad, Bill, was an air force pilot

SCOREBOARD

YOUNGEST PLAYER EVER
ON THE U.S. NATIONAL WOMEN'S
SOCCER TEAM.

LEADING ALL-TIME SCORER
IN NCAA WOMEN'S SOCCER
REGULAR SEASON AND
TOURNAMENT HISTORY.

NATIONAL COLLEGIATE
WOMEN'S SOCCER
PLAYER OF THE YEAR IN 1992.

A NATIONAL AND INTERNATIONAL
SOCCER STAR, HAMM HOPES
TO HELP THE UNITED STATES
BRING HOME THE GOLD FROM
THE 1996 OLYMPICS.

and her mom, Stephanie, was a ballerina. Hamm and her two brothers and three sisters moved whenever the air force transferred her father. She lived in Italy and in Texas and Virginia. Her mom described her in *Sports Illustrated* as "a little ball of fire ever since she was teeny."

Hamm has always been quiet and shy. She had trouble making new friends after her family moved. Sports helped her meet people. Hamm first fell in love with soccer when she lived in Florence, Italy, a soccer-crazed country. She used to see other kids playing in parks and tried to get into the games.

Hamm's brothers and sisters played on a local soccer team in Wichita Falls, Texas, and their father coached and refereed. "Basically the soccer field was where I was baby-sat," Hamm recalls. She began playing soccer when she was five. "I first played in this peewee league," she told *Sports Illustrated.* "Our team record wasn't very good, but I did manage to score a lot of goals." Hamm would play continuously for the next ten years, through elementary and junior high school. Most of the time she was the only girl on the teams. The boys never gave Hamm a hard time, because she was usually the best player on the team.

YOUNGEST STAR. Hamm led her high school team to the state high school title. When she was 14, Hamm joined the U.S. Olympic development team. The coach of the development team, John Cossaboon, called his friend Anson Dorrance, the coach of the powerful University of North Carolina women's soccer team, to tell him that he had discovered a star. Hamm impressed Dorrance the first time he saw her. "Mia was playing right halfback," he remembered in a *Sports Illustrated* interview. "I watched her take a seven-yard run at the ball. And I said, 'Oh, my gosh!' I'd never seen speed like that in the women's game. She had unlimited potential." At age 15

Hamm became the youngest member ever on the U.S. national women's team. Playing at this level was a learning experience. "During fitness sessions, I was dying," she recalled in *Sports Illustrated for Kids*. "I would cry half the time."

TAR HEEL TERROR. After high school Hamm entered the University of North Carolina in 1989. For the next four years she would shine. As a freshman Hamm scored 21 goals and chipped in with 4 assists. For the next three years she was a scoring machine. In 1990 she scored 24 goals and had 19 assists. As a junior in 1992 Hamm set an NCAA single-season record for assists (33) and points (97) and scored an incredible 32 goals. As a senior in 1993 she continued her great play, tallying 26 goals and 16 assists. Hamm was a first-team All-American and led her team in scoring during her last three seasons at North Carolina.

Hamm led North Carolina to four straight NCAA women's soccer championships. The Tar Heels' record during her career was an amazing 92-1-2. The team's only loss was to the University of Connecticut in 1990, a team the Tar Heels defeated in the NCAA finals, 6-0, later that same year. Hamm graduated as the all-time leading scorer in NCAA women's Division I soccer history with 103 goals and 72 assists. She also is the record holder for the NCAA women's Division I soccer tournament, with 16 goals and 9 assists.

BEST IN THE LAND. In both 1992 and 1993 Hamm won the Herman Award, recognizing her as the best female college soccer player in the nation. She received the Honda-Broderick Cup as female college athlete of the year in January 1994. North Carolina has retired her number 19 jersey. Hamm was sad to leave North Carolina. "This is my field of dreams," she confessed in *Sports Illustrated*. "I've had some wonderful years here, but I don't want to sit and look at all the trophies. I don't want to live in the past—I want to live now!"

LIKE MOTHER, LIKE DAUGHTER?

Hamm's mother had visions of her daughter following in her footsteps as a dancer. "I thought because she was so petite, she'd be ideal," Mrs. Hamm recalled in *Sports Illustrated for Kids*. "But she hated it." Good thing for the game of soccer, because Hamm joined a pee-wee soccer team instead.

SOCCER POWERHOUSE

The University of North Carolina women's soccer team has had one of the most remarkable streaks of success in the history of collegiate athletics. Through 1994 they had won 9 straight NCAA championships and 12 of the 13 NCAA tournaments ever held. During one stretch, from 1990 to 1994, they won 92 straight games. Their overall record is 323-9-10. Hamm says a big reason for the team's success is Dorrance. "Obviously he knows what it takes to win and that is very rare," Hamm said. "He makes another kind of investment in his players beyond just training, he cares about them as people. He knows what motivates certain types of players and ties it all in to team chemistry and camaraderie."

Superstar

WORLD CHAMP. Hamm was the youngest player on the U.S. national team that participated in the first-ever women's world championship, in China in 1991. She struggled in the team's first game, having to play outside midfielder instead of her usual position, inside midfielder, because of injuries. "I just didn't want to make a mistake," Hamm told *Sports Illustrated for Kids.* Hamm did not make many mistakes, and she scored the game-winning goal for the United States. She also scored a goal in the next game as the United States won the title.

OLYMPIC DREAMS. Hamm has continued her great play since leaving North Carolina. She was the Most Valuable Player (MVP) at the 1995 U.S. Cup tournament and led the U.S. national team in scoring during 1995 with 19 goals and 18 assists. She was also on the U.S. team that won a bronze medal at the 1995 World Women's Soccer Championship in Sweden. The U.S. Soccer Federation honored Hamm by naming her the 1995 Female Athlete of the Year.

Hamm's next goal is to lead the U.S. national women's team to victory in the 1996 Olympic Games. This is the first time women's soccer will be part of the Olympics.

In 86 international games Hamm has scored 43 goals and dished out 19 assists. Only two players have accumulated more points for the U.S. women's team. "I think she is driven by this passion," Dorrance told *Sports Illustrated,* "to become the best in the world."

OFF THE FIELD. Hamm lives in Chapel Hill, North Carolina, with her husband, Christiaan Corey, a Marine Corps pilot. She likes to play basketball and golf and loves to watch college basketball on television. Her favorite athletes are hockey star

Wayne Gretzky, cyclist Greg LeMond, and track star Jackie Joyner-Kersee. Hamm graduated from North Carolina with a degree in political science. She is currently a spokesperson for Nike.

Hamm's parents now live in Italy, so she only gets to see them twice a year. She still talks to them on the phone, sometimes three times a week. Hamm's parents have always encouraged her to do her best. "Every time I wanted to do something—like play for the National Team—they've always supported me," she told *Seventeen*.

Hamm stays in shape by working out with weights and running. "I'm exhausted after a lot of training sessions," Hamm admitted in *Seventeen*. She tries to eat right, getting all her necessary vitamins, but she does have a weakness for chips and salsa. Hamm is superstitious. She always puts her socks and shoes on the same way before a game.

Hamm is thrilled that soccer is becoming a popular sport for girls, but she says that each person has to make up her own mind about playing sports. "The more I go out and coach kids or watch kids play, the more I see parents pushing them to be something they don't necessarily want to be," Hamm told *Seventeen*. "I think that the decision to play sports—or do anything—has to be your own. It can't be someone else's."

Sources

People, November 1, 1993.
Seventeen, June 1994.
Sporting News, January 17, 1994; January 23, 1995.
Sports Illustrated for Kids, November 1993; June 1995; July 1995.
Additional information provided by U.S. Soccer Federation and the University of North Carolina.

WHERE TO WRITE:
U.S. SOCCER FEDERATION,
1801-1811 S. PRAIRIE AVE.,
CHICAGO, IL 60616.

Anfernee Hardaway

1971—

"When people talk about the greats, I want to be mentioned with Michael Jordan, Magic Johnson, Larry Bird."
—Anfernee Hardaway

Anfernee "Penny" Hardaway almost lost his basketball career before it began. A thief's bullet lodged in his right foot threatened to keep him grounded in a game played much of the time in the air. Hardaway was luckier than many people and the injury was not serious. But then he has always led a charmed life, one that has led Hardaway from the tough streets of Memphis to the National Basketball Association (NBA). Today he teams with Shaquille O'Neal to make the Orlando Magic the best young team in the NBA.

Growing Up

"PENNY." Anfernee Deon Hardaway was born July 18, 1971, in Memphis, Tennessee. His father, Eddie Gordon, never took care of the family. His mother, Fae, traveled to California to pursue a singing career. His grandmother, Louise Hardaway, who was a school cafeteria cook, raised Hardaway. She nicknamed him "Pretty" when he was a baby. The way she said it, however, sounded like "Penny." Soon that was what everybody called him.

The neighborhood in which Hardaway grew up was tough, and his grandmother tried to protect him from crime and the streets. "My grandmother was very strict about where I was and when I had to be home," Hardaway recalls. "I had to be in before dark every night. I'd see guys out walking and hanging out all hours of the night and I'd be thinking, 'Man, I wish I could be out there,' but my grandmother never let me. She was real strict about that and I'm glad about it now." Hardaway's grandmother made sure he spent a lot of time at the Early Grove Baptist Church.

SCOREBOARD

NATIONAL HIGH SCHOOL PLAYER OF THE YEAR (1990).

VOTED STARTER IN NBA ALL-STAR GAME (1995).

NAMED TO ALL-NBA FIRST TEAM (1995).

MAY BE BEST ALL-AROUND PLAYER TO ENTER NBA SINCE EARVIN "MAGIC" JOHNSON.

MAKING THINGS HAPPEN. Hardaway was always tall for his age. He was six feet four inches tall by the time he was 12 years old. Basketball, therefore, was a natural sport for him to take up. Jim Kern, the coach of the Memphis Amateur Athletic Union (AAU) team recruited Hardaway at an early age. "The game was so easy for him," Kern recalls. "He wasn't like most kids tall for their age. He was coordinated, could run, handle the ball, score, rebound, do anything. We didn't call him a guard, forward or center, we just put him out there and said, 'Go.' He made things happen."

Hardaway joined future NBA players Elliot Perry, Vincent Askew, Todd Day, and Tony Dumas on the AAU team. They traveled around the country and won the AAU national tournament when Hardaway was 16. "We would go just about anywhere that would have us," Kern says. "And Penny was the man. I didn't do a whole lot of coaching with him. I think the only thing I ever said to him was 'You've got to shoot more,' but he wouldn't. He wanted everybody on the team to score. He always got a bigger thrill out of setting somebody else up than he did scoring himself."

SCHOOL DAZE. Hardaway attended Treadwell High School in Memphis. He was a star on the court, but he did not take his

schoolwork as seriously as his game. His grades almost cost him a career in basketball. Hardaway had to sit out the middle part of his senior season because of academic problems. "I wouldn't listen to anybody," Hardaway admits. "I don't know what was going on in my head. I guess I thought I was so good at basketball, the teachers would just let me skate in the classroom. Even when I had to sit out, I didn't realize the grades would be a big deal until they told me I couldn't play my first year in college."

Hardaway returned to his team just before the end of the season. He was rusty, however, and Treadwell did not win the state championship. Hardaway finished his senior season averaging 36.6 points, 10.1 rebounds, and 6.2 assists per game. Experts named Hardaway Mr. Basketball in Tennessee, and he was the *Parade* magazine National High School Player of the Year.

HOMETOWN HERO. Hardaway decided to stay close to home and attend Memphis State University. He had to sit out his first season at Memphis State because he did not achieve high enough scores on the American College Test (ACT) college entrance exam. Sitting out was tough on Hardaway. "Imagine walking around your hometown and everybody thinks you're a dummy," Hardaway recounted in *Sport* magazine.

LUCKY TO BE ALIVE. Hardaway almost did not survive his freshman year at Memphis State. One night in 1991 he was returning a wallet to his cousin, LaMarcus Golden. A car pulled up from behind Hardaway when he parked in front of his cousin's house. A man got out claiming he needed directions. What he really wanted was to rob Hardaway and his friends. The thief pulled a gun and made Hardaway lie face-down on the driveway. He could feel the gun on the back of his head. "I thought I was dead," Hardaway admitted in *Sport* magazine.

◀ *Hardaway passes around Chicago Bulls' Toni Kukoc (left rear) and Scottie Pippin during a 1995 play-off game.*

LESSONS LEARNED

The events of his freshman season taught Hardaway some hard lessons. "It was tough, but it was a blessing," Memphis State coach Larry Finch said. "Penny finally realized the price he had to pay to be involved in something he loved. He really made up his mind that nothing was going to keep him from basketball again, and you know what? He made the dean's list his first semester here [at Memphis State]!" Hardaway finished his college career with a 3.4 grade point average while majoring in education.

The thief took their wallets, a gold chain, a ring, and their gym shoes. As he was driving away, the thief fired several shots out of the window of the car. One of these ricocheted off the pavement and lodged in Hardaway's right foot. "That night had an impact on me that will last the rest of my life," Hardaway confessed. "I notice everyone and everything now. I don't take anything for granted. You come from where I come from and you learn to be defensive, real defensive." Luckily, the injury was not serious.

TIGER TERROR. Hardaway was a star at Memphis State. Twice he won the Great Midwest Conference Player of the Year and was a finalist for the prestigious Wooden and Naismith awards in 1993. Hardaway led the Tigers to two consecutive NCAA tournament appearances and to the Final Eight in 1993. He averaged 22.8 points, 8.5 rebounds, and 6.4 assists his final season at Memphis State. "I'm like the biggest thing that ever came out of Memphis—besides Elvis," Hardaway told *People*. "I've been loved everywhere I've ever played." He was a first team All-American. Memphis State retired his jersey.

Superstar

MAGIC PENNY. The Orlando Magic, in one of the luckiest moments in sports history, won the first pick in the NBA Draft lottery for the second year in a row in 1993. The year before the team drafted Shaquille O'Neal, the NBA Rookie of the Year. Orlando fans wanted the Magic to use the 1993 draft pick to take **Chris Webber** (see entry), the powerful leader of the famous "Fab Five" team at the University of Michigan. Shaquille O'Neal, who had played against Hardaway during the filming of the movie *Blue Chips,* convinced the Magic to consider Hardaway.

On draft day the Magic did pick Webber, but quickly traded him to the Golden State Warriors for Hardaway and three first-round draft picks. The two players traded caps on the podium after the announcement of the trade. Orlando realized that Hardaway would be the perfect outside scoring threat to keep teams from double-teaming O'Neal inside. He also would be able to get the big man the ball inside for easy baskets.

The fans in Orlando were not happy and booed the announcement of the trade. The reaction hurt Hardaway's feelings. "You see and hear bad things all your life growing up; you don't want to hear no more when you go someplace new," Hardaway said. "I want the fans in Orlando behind me."

RUNNING ROOKIE. It did not take Hardaway long to win over his new hometown. He started the season at shooting guard, but soon was taking over the point guard position. Hardaway finished the season strong, averaging 16 points, 6.6 assists, and 5.4 rebounds per game. He also had 190 steals, good for sixth place in the league. The Magic, a recent expansion team, was now one of the NBA's elite, winning 50 games for the first time. Hardaway finished second to Webber in the NBA Rookie of the Year voting, but fans in the Orlando Arena had gotten the message about their young star. They hung banners that read, "We Picked the Right One Baby, Uh Huh!"

The NBA named Hardaway to its All-Rookie first team. "Penny did everything we asked of him, but you knew he was only scratching the surface that rookie year," Magic coach Brian Hill said. "He was getting to know his own strengths and weaknesses as well as those of his opponents. I had a feeling he was going to burst into the elite status of guards in the league his second year."

The only low point in Hardaway's rookie season came when Orlando was swept in the first round of the play-offs by the Indiana Pacers. "I never expected that to happen," Hardaway admitted in *Sport* magazine. "That left a bitter taste in our mouths for a long time."

ALL-NBA. During the off-season the Magic signed Horace Grant, a member of the three-time NBA champion Chicago

THE NEXT MAGIC?

People have compared Hardaway to Earvin "Magic" Johnson from the time he was in junior high. There are many similarities between the two players. Both are tall for their position, point guard, and both have the ability to score and help make their teammates better. "He can definitely be another Magic," Seattle Sonics scout Bob Kloppenburg said. "I really believe that. Some of the passes he throws, he makes them look so easy. He has the whole package." The Magic Man himself agrees. "He's absolutely phenomenal," Johnson told *Sport* magazine. "Really, words don't describe how great he is and how great he's going to be." Hardaway knows he still has a long way to go. "It's really nice to hear when people compare me with Magic," Hardaway said in the *1996 Complete Handbook of Pro Basketball,* "but it's because of my height and the fact we both play point guard. You can't really put me in the same class with Magic until I've won the number of championships he's won. I'm not even close to that yet." Not yet, but that is his goal. "I want to be known as one of the greatest players in history," Hardaway confessed in *Sport* magazine. "When people talk about the greats, I want to be mentioned with Michael Jordan, Magic Johnson, Larry Bird."

Bulls. Many people felt Grant, a solid power forward, would bring experience to the young Magic squad. The Magic started fast and never slowed down. They were 35-8 by the All-Star break, the best record in the NBA. Fans elected Hardaway as a starter in the All-Star game. He scored 11 points and had 11 assists in the game.

Hardaway took on more and more of a leadership role as the season went along. "The best players can adjust to whatever their team needs," Hardaway said. "Before every game, I look at the matchups and try and figure out what we need that night. If we need scoring, I'll score. I have to get everybody involved, keep everybody happy. That's really the way I like to play."

The Magic soared to the Atlantic Division title with 57 victories, and Hardaway was a major reason. He averaged 20.9 points and 7.2 assists a game (tenth in the NBA). The NBA named Hardaway to the All-NBA first team. The Magic eliminated the Boston Celtics for their first ever play-off victory. They then defeated the Chicago Bulls, with the recently un-retired Michael Jordan, in six games. They would now face the Indiana Pacers in the Eastern Conference Finals.

The Pacers and the Magic battled for seven tough games. The series went back and forth, with Hardaway and O'Neal battling **Reggie Miller** (see entry) and Rik Smits. The Magic won the first two games, but the Pacers came back to force a final Game Seven. The Magic won that final game, 105-81, reaching the NBA Finals in only their sixth season. "Everybody kept saying we didn't have the experience, we couldn't go all the way," Hardaway told the *New York Times*. "It motivated us, it really did. While everybody was criticizing, we just kept playing ball."

FINALS SWEEP. The NBA finals were a disappointment for the Magic. The Houston Rockets, the defending NBA champions, were too tough. Hakeem Olajuwon and Clyde Drexler led the way to a four-game sweep of Orlando. Hardaway did all he could in the series, averaging 25.5 points per game, but it was not enough. The Magic huddled as the Rockets celebrated. "We huddled up after the game and just looked at the Rockets celebrating, tried to soak in as much as possible and tried to use this as a motivating factor to get back next year and try to be the same way they [the Rockets] are right now," Hardaway explained in *Sport* magazine.

The young Magic team will be back, and Hardaway will be leading them. "I'm going into this off-season the same way I did last year: remembering how we lost, more so than how good a season we had," Hardaway said after the season. "I've been to the state finals in high school, the last eight in the NCAA tournament and the NBA Finals and never won. I don't know how may more chances I'm going to get, but I'm going to find a way to win one."

OFF THE COURT. Hardaway works with Penny's Pals, a program in which corporations and individuals donate money for every dunk Hardaway makes during the season. He also works with the Campaign for Community Values, which helps prevent neighborhood violence an antiviolence project. Hardaway bought a home for his mother and grandmother in Memphis, not far from Elvis Presley's Graceland mansion. He is a spokesperson for Nike. Money has not changed Hardaway, however. "I'm never afraid I'll change," he told *People* magazine. "My grandmother—and my mom, both—will always keep me from getting a big head. Like I said, I'm just a hometown boy."

Sources

Hollander, Zander, ed. *The Complete Handbook of Pro Basketball.* New York: Signet Books, 1995.

People, March 28, 1994.

Sport, June 1995; October 1995.

Sports Illustrated, February 7, 1994; June 19, 1995.

Additional information provided by Orlando Magic.

 WHERE TO WRITE:
C/O ORLANDO MAGIC, ORLANDO ARENA,
ONE MAGIC PLACE,
ORLANDO, FL 32801.

Grant Hill

1972—

rant Hill burst onto the National Basketball Association (NBA) picture as an instant sensation. A fan
favorite from the first moment he stepped onto the
court, Hill became the first rookie to lead the voting for the
NBA All-Star Game. The fame would have been tough for
most people to deal with, but Hill handled the attention with
grace. He also played great, well enough to earn 1994-95
NBA Rookie of the Year honors. Hill has done all this while
living up to the high expectations of his father, former All-Pro
football star Calvin Hill.

Growing Up

FAMILY AFFAIR. Grant Henry Hill was born October 5, 1972,
in Dallas, Texas. He is the child of famous parents. His mother, Janet, is an attorney and consultant, and she once shared a
suite of rooms in college with First Lady Hillary Rodham
Clinton. His father, Calvin, attended Yale University and was

"Off the court, I can be the nicest person in the world. But when I get on the court, whether you're my mother, father, or friend, I want to beat you."

—Grant Hill

SCOREBOARD

STAR OF BACK-TO-BACK NCAA
BASKETBALL CHAMPIONSHIP
TEAMS AT DUKE UNIVERSITY
(1992 AND 1993).

FIRST ROOKIE EVER TO RECEIVE
MOST VOTES IN NBA ALL-STAR
BALLOTING (1995).

1994-95
NBA ROOKIE OF THE YEAR.

ONE OF THE MOST EXPLOSIVE
AND POPULAR YOUNG PLAYERS
IN THE NBA.

an All-Pro football player with the Dallas Cowboys. Calvin Hill was the first Cowboy to ever rush for over 1,000 yards in a season (1972) and led the team to its first ever Super Bowl victory in 1971. His trademark was leaping over defensive players. What Hill remembered most about his dad's football career though, was the injuries he suffered. Young Hill decided he did not want to play football.

The Hill family settled in Reston, Virginia, a suburb of Washington, D.C., after the Cowboys traded Hill's father to the Washington Redskins. Unlike many NBA players, Hill grew up in a very wealthy home. An only child, Hill was held to strict disciplinary standards by his parents and had to follow their rules. His mom's nickname was "The General." Hill could not make phone calls on week nights, and could use the telephone only 30 minutes a day on weekends. He could not leave the neighborhood if his parents were not home, and his homework had to be finished before he could play sports. Hill could not attend dances or parties until he turned 16.

"They were too strict, if you ask me," Hill told the *Sporting News.* "I didn't make any mistakes as a kid because I couldn't. They mapped out my whole life for me to the point where I didn't get to do anything. I tried to negotiate with them, but they were way too smart for me. It made me always want to get [something] over on them, but I rarely did." The major rule in the house, though, was that Hill could not play football until high school. "I didn't want him dealing with the pressure of the comparisons," Calvin Hill explained to *Sporting News.*

DEALING WITH DAD. Hill told the *Sporting News* that he still has unique relationships with his mom and dad: "Both my parents are very proud of me and love me very much, but they just show it in very different ways," Hill explained. Hill's mom is easygoing, very much like her son, but his dad is very intense and competitive. "He's got that football mentality," Hill said. "He wants me to show intensity all the time. But what he doesn't understand is, as much as he wants for me, I want even more. I just don't show it on my face. I keep my emotions inside. But I'm harder on me than he ever could be."

Being the son of a famous father was not always easy. Hill worried that people would like him not as a person but because his dad had been a football star. One time Hill faked being sick because he did not want to be at school when his dad was a guest speaker. He also remembers that he always wanted to be picked up from school in the family's run-down Volkswagen, not the flashier Porsche or Mercedes. "I guess I always wanted to be liked by everybody," Hill recalled in *Sports Illustrated.* "Here my father was in sports, my parents had money, and I'm thinking that if I do well in sports, people will get jealous of me and not like me. I didn't want to seem better than everybody else. Eventually I realized I was better [at basketball]."

"It [his relationship with his dad] was really bad in high school," Hill told the *Sporting News.* "Whatever I scored or whatever I did would never be enough for him. I mean, the thing is, my father doesn't know a thing about basketball. But in a way I'm lucky. It would've been ten times worse if I played football."

Hill played basketball and soccer in high school, but not football. "It's funny, but when I was finally allowed to play football, I didn't feel like playing it anymore," Hill recounted in the *Sporting News.* From the age of 13, basketball was his sport. Hill started for his American Athletic Union (AAU) team that upset a Detroit team led by **Chris Webber** (see entry) and Jalen Rose. When he returned from the championship game, Hill beat his dad in two straight games of one-on-one.

In his four years of high school basketball, Hill helped his team advance to the state finals twice. He averaged 30 points per game in his senior year, and many major colleges recruited him. Hill's mom wanted him to attend Georgetown

University, close to home, and his dad wanted him to play at the University of North Carolina. Showing his independence from his parents, Hill chose Duke University.

BLUE DEVIL STAR. Duke was already a college basketball powerhouse under Coach Mike Krzyzewski. Hill entered Duke in the fall of 1990 and joined the Blue Devils basketball team. As a freshman, he played with a group that included Bobby Hurley (now with the Sacramento Kings) and Christian Laettner (now with the Atlanta Hawks). This team would turn out to be one of the best of all time. They won the 1991 NCAA Basketball Championship, defeating the University of Kansas Jayhawks in the final game. Hill capped off the victory with a thunderous slam after grabbing an off-target pass from Hurley.

MAKING HISTORY. The following year the Blue Devils made history. The last team to have won back-to-back NCAA Basketball Championships was the University of California at Los Angeles (UCLA) Bruins in 1972 and 1973, under their legendary coach John Wooden. Duke once again had an impressive regular season and entered the NCAA Tournament as a favorite to repeat. They faced their most serious challenge in the East Regional Finals game against Jamal Mashburn and the University of Kentucky Wildcats. The Blue Devils trailed with only seconds left. Hill took the ball under his own basket and threw it the length of the court to Laettner. Laettner turned at the top of the key and fired up a desperation shot. It went in and Duke advanced to the Final Four. That was all the Blue Devils needed. They blew out Chris Webber and his "Fab Five" University of Michigan teammates in the championship game, 71-51, to win their second straight national title.

TEAM LEADER. Laettner graduated before the 1992-93 season. Hill averaged 18 points and six rebounds during his junior season, but a broken toe he suffered before the NCAA Tournament slowed him down. Duke was upset in the 1993 NCAA Tournament by the upstart University of California Golden Bears, led by **Jason Kidd** (see entry).

Hill leaps over Charolotte Hornets' Larry Johnson.

Hurley graduated before the 1994 season and now the Blue Devils were Hill's team. He overcame a natural shyness and took on the leadership role. "Now, I feel it's my time," Hill told the *Sporting News,* "and I'm trying to do all I can to lead this team. Whatever it takes to win. There have been games this year where I felt I played well and contributed and didn't score in double figures. I did it in other areas. I decided to do whatever it takes, be it scoring, rebounding, playing defense. I just want to go out there and do that and do it well and try to dominate in those areas. It's not always scoring."

Hill averaged 17.4 points, 6.9 rebounds, and 5.2 assists per game. These numbers were good enough to make him the Atlantic Coast Conference Player of the Year. "A kid like Grant needs to be helped to get to his rightful position, to realize that he's really that good," Krzyzewski told *Sports Illustrated.* "Grant being Grant, he wants to be asked to advance in the line. He'll always be very sensitive toward everyone else in line, even when he's at the head of it." In his senior season Hill demonstrated his versatility, playing point guard, shooting guard, and small forward.

Duke again was a force in the 1994 NCAA Basketball Tournament. In the Southeast Regional Finals they faced Purdue University and **Glenn "Big Dog" Robinson** (see entry), the College Player of the Year. Hill matched up against Robinson and, showing his defensive ability, shut down his talented opponent. Robinson made only 6 of 22 shots as Duke easily won. For the seventh time in nine years, Duke was in the Final Four. Duke once again reached the finals, only to lose to the number-one ranked University of Arkansas Razorbacks, 76-72. Hill scored only 12 points in the championship game, a disappointing end to his successful college career.

Experts named Hill an All-American his last three seasons at Duke. He is the only player in the history of the Atlantic Coast Conference to total at least 1,900 points (1,924), 700 rebounds (769), 400 assists (461), 200 steals (218), and 100 blocked shots (133). His number, 33, has been retired by the school. "Grant Hill is the best player I ever coached, period," Krzyzewski admitted in the *Sporting News.* "But he's the reluctant superstar. He wants to be the best, but he doesn't want to separate himself from the team."

Superstar

PISTON POWERHOUSE. The 1994 NBA Draft was a great one. Milwaukee chose first and picked Glenn Robinson. The Dallas Mavericks, holding the second pick, selected Jason Kidd. The Detroit Pistons, holding the third pick, were thrilled that Hill was still available. "He was impressive in every way," Pistons executive Billy McKinney told *Sporting News.* Hill felt the same way about Detroit. "There was no other place I wanted to play," Hill said. The Pistons drafted Hill and quickly signed him to an eight-year, $45 million contract. He also quickly signed contracts to endorse Fila athletic wear, Chevrolet automobiles, and Sprite soda.

ALL-STAR LEADER. Hill was an instant sensation. Crowds in every basketball arena in the country greeted the rookie with cheers. The biggest thrill for Hill during his rookie season was the response he received from the voters for the NBA All-Star Game. Hill received more votes than any other NBA player, the first time a rookie had ever achieved this feat.

ROOKIE OF THE YEAR. Despite missing several games because of a foot injury, Hill led the Pistons in scoring with a 19.9 points per game average. Because of his outstanding rookie season, Hill seemed like a sure bet to win the NBA Rookie of the Year award. Surprisingly, Hill tied with Jason Kidd when the votes were counted. His coach at the time, Don Chaney, knew who the best rookie was. "Grant is headed for stardom," Chaney told *Time* magazine. "You can't talk it, and you can't teach it. The fans are getting hungry—hungry—and are getting tired of immature athletes. They want something better."

Soon basketball fans were comparing him to all-time great NBA players, but Hill said that was ridiculous. "Oh, man, forget all that stuff," Hill said in the *Sporting News*. "I really hate it. And, besides, it's so stupid. I'm not that good, really. Those guys have done great things. I haven't done anything yet." Hill does not sell himself short, though. "I want to be the best there ever was," he said. "That's the only thing that motivates me. Everybody asks me if I want to be the next Magic [Johnson] or Michael [Jordan]—and they're great players and they've accomplished a great deal—but I don't

HERO WORSHIP

During his rookie season Hill got to meet one of his childhood heroes, Julius "Dr. J" Erving. "We played Philadelphia and Julius Erving called me over and talked about half an hour, forty minutes after the game," Hill told the *Los Angeles Times*. "I couldn't believe Dr. J was talking to me, to give me advice, this and that. He gave me his phone number and I was like a little kid. I got on the bus to go to the airport, I was calling his number with my cellular phone to make sure it was the right number—and hanging up when the answering machine answered. I just couldn't believe it was Dr. J's number."

NICE GUY?

All the talk about how nice he is amuses Hill. Off the court, maybe, but when the game is on he wants to win. "You can't be nice on the court and win," he explained to *USA Today Weekend.* "Off the court, I can be the nicest person in the world. But when I get on the court, whether you're my mother, father, or friend, I want to beat you. I want to beat you bad. I'm not going to cheat. I'm not going to play dirty. I'll do anything within the rules to win."

want to limit myself to just that. Why should I? And I have people saying I'm crazy if I think I'm going to be better than them. But that's what I'm shooting for. The highest a player can get."

OFF THE COURT. Hill lives near the Pistons' Palace of Auburn Hills arena. He plays piano and is a fan of actor Eddie Murphy and singers Bobby Brown and Janet Jackson. Hill's favorite food is shrimp fried rice, which he sometimes eats five times a week. He does not drink—in fact he has never touched a drop of alcohol. Hill earned his bachelor's degree from Duke in 1994. He has provided $120,000 to fund a summer basketball program for Detroit boys and girls ages eight through 16.

"I feel I'm blessed with a lot of positives in my life," Hill confessed in the *St. Louis Post-Dispatch.* "I've been around a lot of very good people. So it's more of a credit to my parents and people that have been around me. By no means am I perfect. I think that's an image that's been created because of my parents, and being at Duke, and just being a good person. That's something I take a lot of pride in."

Sources

Esquire, February 1995.
GQ, April 1995.
Los Angeles Times, January 5, 1995.
People, January 23, 1995.
Sporting News, April 4, 1994; April 11, 1994; August 29, 1994; January 16, 1995.
Sports Illustrated, February 1, 1993.
Sports Illustrated for Kids, June 1995.
St. Louis Post-Dispatch, March 24, 1994.
Time, February 13, 1995.
USA Today Weekend, December 16-18, 1994.
Additional information provided by Detroit Pistons.

WHERE TO WRITE:
C/O DETROIT PISTONS, THE PALACE OF AUBURN HILLS,
TWO CHAMPIONSHIP DR.,
AUBURN HILLS, MI 48326.

Michael Irvin

1966—

Michael Irvin has always had a big appetite. Growing up in a family of 19, Irvin had to fight for food. Today, Irvin eats up defensive backs as one of the premier receivers in the National Football League (NFL). Irvin teams up with quarterback Troy Aikman and running back Emmitt Smith to give the Dallas Cowboys a potent offensive attack. This attack has made the Cowboys a three-time Super Bowl champion (1993, 1994, and 1996) and the best team of the 1990s.

"When I step on the field, I have the attitude that I'm the best receiver on the field."
—Michael Irvin

Growing Up

BIG FAMILY. Michael Jerome Irvin was born March 5, 1966, in Fort Lauderdale, Florida. His father, Walter, was a roofer and Baptist preacher. His mom, Pearl, was in charge of taking care of the Irvins' 17 children. Irvin has six brothers and 10 sisters, 14 of whom are older than he. Irvin's father worked long hours, often leaving the house at five o'clock in the

SCOREBOARD

LED NFL IN RECEIVING YARDAGE IN 1991 (1,523 YARDS).

FIVE-TIME SELECTION TO PRO BOWL GAME (1991-95).

MEMBER OF BACK-TO-BACK DALLAS COWBOYS SUPER BOWL CHAMPIONS (1993, 1994 AND 1996).

IRVIN SURVIVED A TOUGH CHILDHOOD TO BECOME ONE OF THE NFL'S MOST DANGEROUS OFFENSIVE WEAPONS.

morning and returning late at night. Mr. Irvin worked on his construction job six days a week and preached for the Primitive Baptist Church on two Sundays a month. Despite being tired, he came home from work and played marbles with his children.

"He was as dark as I am, but he would come home just white from all the cement," Irvin recalled in *Sporting News*. "He would come out and play marbles with us. It'd be right before it got dark, and we'd be out there, playing. He always cheated! He'd always try to shoot with the hunk, the big marble."

The Irvin house had only three bedrooms. Irvin shared one with his brothers, and his sisters shared another one. He did not have a bed to himself until he went to college. His father worked hard on the house to create more sleeping space. "He filled in every hole to make places to sleep," Pearl Irvin recalled in *Sports Illustrated*. The children learned not to complain about what they did not have. "You dealt with what you needed, not what you wanted," Irvin explained in *Sports Illustrated*. Christmas usually came and went without presents. Irvin lied to his friends, telling them that his presents were at his grandparents' house.

FOOD FIGHTER. Irvin always had a big appetite. As a child he snuck food from the kitchen when the rest of the family was asleep. "He was a hog, he ate everything," his sister Renee told *Sports Illustrated*. Irvin's mom grew vegetables in the backyard and stayed up late making the next day's meal.

Irvin fought with his brothers and sisters over food, beds, and attention. He learned quickly that he had to be loud to make himself noticed. "Michael does like attention," his mom admitted in *Sports Illustrated*. "I have noticed that about my son." The Irvin children also fought over the family's one fan, important in the hot Florida summers. "We couldn't afford two fans," Irvin recounted in *Sporting News*. "How much do fans cost? I always would have to be the one to go steal the fan from the girls' room. You had to 'call' the fan after six in the morning, like, 'We get the fan tonight.' My sisters always seemed to be able to call the fan, and I always would go steal it. We'd get it going, now we're O.K., and we sleep. Of course, my sisters start to get hot, and they come in and steal it right back."

HARD WORK. Making ends meet was hard for Irvin's family. When Irvin outgrew his gym shoes, his dad cut off the toes and made him wear them that way. The family could not afford to buy new ones. All the children did chores, and Irvin began working with his father on construction jobs at age 13. His father took food and rent money out of his son's pay.

Irvin played football and basketball and ran track in junior high. His sister Pat took a temporary job to earn enough money to buy her brother new gym shoes. His brother Willie became his trainer. Willie Irvin bribed his brother with food to get him to run several miles a day.

TROUBLE. Irvin became envious of things other children had in high school. Piper High School suspended Irvin at the end of his sophomore year for getting into trouble. "I was hanging with the wrong crowd, guys who had no goals, who were just fluttering," Irvin admitted in *Sports Illustrated*. His father began worrying about his son and looked for a private school for Irvin to attend. He finally settled on Saint Thomas Aquinas High school, a middle-class Catholic school. Irvin sat out his junior year of athletics because of the transfer.

Irvin now says that sitting out one year of athletics was the best thing that could have happened to him. He liked Saint Thomas Aquinas, and the teachers and other students took an interest in him, something he felt he had been missing before. "I realized there were people willing to help me," Irvin told *Sports Illustrated*. "I was around kids who had plans. I said, 'Man, this is what I've been missing.'"

DEALING WITH DEATH. During this year Irvin also had another difficult experience. Doctors diagnosed his father, who seemed indestructible, with cancer. Irvin drove his father to

After making a 36-yard touchdown, Irvin celebrates.

the hospital and spent many hours talking with him. The experience gave him new determination to be a good person. His father's ability to laugh in the face of his illness impressed Irvin. "When people see you joking, they don't see a weakness," Irvin stated in *Sports Illustrated*. "When I talk about how strong my father was, that's what I mean. You never saw the man's weakness."

His father died while Irvin was at football practice. When he heard the news, Irvin ran away from home. No one heard from him for hours. Finally, someone from Saint Thomas called and told the family Irvin was there. He had been crying with one of the school's priests. Irvin became determined at that point that no one in his family would ever have to work as hard as his father had. "Football was the trampoline," Irvin explained in *Sports Illustrated.* "It was going to bounce me right over the top."

TWO-SPORT STAR. Irvin earned All-State honors at Aquinas High School in both basketball and football. He was a basketball forward and won several slam-dunk contests. His football team was undefeated in Irvin's senior year and won the state championship.

HURRICANE. Irvin stayed in his home state when it came time to go to college in 1984. He attended the University of Miami, a college football powerhouse. His coach at Miami was Jimmy Johnson, later to be his coach with the Cowboys. In just three seasons as a starter Irvin set Miami career records for catches (143), receiving yards (2,423), and touchdown receptions (26). The Hurricanes won the national championship in 1987, and Irvin caught the winning touchdown pass in their Orange Bowl victory over the University of Oklahoma.

It was at Miami that Irvin began to get his reputation for being a hotdog. He earned the nickname "Playmaker," and when he made a great play he let everyone know about it. "I said crazy things," Irvin confessed in *Sports Illustrated for Kids.*

DALLAS DRAFTEE. The Dallas Cowboys selected Irvin in 1988 with the eleventh pick overall in the NFL Draft. The Cowboys had a long history of greatness, but when Irvin joined the team they were not very good. The 1988 season was the last for legendary coach Tom Landry. Irvin started at wide receiver when the season began, and he proved to be an instant threat. He caught 32 passes for 654 yards, an impressive 20.4-yard average per catch. Irvin also hauled in five touchdown passes. The Cowboys, however, finished a miserable 3-13.

NEW OWNER, NEW COACH. Three major changes took place in Dallas before the 1989 season. Jerry Jones, a millionaire businessman, purchased the team. Jones fired Landry and hired his former college roommate, Johnson. The Cowboys then used the first pick in the NFL Draft to select quarterback Troy Aikman from the University of California at Los Angeles (UCLA).

Johnson's taking over the Cowboys thrilled Irvin. He claimed that Johnson knew him better than anyone else. Johnson may have wanted to win even more than Irvin. "With Jimmy, it was different," Irvin explained in *Sport* magazine. "You felt like if you didn't make it [a first down], he was going to die. You'd see him on the sideline and you'd think, if we don't get this first down it's going to kill him. So you'd get it. That's what Jimmy could do."

Irvin started fast in 1989, but his season came to a crashing halt in the sixth game when he tore up a knee against the San Francisco 49ers. The injury lingered into the 1990 season, and the Cowboys considered trading Irvin. Johnson claims he never considered dealing his speedy wide receiver. "There's not another receiver in the league I'd even consider trading Michael Irvin for," Johnson told *Sport* magazine. "I think number one, he is a great player. I think he is a great competitor, a great practice player with great work habits, and I think that carries over to the rest of the players. The other thing is, personally I like him."

Superstar

TURNING THINGS AROUND. The Cowboys finished 1-15 in 1989 and 7-9 in 1990. Irvin and the rest of his Dallas teammates decided that their losing streak had to end. The Cowboys were 6-5 more than halfway through the 1991 season but then exploded for five straight victories to earn a play-off spot. The triple threat of Irvin, Aikman, and running back Emmitt Smith led the way. Irvin exploded for the best season of his career, catching 93 passes for 1,523 yards (number one in the NFL) and eight touchdowns. The Cowboys won their

IRVIN AND RICE

The player to whom Irvin is most often compared is the great Jerry Rice of the San Francisco 49ers. Both players are tall and fast and specialize in making tough catches. Rice has played several years longer than Irvin, but their first seven seasons are compared below.

	Receptions	Yards	Touchdowns
Irvin	416	6,935	40
Rice	526	9,072	93

first play-off game, 17-13, against the Chicago Bears but then lost 38-6 to the Detroit Lions. Irvin, playing in his first Pro Bowl game following the season, caught eight passes for 125 yards. Reporters named him the game's Most Valuable Player.

SUPER STEAMROLLER. No team could stop the Cowboys the next two seasons. Dallas ran over the competition on the way to back-to-back Super Bowl championships. Irvin continued to run by defensive backs. He caught 78 passes for 1,396 yards in 1992 and 88 passes (third in the NFL) for 1,241 yards (second in the NFL) in 1993. Each season Irvin caught seven touchdown passes. He came up big in Super Bowl XXVII, catching two touchdown passes in a mere 15 seconds against the Buffalo Bills. The touchdowns gave the Cowboys a 28-10 halftime lead on the way to a 52-17 victory.

SHOCKER. Jerry Jones, in a surprise move, fired Johnson after the Cowboys' second Super Bowl victory. He replaced Johnson with Barry Switzer, formerly coach of the University of Oklahoma Sooners. The decision upset Irvin more than it did any of the other Cowboys. He went to see Jones and demanded a trade. "I had been through the losing, and I wasn't going back," Irvin recalled in *Sport* magazine. "I've been through 1-15 and 3-13 seasons, and I would not, and will not, have any part of that. We were used to winning under Jimmy. If my car is running fine, I don't take it to the shop. I keep driving it until it breaks. And we should have kept driving that machine until it broke."

Irvin decided to stay in Dallas. "There was a certain point when I wanted to leave, but my commitment to my teammates—both as teammates and as friends—became my biggest liability," Irvin admitted in *Sport* magazine. "I truly love being with them. I can't help it." Irvin also helped keep the Cowboys focused and not worried about their own statistics or contracts. "If we're bickering and having problems," Irvin told his teammates, "then nobody gets anything. I'd rather take half of somebody's something than have my own nothing. You'd rather have a part of something big—even a little part—than your very own nothing."

THREEPEAT DEFEAT. In 1994 the Cowboys had the chance to set two records. They set out to become the first team ever to win three straight Super Bowls and the first franchise to win five Super Bowls in its history. Irvin caught 79 passes for 1,241 yards (eighth in the NFL). Personal glory did not interest Irvin, however. "There are no statistics on Super Bowl rings," Irvin declared in the *Dallas Morning News*. "It takes one game in the play[-]offs to lose what has taken three years to build. Think about what it has taken to reach this point and one play can lose it. It can go like that, something we worked so hard for. We know we have a chance to do something that has never been done and nobody on this team wants to feel like that didn't happen because they didn't make a block or they dropped the ball."

The Cowboys' dream of a third straight Super Bowl came up short in 1994. The Cowboys lost 38-28 to the eventual champions, the San Francisco 49ers, in the National Football Conference (NFC) Championship Game. Irvin caught 12 passes for 192 yards, both championship game records. The loss was hard to accept, and Irvin and Smith were seen crying on the sideline. "I remember sitting down right before the end of the game and thinking, 'I cannot believe we are at this point,'" Irvin told *Sport* magazine. "I won't let it [the feeling of losing] go. I want to remember how bad it feels to walk off that field and not be the best. We're not champions. We're not being chased, we're chasing."

LOYALTY. Irvin could have left the Cowboys after the season, but instead signed a five-year contract. "This is the team I won two Super Bowls with," Irvin admitted to *Sport* magazine. "This is the same team I went to battle with time and time again. You always hear that there's no loyalty anymore. Well, I think that's all there is." Irvin and Smith are friends and have a ritual they go through each game before going onto the field. "It's you and me," Irvin tells Smith. "Let's go make things happen." Smith then slaps Irvin on the shoulder pads and says, "It's you and me, Michael. Just you and me. Let's go do it."

Even though the Cowboys did not repeat as champions, Irvin still supported Switzer. "Any other rookie coach comes in and takes a team to the championship game, he gets all kinds of praise," Irvin told *Sport* magazine. "But what they're saying here is, we should have been there anyway. The truth is, Barry did a great job just keeping things together."

NEW DETERMINATION. Irvin entered the 1995 season with renewed determination to win the championship. "Michael has been strictly business, on and off the field," Cowboys' receivers coach, Hubbard Alexander, told *Sporting News*. "He's not as jovial as he usually is. I've never seen him like this since I've been around him. He's still working as hard as ever; it's just that he's going another way now, trying to make this thing happen." When wide receiver Alvin Harper left to join the Tampa Bay Bucaneers before the season, Irvin's job became more difficult. Now teams could double-team Irvin and try to take him out of the Cowboys offense.

The Cowboys started fast and established themselves as the team to beat, especially after signing All-Pro defensive back Deion Sanders. Soon, however, the team began to struggle. They lost to the San Francisco 49ers and later lost a tough game to the Philadelphia Eagles after a controversial fourth-down call by Switzer. Dallas turned things around, however, and finished 12-4, good enough to earn the team home-field advantage throughout the play-offs.

TOUGH ENOUGH

Irvin has earned his reputation as one of the toughest receivers in the NFL. "When I step on the field, I have the attitude that I'm the best receiver on the field," Irvin revealed in *Sport* magazine. "It means the best state, the best game, the best blocks. I step on the field with the intent to be the best receiver. I do a lot of dirty work. I catch a lot of under routes in front of the linebackers. I'm willing to go catch the football wherever it is thrown. If I don't make a catch, it's not because I don't go after it." Known for his trash-talking, Irvin has tried to cut back on his boasting and let his play do the talking. "I want to be looked at as a professional," Irvin explained in *Sports Illustrated for Kids*. He will never be completely quiet, however. "Everybody says 'Look at that hot dog,'" Irvin stated in *Sports Illustrated*. "I'm just having fun. They all take me wrong."

Irvin had another remarkable season in 1995. He caught 111 passes for 1,603 yards and ten touchdowns. Irvin tied an NFL record with eight straight 100-yard games and eleven 100-yard games overall. "He's had a fantastic year," Hubbard Alexander explained in *Sporting News*. "I mean, his numbers alone show that. And that's really great when you consider how he's been looking at a lot of double coverage. This is the best year he's ever had."

THREE IN FOUR. The Cowboys rolled over the Philadelphia Eagles, 30-11, in their first play-off game. In the NFC Championship Game, Dallas faced the Green Bay Packers, who had defeated the 49ers the week before, knocking the defending champions out of the Super Bowl race. The Cowboys defeated the Packers, 28-27, and qualified for their third Super Bowl appearance in three seasons. "It's where we belong," Irvin told *Sports Illustrated*. "It's where we're at our best. It's where we need to be." Irvin caught seven passes in the game for 100 yards and two touchdowns.

Super Bowl XXX was held in Tempe, Arizona, and featured two of the NFL's great franchises. Both the Cowboys and the Pittsburgh Steelers had won four Super Bowls and Dallas had the chance to do what no team had done before—win three Super Bowls in four seasons. The Cowboys took a 13-0 lead against the Steelers, with seven points coming on a touchdown pass to Irvin. Irvin caught five passes for 76 yards in the first half.

The Steelers changed their defensive strategy at halftime. They put All-Pro cornerback **Rod Woodson** (see entry) on Irvin, despite the fact that Woodson had just returned to the lineup after knee surgery. Woodson did a great job on Irvin, holding him without a catch in the second half. Fortunately for Dallas, Steelers' quarterback Neil O'Donnell threw two second-half interceptions to cornerback Larry Brown that led to 14 points for the Cowboys. Dallas won the game 27-17. They were the Super Bowl champions for the third time in four years.

OFF THE FIELD. Irvin, his wife Sandi, and their daughter, Myesha, live in Carrollton, Texas. He bought his mom a house and a car. He also maintains a scholarship in his father's name at Saint Thomas Aquinas and encourages all of his male relatives to attend the school.

Irvin earned his degree in business management from Miami. He is the host of the *Michael Irvin Show,* a weekly television show that runs throughout the football season. Irvin appears on "Stay in School" posters sponsored by the Dallas All-Sports Association. He has a big appetite and likes to eat a lot. "I crave things," he admitted in *Sports Illustrated.*

Unfortunately, Irvin also has an appetite for trouble. On April 1, 1996, Irvin and two other people were indicted on charges of cocaine and marijuana possession. Irvin was released on bond and is awaiting trial. If convicted, Irvin faces up to 20 years in prison and a $10,000 fine. If acquitted, Irvin may have to work extra hard both on and off the football field to regain the respect of fans.

Sources

New York Times, March 31, 1996.
Sport, January 1994; July 1994; July 1995.
Sporting News, January 24, 1994; January 31, 1994; February 7, 1994; January 16, 1995; January 23, 1995; December 25, 1995; January 8, 1996; January 15, 1996; January 22, 1996; February 5, 1996.
Sports Illustrated, October 25, 1993: February 7, 1994; January 16, 1995; January 23, 1995.
Sports Illustrated for Kids, October 1994.
Additional information provided by Dallas Cowboys.

WHERE TO WRITE:
C/O DALLAS COWBOYS, COWBOYS CENTER,
ONE COWBOYS PKWY.,
IRVING, TX 75063.

Jaromir Jagr

1972—

"Scoring goals, winning the games, and celebrating after that, that's why you play."
—Jaromir Jagr

Jaromir Jagr arrived as a star for the Pittsburgh Penguins during the 1994-95 National Hockey League (NHL) season. Injuries forced the Penguins' captain and superstar, the remarkable Mario Lemieux, to miss the entire season. Jagr, who had played in the shadow of his more famous teammate, had his chance to shine. He took advantage of the opportunity, tying for the NHL scoring title and becoming a team leader. Jagr hopes to rejoin Lemieux and make the Penguins the most dangerous hockey team in the world.

Growing Up

LOOKING FOR THE TRUTH. Jaromir Jagr (YAR-ah-meer YAH-guhr) was born February 15, 1972, in Kladno, Czechoslovakia. His father, Jaromir, was a coal mine administrator. His mother's name is Anna. Jagr grew up under the Communist government of Czechoslovakia. He relied on his grandmother, Jarmila, to tell him the truth about his country's history. Jagr's grandfather, also named Jaromir, had his farm taken away when the Communists took over in 1948 and was put in jail for more than two years. "In school we were always taught the Soviet doctrine [story]," he recalled in *Sports Illustrated*. "The USA was bad and wanted war. Russia was our friend and was preventing the United States from bombing us. Even my father didn't tell me the truth, because he was afraid I would say something in school that would get us into trouble. But my grandmother, she told me the truth."

Jagr grew up with strong pro-American feelings as a result of his grandmother's lessons. When he was 12, he carried a picture of then U.S. President Ronald Reagan torn out of a magazine to school in his grade book every day. Jagr's teachers punished him for doing so and warned him he might get into trouble. He also had American flag stickers on his car. Jagr taped two posters to his wall: the great one, Wayne Gretzky, and tennis star Martina Navratilova, who had defected from Czechoslovakia to the United States to pursue her professional career. Jagr dreamed that one day he, too, could compete in the West.

LEARNS FROM DAD. Jagr showed talent for hockey at an early age. At age five, he began to play with his dad. The Jagr family was poor, so his dad tried to help him learn the game any way he could. Father and son would play after school among the chickens in the dirt between their house and the family barn. Mr. Jagr also built his son a barbell from an old tractor axle so that the boy could work on his upper-body strength.

The elder Jagr encouraged his son to play on older boys' teams to help him find his real skill level. "He [his father] knew a friend who was a coach," Jagr recalled in *Sports Illustrated for Kids*. "He brought me there to try and skate. I was two years younger than the other guys." Playing with older players forced Jagr to work harder. "I probably spent three

SCOREBOARD

LED NHL IN SCORING (1994-95).

FINISHED SECOND IN VOTING FOR 1994-95 HART MEMORIAL TROPHY AS NHL MOST VALUABLE PLAYER (MVP).

HELPED LEAD PENGUINS TO BACK-TO-BACK STANLEY CUP TITLES (1992 AND 1993).

JAGR AND MARIO LEMIEUX MAKE THE PITTSBURGH PENGUINS ONE OF THE NHL'S MOST EXPLOSIVE TEAMS.

DEFINING DEFECTING

Before the overthrow of the Communist governments of eastern Europe, many athletes defected, or left their countries without the permission of the Communist governments. Although these athletes could make more money and have their freedom in the West, there were some bad things about defecting. An athlete who defected could not return to his home country, and many times the athlete's family would lose their jobs, get arrested, or be physically harmed by the government. Fortunately, the many great athletes of eastern Europe no longer have to choose between freedom and their families, because of the overthrow of the Communist governments in eastern Europe.

times more time on the ice than the other players," Jagr explained.

ESCAPE ROUTE. Hockey was Jagr's way to escape from his homeland. The Communist government of Czechoslovakia would not allow people to leave the country, even to visit other countries on vacation. The government did, however, allow star athletes to travel to competitions around the world. "That's the only way you could see other countries," Jagr explained in *Sports Illustrated for Kids*.

Jagr played in the Czech hockey major league with the team Poldi Kladno when he was 15. When he was 16, he was making more money than his father, and when he was 17, in 1989, he earned a spot on the Czech national team. Jagr played for his country in the 1990 world championship tournament, in which a victory over Team Canada and some of the NHL stars who were his idols built up his confidence. NHL scouts got a firsthand look at how good Jagr was.

PENGUIN PICK. Thanks to the Czech revolution of 1989, Jagr had his chance. The overthrow of the Communist government led to the formation of two new countries. The two new countries were the Czech Republic (where Jagr lived) and Slovakia. When Jagr attended the 1990 NHL entry draft in Vancouver—at which Pittsburgh selected him fifth overall—it marked the first time a Czech player had attended the draft without needing the permission of the government. Jagr was now in the NHL at age 18. "My parents told me that I should stay here [in the Czech Republic] and finish school," Jagr confessed in *Sports Illustrated*. "But I said I want to play the best hockey in the world."

MEETS PRESIDENT. Jagr had an impressive rookie season in the NHL in 1991-92. He tallied 27 goals and 30 assists, earned a spot on the league's All-Rookie team, and helped the Penguins to their first Stanley Cup championship. Jagr and his teammates visited the White House and met President George Bush, a thrill for someone who used to carry a president's picture with him.

HOMESICK. Despite his success, Jagr was homesick. He missed his family, friends, and country. Jagr lived with a Czech-speaking family, and in the first half of the season was unhappy and "slipping farther and farther away," as Pittsburgh general manager Craig Patrick recalled in *Sports Illustrated.* Pittsburgh coaches tried to help, but Jagr did not understand what they were saying and thought they were criticizing him. So Patrick traded for a veteran Czech player, Jiri Hrdina, to become something of a mentor to his prized rookie. "Jags was really down low when I got there," Hrdina told *Sports Illustrated.* "He wasn't going to go home or anything, but he felt alone. I could talk to him about his problems. He's a very smart guy for his age."

Having someone to talk to helped, and in the second half of the season Jagr accounted for 37 of his 57 points. He also scored his first hat trick—scoring three goals in one game—against Boston on February 2, 1991. Jagr set a rookie record for the Stanley Cup Finals with five assists.

TAKES OVER. Jagr's second season in the NHL firmly established him as one of the league's stars. His regular season statistics improved to 32 goals and 37 assists. Jagr got more ice time when the Penguins traded right-winger Mark Recchi near the end of the season. He was forced to step up in the second round of the play-offs when Penguins star Mario Lemieux broke his hand and had to miss several games. Jagr became the main man in the Penguins' offense, leading the team past the New York Rangers, then the Boston Bruins, both in best-of-seven series, to put the Penguins back in the Stanley Cup Finals. Four times during these series Jagr scored game-winning goals.

Lemieux returned to the lineup for the Stanley Cup Finals. Pittsburgh, with both offensive guns blazing, swept the

Chicago Blackhawks in four straight games. The Penguins had successfully defended their championship. Jagr finished the play-offs with 11 goals and 13 assists, but his leadership in Lemieux's absence made the difference in the Penguins' play-off run. His more famous teammate agreed. "Jaromir's probably going to be the best player in the world in a couple of years," Lemieux predicted during 1992 in *Sports Illustrated*.

POPULAR PENGUIN. Jagr's popularity in Pittsburgh had grown by the end of the 1991-92 season. It was during this season that someone rearranged the letters in "Jaromir" to spell "Mario Jr.," and Penguins fans treated him as almost the equal of Lemieux. Jagr's long hair and youthful looks made him a hit with the female fans in particular.

One night Penguins radio announcer Mike Lange mentioned that Jagr liked Kit Kat bars. Soon Jagr began receiving hundreds of the chocolate wafers from admirers, mostly young women. "I will eat them all," Jagr told the *Detroit News*. "I have over 1,000 Kit Kat bars." The city's top-rated FM radio station, WDVE, even made him its on-air weather personality. The station began running "Jaromir Weather" on its morning show. After each of his first two seasons, Jagr went back to spend the summer with his family in Kladno, where he was even more popular.

His popularity did not make Jagr completely happy. Since the Penguins would not allow players under age 20 to live on their own, Jagr lived with an English-speaking family his second year. He did not feel comfortable talking to the media because his English was not very good. The Penguins supplied him with an English tutor, but Jagr told the *Detroit News* that he was learning the language a different way. "I watch TV. I like the Bundys.... I don't take lessons. I'm too lazy for that." Jagr began to get into trouble, usually because he drove too fast, and requested a trade. In one several-month stretch he received 24 speeding tickets.

Superstar

PENGUIN POWERHOUSE. Jagr decided to stay in Pittsburgh and became one of the NHL's best players the next two seasons. He tallied 34 goals and 60 assists in 1992-93, and 32 goals and 67 assists in 1993-94. The Penguins lost in the early rounds of the play-offs both years, but Jagr's reputation continued to grow. Pittsburgh became Jagr's team during the 1993-94 season because Lemieux missed most of that year with Hodgkin's disease. The Penguins rewarded his leadership with a five-year, $19.5 million contract.

ATTITUDE ADJUSTMENT. Jagr improved his attitude along with his play. He became more popular with the media as his English improved, and he also stopped pouting after bad games. "When I was 18 I thought hockey was all that mattered," he admitted in *Sports Illustrated*. "But no more. Now I know how important life is. Hockey is still great and a lot of fun and a great job, but it's not everything in life. I used to think, if I play a bad game, my life is over. Now I realize that if I play a bad game, well, so what? Life is still good." Jagr also showed his leadership in practice. "I spend a lot of time here at the [Pittsburgh] Arena," he told *Sports Illustrated for Kids*. "I'm always the last to leave."

TEAM LEADER. Lemieux announced that he would sit out the 1994-95 season to recover from his Hodgkin's disease and rest a sore back. The announcement put Jagr's leadership to a test. "He [Jagr] just has much more of a sense of responsibility this year," Pittsburgh coach Ed Johnston told *Sports Illustrated*. "He has slowed the pace of his life down, and now he's become more focused on what's important." Jagr's leadership impressed teammate John Cullen, who said in *Sports Illustrated,* "I think he looks around now and says, 'Hey Mario's gone, maybe this is my show now.' I think he's really enjoying himself."

A dispute between the players and team owners shortened the 1994-95 season to 48 games. Jagr took advantage of the break and played in Czechoslovakia and Italy. The extra games made Jagr ready when the new season started. "With Mario out, we needed someone else to step forward, and he has," Johnston revealed in *Sport* magazine. Injuries to winger Kevin Stevens and goalie Tom Barrasso made Jagr's job even more difficult.

ONE—TWO PUNCH

Lemieux returned to the Penguins' lineup for the 1995-96 season, and Pittsburgh promised to be an offensive powerhouse. Many people compare the two players. "They've got different styles, but Jagr does remind you of Mario in a lot of ways," teammate Kevin Stevens said in *Sports Illustrated.* "He's got the same kind of presence on the ice." Another teammate, John Cullen, told the same publication that you cannot take your eyes off Jagr. "When you're sitting on the bench, it's just like it was with Mario," Cullen said. "You watch. You can't help. You know Yaggs can get the puck and just take over the game. You don't want to miss it."

When he was 13, Jagr first saw Lemieux play, in the world championships in Prague, Czechoslovakia. "It was very tough for me to play with Mario," Jagr confessed in *Sports Illustrated.* "You know, sometimes you just have so much respect for a guy and you look up to him so much that you can't believe you're really playing with him. Every student needs a teacher, and he was my teacher." Jagr does not believe the comparisons that some experts make between himself and Lemieux. "Mario is my idol," he admitted in *Sport* magazine. "I can never be like him. I only try to do my best."

LEAGUE LEADER. Jagr tied Eric Lindros of the Philadelphia Flyers for the league lead in scoring (combined goals and assists). He finished the season with 32 goals and 38 assists. Jagr accomplished this despite being a marked man, the one player the other team knew they had to stop. "He should practice with a 100-pound dummy strapped to his back, because that's the way he has to play in the games," teammate Shawn McEachern told *Sports Illustrated.* Jagr won the Art Ross Trophy as the league's leading scorer, because he scored one more goal than Lindros. "He knows the game better than anyone on the team," Johnston told *Sports Illustrated.* "He's very smart out there. He knows the little things, things you can't teach. He knows how to play the angles and how to protect the puck."

OFF THE ICE. Jagr lives in the suburbs of Pittsburgh. His mother has moved from Czechoslovakia and now lives with him, and his father visits twice a year. Jagr says he still thinks a lot about his home country and is a hero there. "If I could bring Czechoslovakia here, I would be happiest," Jagr confessed in *Sports Illustrated for Kids*. His number, 68, stands for 1968, a year the people in Czechoslovakia revolted against the Communist government. That revolution failed, but it set the stage for later success.

Jagr enjoys what he does, as he told *Sports Illustrated for Kids:* "Scoring goals, winning the games, and celebrating after that, that's why you play."

Sources

Detroit News, May 27, 1992; May 28, 1992.
Sport, July 1995.
Sporting News, September 20, 1992; October 12, 1992.
Sports Illustrated, October 12, 1992; March 13, 1995.
Sports Illustrated for Kids, May 1995.
Additional information provided by Pittsburgh Penguins.

WHERE TO WRITE:
C/O PITTSBURGH PENGUINS,
CIVIC ARENA,
PITTSBURGH, PA 15219.

Michael Johnson

1967—

"The only one who can beat me is me."—Michael Johnson

In 1996 Michael Johnson hopes to attempt a feat no one has ever accomplished. He wants to become the first sprinter to ever win gold medals in the 200- and 400-meter dashes at the same Summer Olympics. Johnson, the number-one-ranked sprinter in both events, made history in 1995 by accomplishing this feat at the World Track and Field Championships. Unfortunately, he may not get the chance to pull off this rare Olympic double feat. The Olympic schedule for the two races overlaps, leaving Johnson with no choice but to compete in one or the other. A world indoor record holder in the 400-meter dash, Johnson will likely be one of the most watched track and field athletes at the 1996 Summer Olympics in Atlanta, Georgia.

Growing Up

SPEEDY READER. Michael Johnson was born September 13, 1967, in Dallas, Texas. He is the youngest of five children.

His parents stressed that education and good grades are important. Each of Johnson's four siblings finished college. Johnson attended classes for gifted children. He wore black horn-rimmed glasses that made him look like the class brain, and other children called him a nerd. Rather than dreaming of becoming a star athlete, Johnson wanted to be an architect.

Johnson did not start running track until he was a teenager. "I first competed in track at Atwell Junior High in Dallas, and then just because it was something fun to do," Johnson remembered in *Boys' Life*. "I ran the 200 and the sprint relay, but I wasn't outstanding and had no big plans for high school track."

SCOREBOARD

FIRST SPRINTER IN HISTORY TO WIN BOTH 200- AND 400-METER DASHES AT THE WORLD TRACK AND FIELD CHAMPIONSHIPS (1995).

WORLD INDOOR RECORD HOLDER IN 400-METER DASH (44.63 SECONDS).

TOP-RANKED SPRINTER IN BOTH 200- AND 400-METER DASHES.

JOHNSON HOPES A SCHEDULE CHANGE WILL ALLOW HIM TO COMPLETE A RARE DOUBLE VICTORY AT THE 1996 SUMMER OLYMPICS IN ATLANTA, GEORGIA.

RUNS FOR FUN. Johnson did not run track his first two years at Skyline High School so that he could concentrate on his studies. He tried out for the track team as a junior and received some good advice from his coach, Joel Ezar—relax and enjoy running. "Track is a big sport in Texas, but he [Ezar] didn't put pressure on me," Johnson explained in *Boys' Life*. "I ran the 200 and both relays [400 and 1,600]. I never went to a meet intent [determined] on running some great times and trying to impress college coaches and get a scholarship. As a result, I never felt burned out."

Johnson won the district title in the 200 meters as a senior but lost at the state meet. "I believe Michael has done so well because he wasn't always No. 1 in high school," his future college coach at Baylor University, Clyde Hart, related in *Boys' Life*. "He knew what it was like to lose, then go back to work and stay at it. He decided that if he used everything he had in himself, that some day he would be No. 1."

BAYLOR BULLET. Johnson attended Baylor University, but track still was not his priority. "I loved track, but at the time, it was a way to get to a better college," Johnson confessed in

Boys' Life. "I wasn't as concerned with track as with education." Johnson shocked Hart when he broke the school record in the 200 meters in his first race. "We knew he'd be solid, but we had no idea he'd be that good," Hart admitted in *Newsweek.* "He turned out to be an incredible combination of strength and relaxation on the track."

BAD LUCK BEAR. Johnson had a tough year in 1988. Already a ranked sprinter, he suffered a major setback. "Michael had lots of setbacks and injuries his first two years in [college]," Hart recalled in *Boys' Life.* "Everything that could go wrong, did go wrong. But when he fell and broke his leg during the NCAA [National Collegiate Athletic Association] Championships it was the worst luck yet."

The injury, a stress fracture in his left leg, occurred just six weeks before the 1988 Olympic Trials. Seeing his Olympic dream slipping away, Johnson worked to keep his legs strong. Wrapping the leg securely with tape, he trained in a swimming pool and gradually forced himself to run on the track. Despite his effort, Johnson could not regain his usual speed by the time of the Olympic Trials. He finished dead last in his first-round race, eliminating him from the competition.

Instead of being disappointed by his bad luck, Johnson used the experience in a positive way. "The race told me I could come back and compete with the best if I worked hard enough," Johnson stated in *Boys' Life.* Hart told the same magazine the race was "probably the best 55 seconds Michael ever invested. Michael came back with a new resolve [determination]."

NUMBER ONE. In 1990 Johnson became the first athlete ever to be ranked number one in the 200- and 400-meter sprints in the same year. To show this was not a fluke, he repeated the feat in 1991. Running against the toughest competition in the world, Johnson did not loss a race in the summers of 1990 and 1991. His biggest triumph came at the 1991 World Track and Field Championships, where he won the 200 meters.

Johson is victorious at the 1995 World Track and Field Championships.

MORE BAD LUCK. Because of his success, Johnson decided to try out for the U.S. Olympic track team in both events in 1992. "It will be tough, trying to win both the 200 and the 400 because you have to run so many heats to reach the finals in both," Johnson explained in *Boys' Life*. "But I really believe I have a shot."

Bad luck continued to follow Johnson at the 1992 Summer Olympics in Barcelona, Spain. Before the Olympics began, Johnson ate something that made him very sick. He couldn't train for two weeks and had not worked his way back into shape by the time he needed to race. In the semifinals of the 200 meters, Johnson finished a disappointing sixth. He did not qualify for the finals. "I'm just disappointed I didn't get to do my best," Johnson said after the race. He did win an

Olympic gold medal, running the anchor (final) leg of the victorious U.S. 1,600-meter relay team.

STILL THE BEST. In both 1993 and 1994, Johnson earned U.S. track's Athlete of the Year honor. In 1993 he won the 400 meters at the World Track and Field Championships. Johnson maintained his number one rating in both the 200- and 400-meter sprints through 1994 and 1995. In March 1995 Johnson lowered his own indoor 400-meter world record by running 44.63 at the USA/Mobile Indoor Championships.

Superstar

U.S. RECORD. In June 1995 Johnson became the first runner in almost 100 years to win both the 200 and 400 at the U.S. Track and Field Championships. His time in the 400 (43.66 seconds) was the fastest ever run in the United States, and he beat the second-place finisher, world record holder Butch Reynolds, by ten meters. Johnson might have set the world record, but he celebrated just before crossing the finish line, doing a high-stepping dance he called "my Deion Sanders thing."

MAKES HISTORY. Johnson attempted to become the first sprinter ever to win both the 200- and 400-meter sprints at the World Track and Field Championships held in August 1995 in Goteborg, Sweden. "In order to be considered the best in the world by everyone, I'll have to run both at the world championships," Johnson said in the *New York Times*. "Hopefully, people will really understand what I'm doing and better appreciate it."

In the 400 meters Johnson ran the best race of his life, winning by seven meters. When he looked at the clock after crossing the finish line, he discovered he had missed the world record by the smallest of margins—one-tenth of a second. Johnson's 43.39 was the second-fastest time ever. "At first it was upsetting, but I'm happy," Johnson said after the race. "I'm extremely pleased with 43.39."

Johnson's work was not done, however. "I came in here with the objective of winning the gold medal at 400 and at

DOUBLE TROUBLE

The 200- and 400-meter sprints are similar in some ways, but different in others. The 200-meter race is an all-out sprint that usually lasts about 20 seconds. The 400 meters, because it is twice as long, requires both speed and endurance. Many runners, such as the legendary Jesse Owens and Carl Lewis, have run both the 100- and 200-meter dashes, but no one has achieved what Johnson has in his career. "I've been blessed with an ability to sprint, and also with some endurance," Johnson explained in *Runner's World.* "I've studied both events. I didn't follow the traditional lines of a sprinter, who typically runs the 100 and 200 or just the 400." Training for both races is difficult, and some experts think Johnson should concentrate on only one. To win both races he needs to compete in seven races, running flat out against the fastest men in the world, all in the space of a few days. "The body can only take so much," U.S. Olympic track and field coach Erv Hunt told *Newsweek.* "But this guy is almost superhuman." Johnson feels the reward is worth the pain. "Sure there's a risk involved, but that's what makes it fun for me and exciting for the fans," Johnson stated in *Newsweek.*

200 meters," Johnson told the *New York Times.* "As far as I'm concerned, this is the halfway point." Johnson had only 15 hours of rest between the 400-meter final and the first heat of the 200 meters.

Fatigue could not stop Johnson from making history. He blew away the competition and tied his personal best time of 19.79 in the 200-meter dash. Johnson thus became the first sprinter to ever win both events in a single world championships. He added a third gold medal as part of the U.S. 1,600-meter relay team.

THE FUTURE. Johnson continues to have bad luck with the Olympics. Because the Olympic schedule calls for the semifinals of the 200 meters to take place only three hours before the 400-meter finals, Johnson must choose the event in which he wants to compete at the 1996 Summer Olympics in Atlanta, Georgia. He asked the International Amateur Athletic Federation to change the schedule, but the organization turned down his request. Johnson believes he would be too worn out to do his best in either race if he tried to run in both.

WHY SO GOOD?

Johnson has an unusual style, running upright instead of crouched over. His high school coach said he ran "like a statue." None of his coaches have tried to change his style, because of his success. Johnson is very intense when he runs and rarely shows emotion. He looks mean on the track, but he says he is only concentrating. "They say I look mean," Johnson explained in *Runner's World.* "My focus is on winning. At that point, I can't 'like' my opponents." Most important, Johnson works hard, training up to four hours a day running and lifting weights. "He outworks everybody to get strong," Hart told *Newsweek.*

"Whichever race I don't run will be a joke, and I won't be the only one who will be disappointed," Johnson complained in *Sports Illustrated.* His victory at the world championships, and the media attention Johnson's Olympic double would create, may force a change in scheduling.

OFF THE TRACK. Johnson is a spokesperson for Nike. He earned his business administration degree at Baylor. Johnson has not lost a 400-meter race since 1990 and is a threat to break the world records in both of his specialties. For now, Johnson focuses on his goal. "I can't let anything or anyone distract me," Johnson explained in *Newsweek.* "The only one who can beat me is me."

Sources

Boys' Life, May 1992.
Jet, January 31, 1994; August 28, 1995.
Newsweek, July 31, 1995.
New York Times, June 18, 1995; June 19, 1995; August 6, 1995; August 9, 1995; August 10, 1995.
Runner's World, July 1995.
Sports Illustrated, June 26, 1995; August 21, 1995.
Sports Illustrated for Kids, September 1995.
Additional information provided by USA Track and Field.

WHERE TO WRITE:
C/O U.S. TRACK AND FIELD,
ONE HOOSIER DOME, STE. 140,
INDIANAPOLIS, IN 46225.

Randy Johnson

1963—

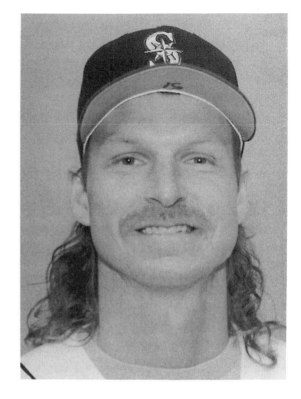

R andy Johnson stands out in a crowd. His six-foot-ten-inch height makes him the tallest player to ever play in the major leagues and has earned him the nicknames "Big Bird" and "Big Unit." It is his 100-mile-an-hour fastball and unhittable slider, however, that have made him the most dominating pitcher in the American League. Johnson has led the major leagues in strikeouts for four straight seasons, a feat not even his idol and mentor, Nolan Ryan, could match. Johnson so dominated the American League in 1995 for the division-winning Seattle Mariners that baseball experts gave him the Cy Young Award, which is awarded annually to the league's best pitcher. Johnson has proved that tall is not all for him as a pitcher or as a person.

Growing Up

NO CONTROL. Randall David Johnson was born September 10, 1963, in Walnut Creek, California. His father's name was

"When you can throw 97 miles an hour and put the ball over the plate any time you want, it's fun."
—*Randy Johnson*

SCOREBOARD

1995 AMERICAN LEAGUE CY YOUNG AWARD WINNER.

LED MAJOR LEAGUES IN STRIKEOUTS FOUR STRAIGHT SEASONS (1992-95).

FOUR-TIME AMERICAN LEAGUE ALL-STAR (1990, 1993-95).

JOHNSON USED HIS FATHER'S DEATH AND A LEGEND'S ADVICE TO BECOME THE BEST PITCHER IN THE AMERICAN LEAGUE.

Bud and his mother's name is Carol. Johnson could always throw the ball hard but had a hard time controlling it. He would tape a strike zone to his garage door and pretend to pitch tennis balls to his major league heroes. When he was finished, his dad would come out and check to see how many ball marks were inside the strike zone. There never were very many.

TALL TEASING. Johnson's career in Little League got off to a rocky start. He showed up late for his first game, could not find his team, and returned home to his mom in tears. Johnson grew seven inches between the ages of seven and 12. He was an easy target for teasing because of his height. "I used to be a real outgoing person when I was younger," he recalled in *Sports Illustrated*. "But then I started getting noticed a lot because of my height. I felt like I was in a three-ring circus and didn't know how to handle it."

Johnson attended Livermore High School. He was a two-sport star. In basketball Johnson led the East Bay Athletic League in scoring twice and was the baseball team's star pitcher. He left high school with a bang, pitching a perfect game in his last game. (A perfect game occurs when no opposition batters reach base.) He graduated from Livermore in 1982 and received a combined baseball and basketball scholarship to attend the University of Southern California. Johnson played both sports his first two years at Southern Cal but concentrated solely on baseball in his junior year.

JOHNSON RULE. The Montreal Expos picked Johnson in the second round of the 1985 major league baseball draft. He was always highly emotional. Early in 1988 the Expos sent scouts to watch him pitch for the Indianapolis Indians, their top farm

The baseball is a blur as Johnson releases it. ▶

Randy Johnson | **190**

club. During the game a line drive hit Johnson on his left wrist. Afraid that his chance to impress the major league scouts was gone, Johnson punched the team's bat rack. It turned out that his left wrist was fine, but he broke a bone in his right hand because he had gotten so mad. The Expos created the Randy Johnson Rule after the incident. From that day on, any player who did something foolish to injure himself would be fined.

Johnson, at six feet ten inches tall, became the tallest player in major league history when the Expos called him up to the majors in September 1988. "He doesn't look that big up there," his teammate Tim Raines told *Sports Illustrated.* "Just about nine feet tall." Johnson got off to a good start, going 3-0 with a 2.42 earned run average (ERA). He started the 1989 season with the Expos, but then things went sour. He was 0-4 with a 6.67 ERA when the Expos sent him back to the minors. Control was Johnson's problem. He walked 26 batters in 29 innings.

SWITCHES LEAGUES. The Expos were in contention in the National League East Division. The Expos, seeking an established pitcher for the stretch drive, traded Johnson and pitcher Brian Holman for star left-hander Mark Langston on May 25, 1989. Johnson joined the Seattle Mariners and posted a 7-9 record with a 4.40 ERA.

ALL-STAR. Johnson went 14-11 in 1990, and the American League named him to his first All-Star game. (He did not pitch.) He also had one of his greatest thrills, pitching a 2-0 no-hitter against the Detroit Tigers. Johnson threw 134 pitches in the game, 50 of which traveled 94 miles per hour or faster. He called his parents after his big moment. "I talked to my mom, she was crying," Johnson recalled in *Sports Illustrated.* "My dad, my biggest critic, wanted to know why I walked six."

Johnson continued to be consistent the next two seasons. He won 13 games in 1991 and 12 games in 1992. Johnson led the majors in strikeouts in 1992 for the first time (241), but he also led the majors in walks for the third straight season.

Johnson realized he would have to learn to control the ball and himself if he were ever going to realize his potential. Many times he would sulk over bad calls by umpires or errors by his teammates.

Johnson also liked to clown around on the bench. He wore a Conehead costume in the dugout and another time poured a gallon of milk over a teammate's head. On one occasion he waved to the crowd and a fake arm fell out of his sleeve. "That's just Randy," his college coach, Rod Dedeaux, told *Sports Illustrated*. "He was never putting on a show." His teammate and former roommate Jay Buhner told the same magazine, Johnson's "not the kind of guy you turn your back on." Even his mother, Carol, says, "I think he spends too much time with nothing to do."

Superstar

TURNING THINGS AROUND. Two events, one personal and one professional, turned around Johnson's career and his life. Tragedy struck Johnson on Christmas Day 1992. He was flying home to spend the holidays with his parents. His father, Bud, suffered a heart attack and was dead by the time Johnson reached the hospital. Johnson laid his head on his father's chest and cried. His father's death made Johnson consider quitting baseball. "After he passed away, I seriously thought about giving up baseball," Johnson confessed in *Sport* magazine. "Baseball meant so little. I enjoyed the thrill of telling my dad how good I was on a given night. When he passed away, I realized I had no one to call. Part of me had died too."

Luckily for him, his mother talked him out of his hasty decision. Losing his dad was a turning point for Johnson. He became a practicing Christian and drew a cross and the word *dad* on the palm of his glove. He would look at this design when he needed strength on the mound. "My heart got bigger," Johnson admitted to *Sports Illustrated*. "Determination can take you a long way. After my dad died I was convinced I could get through anything. I don't use the word pressure anymore. That's for what he [his dad] went through. Life or death. I use the word challenge. And I'll never again say, 'I can't handle it.' I just dig down deeper." Johnson now had a reason to pitch. "My dad's dream was for me to be a great major league pitcher," Johnson explained in *Sport* magazine. "I'm living that dream."

BEST ADVICE. Johnson learned from the best about how to control his fastball. One day in the bull pen the great Nolan Ryan and Texas Rangers pitching coach Tom House gave Johnson advice on how to throw the ball over the plate and walk fewer batters. Ryan had had the same problem early in his career. He only became successful when he learned to make the batters swing at his unhittable pitches. "Nolan said he saw a lot of himself in me—an unproven pitcher who has shined sporadically [occasionally]," Johnson told *Sports Illustrated*. "Nolan walked a lot of guys in his career, and he told me how he dealt with it. It was really beneficial." Ryan told the same magazine, "Randy has the most potential of any pitcher in baseball. He has a slider that right-handed hitters can't hit." Johnson still calls Ryan for advice, and the two fireballers worked together on a video called *Fastball*.

PUTTING IT TOGETHER. Johnson put his new attitude and delivery to the test in 1993. He had his best season yet. Johnson earned a brilliant 19-8 record, 3.24 ERA, and struck out a major league-leading 308 batters in only 255 innings. He only walked 99, breaking his string of years leading the majors in walks. Johnson became an All-Star for the second time, and this time he pitched two scoreless innings. Johnson had arrived as one of the best in the business. "Every time he goes out there," former Mariners catcher Scott Bradley told *Sports Illustrated,* "he has a chance to throw a no-hitter."

Johnson tied an American League record for left-handed pitchers in 1993 when he struck out 18 batters in a single game. He was also part of one of the funniest moments of the season. Johnson was pitching in the All-Star game against John Kruk of the Philadelphia Phillies. The first pitch to Kruk went over his head and hit the screen behind the plate. Kruk, usually tough at the plate, meekly went down on strikes.

TALL TALES

Johnson's height has always been an issue in his career. During one game in the minor leagues the announcer kept calling him the world's tallest pitcher in a way Johnson told *Sports Illustrated* "made it sound as if I was a freak." The reaction was no different when Johnson reached the major leagues. "Before my first big league start, I had to take pictures with [five-foot-six-inch tall] John Cangelosi," Johnson told *Sports Illustrated*. This attention to his height often bothers Johnson, as he told *Sports Illustrated*: "It's amazing how I can walk down the street or in a mall, and the people just stare at me. Sometimes people come up to me and ask me if I play basketball. Usually I tell them yes. And, yes, they really do ask about the weather up there."

Being so tall has its advantages and disadvantages for a pitcher. Johnson's height gives him the leverage to throw the ball as hard as he does. Johnson also has a much greater reach than other pitchers and thus releases the ball closer to home plate. "He's all arms and legs out there, so you can't pick up the ball easily," Toronto Blue Jays All-Star second baseman Roberto Alomar told *Sport* magazine. "He's coming from less distance because he strides out there so far and because of his arm length," former Blue Jays catcher Pat Borders told the *Sporting News*. The disadvantage is that his height makes it much more difficult to keep together his entire pitching motion. Johnson learned to appreciate being tall. "Now I know it's been a gift from God to be this tall and to be left-handed and to have a fastball," Johnson confessed in *Sports Illustrated*.

"After that first pitch," Kruk said, "my goal was to come out alive."

STRUCK OUT. The 1994 season was frustrating for baseball players, owners, and fans. A players' strike, which ended the season in August, hurt many players who were having great years. One of them was Johnson. He compiled a 13-5 record, lowered his ERA to 3.19, and led the major leagues in strikeouts for the third straight season with 204 in 172 innings. Johnson began to receive recognition as one of the best pitchers in the major leagues. He was named to his third All-Star team and finished third in the voting for the American League Cy Young Award, given annually to the league's best pitcher. (David Cone of the Kansas City Royals won the award.)

STRIKEOUT STREAKS

Only nine pitchers have led the major leagues in strikeouts for three or more seasons, as shown below.

Pitcher	Club	Years
Rube Waddell	Philadelphia Athletics	1903-07
Walter Johnson	Washington Senators	1912-14
Dazzy Vance	Brooklyn Dodgers	1923-25
Lefty Grove	Philadelphia Athletics	1929-31
Dizzy Dean	St. Louis Cardinals	1932-35
Bob Feller	Cleveland Indians	1938-41
Sam McDowell	Cleveland Indians	1968-70
Nolan Ryan	California Angels	1972-74
Randy Johnson	Seattle Mariners	1992-95

FINALLY! The future of baseball in Seattle did not look bright after the 1994 season. The Mariners, formed in 1976, had never been to the play-offs and had only finished above .500 one time. The team's ownership told the city that if it did not build the team a new stadium, the Mariners would move. The situation became worse when star center fielder Ken Griffey Jr. injured his wrist trying to make a catch. It appeared to Mariner fans that the season and the team might be lost.

Amazingly, however, the Mariners did not quit. Despite trailing the California Angels by 11 games on August 9 in the American League West Division, Seattle kept chipping away at the lead. Johnson was the biggest reason for the Mariners' success. He finished the regular season with an awesome 18-2 record, 2.48 ERA, and a record-tying fourth straight major-league strikeout title. He fanned 294 batters in just 214 innings of work. This was a remarkable rate of 12.35 strike-outs per nine innings, breaking the major league record set by his tutor, Ryan. The Mariners' record in games Johnson started was 27-3. Johnson was the starter for the American League All-Star Game, going two innings without giving up a hit and striking out three.

PLAY-OFF BOUND. Time after time down the stretch Johnson won big games. He was 7-0 with a 1.45 ERA in his final ten starts. Griffey returned to the lineup and the Mariners surged, taking the division lead before finishing in a tie with the Angels on the last day of the season. The Mariners would have to win a one-game play-off to capture the first division title in their history. Manager Lou Pinella gave the ball to his "Big Unit" and sat back and watched. Johnson was overpowering, striking out 12 and giving up just three hits in a 9-1 victory. The losing pitcher for the Angels was Mark Langston, the player for whom Montreal had traded Johnson. The Mariners were in the play-offs.

REFUSE TO LOSE. For the first time ever the major league play-offs involved a wild-card team. (A wild-card team is one that has the best record among teams that do not win a division title.) The New York Yankees were the American League wild-card team in 1995, and they were the Mariners' first ever play-off opponent. The Yankees won the first two games of the five-game series in Yankee Stadium, and it looked like the Mariners' play-off run might be very short.

No one counted on the support the Mariners would get from their fans in Seattle, the site of the last three games of the series. Mariner fans cheered their team and carried posters with the slogan "Refuse to Lose" on them. Johnson got his first start of the series in Game Three, a must-win game for the Mariners. He did not let his team down, pitching seven innings in a 7-4 Seattle win. The Mariners won Game Four, setting up a decisive fifth game.

Both managers pulled out all the stops. Late in the game Yankees manager Buck Showalter used former Cy Young Award winner Jack McDowell in relief, while Pinella once again called on Johnson. With only one day's rest, Johnson shut out the Yankees for three innings. Finally, Seattle scored in the eleventh inning to give the Mariners a 6-5 win. Johnson earned the victory in the game, his third straight in games where the Mariners faced elimination. In those games Johnson was 3-0, with an ERA of 1.89 and 28 strikeouts in 19 innings.

CHAMPIONSHIP STRUGGLE. The Mariners faced the Cleveland Indians in the American League Championship Series. The Indians were a powerful team in 1995, winning 100 of 148 games. The two teams split Games One and Two, and Johnson got the call in Game Three. He pitched brilliantly, holding the high-powered Indian attack to only two runs in eight innings. Johnson would have won the game if not for an error by right-fielder Jay Buhner that allowed the tying run to score in the eighth inning. The Mariners, however, won the game in the eleventh inning when Buhner, the goat of the game, hit a game-winning home run.

The increased workload in the play-offs was wearing Johnson out. "I need a rest," Johnson admitted to the *New York Times* after Game Three. "I can't keep going out there. You guys think I have a rubber arm and I'm invincible. Quite frankly, I'm not." The Mariners lost Games Four and Five and once again faced elimination, trailing three games to two. Johnson pitched Game Six but was clearly exhausted. He did his best, pitching seven innings and giving up four runs. Unfortunately, Seattle could not score, losing the game, 4-0, and the series.

THE BEST. Baseball writers honored Johnson following the season by giving him the 1995 American League Cy Young Award, symbolic of his being the best pitcher in the league. Johnson received 26 of 28 possible first-place votes. "He is the number one dominating pitcher in baseball," Pinella, told *Sports Illustrated.* "I don't even know who's number two. I've never seen anybody like him."

OFF THE FIELD. Johnson lives in Bellevue, Washington, with his wife, Lisa, and their daughter, Samantha. "He just melts around her," Lisa Johnson told *Sports Illustrated,* explaining Johnson's relationship with his daughter. "Nothing else is so important to him anymore. When he's away he phones every night and talks to her."

Johnson enjoys playing the drums and once practiced with the group Soundgarden. He also made a brief appearance in the film *Little Big League*. Johnson is an accomplished photographer and has been taking pictures since he was about seven years old. He likes to take pictures in every city to which he travels. In 1990 some of Johnson's pictures were featured at the Art Expo in Los Angeles, California. He once sold some pictures to raise money for the homeless. Johnson says photography is a lot like baseball. "In both activities, you have to stay focused," Johnson joked in *Sports Illustrated for Kids*.

Johnson is very intense before he pitches. No one can talk to him before a start. "I pretty much don't talk to him," his wife told *Sports Illustrated*. Teammate Mike Blowers told the same magazine, "I don't even bother saying hello." Johnson also has to have the same breakfast before every start—two scrambled eggs, three pancakes, a small glass of orange juice, and a small glass of milk.

Being able to throw a ball 100 miles an hour carries responsibilities. "I throw hard, and I can be wild," Johnson admitted in *Boys' Life*. "Batters have to stay on their toes." His former teammate Scott Bradley agreed: "Let's face it, he's not a comfortable at bat." Johnson scares even himself. "That's one reason I don't pitch inside," Johnson admitted in *Sports Illustrated*. "I don't like to throw the ball up and in because of what the outcome might be. My control is not that good." His teammate Mike Blowers agrees. "Deep down he has this terrible fear of seriously hurting someone one day," Blowers told *Sports Illustrated*. Johnson uses his reputation for being wild to his advantage, giving batters something to think about when they step in against him.

Johnson told *Sports Illustrated for Kids* why he loves playing baseball: "When you can throw 97 miles an hour and put the ball over the plate any time you want, it's fun."

Sources

Boys' Life, June 1995.
Detroit News, November 15, 1995.
New York Times, October 3, 1995; October 15, 1995.
Sport, June 1994.

Sporting News, July 11, 1994.

Sports Illustrated, March 20, 1989; June 11, 1990; October 8, 1990; August 26, 1991; May 4, 1992; April 19, 1993; June 13, 1994; June 26, 1995; October 2, 1995.

Sports Illustrated for Kids, August 1994; September 1995.

Additional information provided by Seattle Mariners.

WHERE TO WRITE:
C/O SEATTLE MARINERS,
P.O. BOX 4100,
SEATTLE, WA 98104.

Roy Jones Jr.

1969—

The ring in which Roy Jones Jr. learned to fight was located by the river behind his family home. There Jones developed the speed and power that helped him win the super middleweight boxing title and become the best fighter, pound-for-pound, in the world. The road to the top has not always been easy. He did not reach his full potential until he broke away from the father who trained and controlled him. The trip from that ring by the river to manhood proved to be the most difficult fight of Jones's life.

"I can't imagine what it would take to beat Roy Jones."
—Ross Greenburg, executive producer, HBO Sports

Growing Up

TOO TOUGH? Roy Jones Jr. was born in January 16, 1969, in Pensacola, Florida. He grew up in Barth, Florida, 25 miles north of Pensacola. His father's name is Roy Sr. and his mother's name is Carol. His father, an aircraft electrician at Pensacola Naval Air Station, earned a Bronze Star in Vietnam for rushing through enemy fire to save an injured soldier.

SCOREBOARD

DEFEATED JAMES "LIGHTS OUT" TONEY IN 1994 TO WIN SUPER MIDDLEWEIGHT TITLE.

UNDEFEATED IN 29 PROFESSIONAL FIGHTS.

SILVER MEDAL WINNER AS LIGHT MIDDLE WEIGHT AT 1988 SUMMER OLYMPICS.

JONES OVERCAME AN ABUSIVE FATHER TO BECOME THE BEST BOXER, POUND-FOR-POUND, IN THE WORLD.

Roy Jones Sr. set out to teach his son to be tough at an early age. He gave Jones a shotgun when his son was six years old and had him riding a tractor at seven. Despite Jones's not being able to swim, his father threw him into water over his head. "You're too much like your mother," Roy Sr. would complain every time his son ran to his mother, according to *Sports Illustrated*. "You'll never do nothin' if you're scared."

BEGINS BOXING. Jones began fighting when he was five years old. His father trained Jones and other area boys in a makeshift ring behind the family home. Roy Sr. boxed professionally and went three rounds with the legendary middleweight champion Marvin Hagler. Many of Roy Sr.'s pupils did not have fathers and got into trouble. He worked extra jobs to buy equipment for his boxers and to pay to send them to boxing tournaments in Louisiana, Mississippi, and Georgia. Roy Sr. eventually sold the family farm and moved to Pensacola. There he opened the Escambia County Boys Club boxing program in an abandoned building. "You could give your two-week-old baby to that man, go on vacation and not think twice," Doris Grant, a local mother, told *Sports Illustrated*. "Big Roy'd take care of it."

AFRAID OF FATHER. Although Roy Sr. took good care of other people's children, he treated his own son badly. "Seemed closer to the other kids than he was to me," his son recalled in *Sports Illustrated*. He beat Jones for all sorts of mistakes, inside the ring and out. Roy Sr. hit his son with electrical cords and plastic pipes. "He'd slap Little Roy, punch him, scream at him," Nelson Fountain, a fellow boxer, stated in *Sports Illustrated*. "You'd never know it was his own son." Many children were too afraid of his father to come over to play, and the family lived far away from most people. Jones made friends with the animals around his house. There were dogs, a bull, horses, and a goat.

Jones (left) uppercuts Merqui Sosa during a 1996 fight.

"After a while I didn't care about gettin' hurt or dyin' anymore," Jones recalled in *Sports Illustrated*. "I was in pain all day, every day, I was so scared of my father. He'd pull up in his truck and start lookin' for something I'd done wrong. There was no escape, no excuse, no way out of nothin'. Every day it was the same: school, homework, farmwork, trainin'. Gettin' hurt or dyin' might've been better than the life I was livin'. So I turned into a daredevil. I'd do anything. Didn't make much difference. Used to think about killin' myself anyway."

BE GREAT AT SOMETHING Jones's mother tried to help, but she admits her son had a rough childhood. "Wasn't the ideal way to raise a kid," Carol Jones admitted in *Sports Illustrated*. "But I can't say it was bad." The younger Jones decided to show his father how tough he could be. "I prayed to God, just don't let me be average," Jones explained in *Sports Illustrated*. "Let me be great at something. Because I knew if I was average, he'd dominate me all my life."

RING SUCCESS. By the time Jones turned ten, he was fighting boxers who were bigger and older than he was. He won the National Junior Olympics title at 119 pounds by the time he was 15. In both 1986 and 1987 Jones won the Golden Gloves championship, and in 1986 he won a bronze medal at the Goodwill Games.

Despite Jones's success, his father did not let up on him. "About 17 I realized that a lot of the beatings I got, I didn't deserve," Jones explained in *GQ*. "The beatings as far as discipline—well, I needed them. In training, though, I realized that lots of times I got beat just because of the way that people felt that day. There was nothing I could do about it. There was no way I could tell what day it was going to be."

OLYMPIC EXPERIENCE. Jones won the 1988 Olympic Trials as a light middleweight and then defeated Frank Liles in the Olympic Box-Offs, the competition that determined the U.S. Olympic boxing team for the 1988 Summer Olympics in Seoul, South Korea. At 19, he was the youngest member of the team. At the Olympics, Jones finally had the freedom he never had at home. He played basketball and talked to girls. Jones did not neglect his training, but he felt better about it because he wanted to do it to win a gold medal. "Finally in my own world, by myself, like any other man," Jones explained in *Sports Illustrated*.

Jones also made a new friend at the Olympics. As a member of the U.S. national team, Jones worked with coaches other than his father for the first time. Alton Merkerson, an assistant coach on the U.S. team, helped the young fighter. Merkerson called himself a "democratic" trainer, and he suggested things Jones could do differently, but did not order him to do anything. Jones liked his new coach's style, so different from that of his father.

SHOCKER IN SEOUL. The preliminary rounds flew by for Jones. "You're different from the other American boxers," a member of the U.S. women's basketball team told Jones, according to *Sports Illustrated*. "They all look like they're in a war. You don't get hit. It's like you're floating in and out." Other fighters on the U.S. team looked up to Jones as the leader of their squad, even though he was the youngest fighter.

The young fighter cruised to the final, where he devastated South Korea's Park Si Hun. Jones outpunched his opponent 86-32, but in a shocking decision he lost the fight and the gold medal. Three of the five judges voted for the Korean fighter. The decision shocked boxing experts and fans, and even Park Si Hun whispered in Jones's ear, "I lost the fight." Despite the decision, Jones earned the award as the outstanding fighter in the Olympics. The amateur boxing community banned the judges who voted against him from judging fights for two years.

Superstar

PRO PUNCHER. Returning from the Olympics, Jones decided to turn professional. The best boxing trainers in the world wanted to work with him. Jones, at the urging of his mother, decided to let his father continue as his trainer. Jones won his first four professional fights, scoring technical knockouts against each opponent. (A technical knockout occurs when the referee decides a fighter is unable to continue.)

Jones defeated several more unknown fighters, building up an outstanding record but not earning a championship match. For some reason Roy Sr. did not want him to fight contenders for the title. The lack of quality fights bothered Jones. "I wasn't happy," Jones admitted in *Sports Illustrated*.

"It started affecting my sleep. I'd stay up nights thinking, Should I get out of this sport?"

Roy Sr. continued to abuse his son, causing the boxer to begin carrying a knife to defend himself. "He'd keep screamin' in my face in front of people, tryin' to pick a fight with me, just to prove he could still beat me," Jones recounted in *Sports Illustrated.* "But I wasn't gonna fight him. I had too much respect to fight him. I'd just kill him. Or he'd kill me. That's the fear I had in my heart."

TOUGH DECISION. Finally, in August 1992, Jones broke free. "I told him I wanted to pick my fights," Jones related in *Sports Illustrated.* "I guess he didn't like that." Jones knew the break was necessary. "I knew I had to go," he admitted to *GQ.* "It wasn't that he scared me so much anymore but that I was scared of maybe having to kill my dad one day. I wasn't going to sit there and take a beating."

Jones called his former Olympic coach, Merkerson, to be his trainer. "When Roy came to me, he was fighting all over the place, like a human whirlwind," Merkerson told *Sports Illustrated.* "He's begun to slow down, to not waste punches, to be more patient. Roy's not only got the quickest hands in boxing, but the quickest mind."

To manage his career, Jones looked to attorneys Fred and Stanley Levin. The two had raised money in the past to help support Roy Sr.'s boxing program, and Stanley acted as a father figure for Jones. Moving out of the trailer next to his father's house, Jones bought his own home. He also had fun. "Lettin' out the kid in me that I hardly ever could as a kid," Jones stated in *Sports Illustrated.*

STRAIGHT TO THE TOP. In January 1992 Jones finally fought a contender, Jorge Vaca. He beat him in one round. In his first fight after breaking away from his father, Jones defeated Glenn Thomas. Jones won the International Boxing Federation super middleweight title in 1993 by defeating Bernard Hopkins. Despite winning the title, boxing experts still did not give Jones much respect. "Roy Jones has avoided all the toughest opponents," announcer Larry Merchant of HBO said. "We don't know if he's a superstar or a fraud."

CHAMPION. The chance for Jones to finally prove himself came in November 1994. The super middleweight championship fight featured Jones against James "Lights Out" Toney in Las Vegas, Nevada. Toney was undefeated in 48 professional fights against the toughest competition in the world.

From the opening bell Jones took the fight to Toney. He moved quickly around his slower opponent, banging away with both hands. Jones knocked Toney down in the third round and won the decision in a performance *Ring* magazine called the most dominant big-fight performance in 20 years. Toney won only six of a possible thirty-six rounds on the cards of three judges. "My hands are fast, my feet are quick, but I knew I also had to show a championship heart," Jones told *Sports Illustrated* after the fight.

THE BEST. Jones successfully defended his title in June 1995 against Vinnie Pazienza. The fight became a mismatch, and Jones begged the referee to end the fight in the sixth round before he finally finished off the two-time former champion. Experts now recognized Jones as the best fighter pound-for-pound in the world. His record stood at 29-0, and he held the super middleweight championship.

Jones has a rare combination of speed and power. "I've never seen that kind of punching power and speed in one man," Ross Greenburg, executive producer of HBO Sports, remarked in *Sports Illustrated*. "I can't imagine what it would take to beat Roy Jones." Boxing analyst Gil Clancy agreed in *GQ:* "He's smart and he's fast, but he hits so hard. He does things I've never seen before."

HEAVYWEIGHT CHAMP? Jones is always looking for new challenges. He has even considered facing Mike Tyson, the

A ROOSTER NOW

Jones raised roosters as a child, but his father would make him fight them against other roosters in a cruel exhibition that is illegal in many states. He still takes care of 400 roosters and chickens, and explained in *Sports Illustrated* the similarities between his life and the way roosters need their independence. "Look how this rooster walks in his cage," Jones explained to the reporter. "See that. It's his cage. He owns it. It's his world. Every other male has to respect that. I spent all my life in my dad's cage. I could never be 100 percent of who I am until I left it. But because of him, nothing bothers me. I'll never face anything stronger and harder than what I already have."

COUNTRY BOY

Even though he has seen the bright lights of the city, Jones likes to live in the country, as he told *GQ:* "Being from the country gives you time to see different aspects of life. Like owning horses or owning dogs. Handling roosters. Raising goats or raising pigs. How to plant your own garden, or get your animals to slaughter and make your own meat. It makes you more of an adult. Once you get to the city, all you see is the meat. You never see the cattle. You see the greens and the carrots. You never see the trees that bore them, or the plants that bore them, or the farm that raised them. You only see the finished product. In the country, you can see the whole cycle."

best heavyweight in the world. "I could beat him," Jones bragged in *Sports Illustrated*. "I could reach him. I want to do something no one thinks I can do. That's what a champion does. A warrior is someone who'll fight to the dying end—that's what my father is. But a champion is someone who'll find a way to adapt to any situation and win. That's what I am." Until a fight with Tyson takes place, Jones knows whom he has to compete against. "All I can do is train for the best possible fighter I could possibly face—myself," Jones explained to *Sports Illustrated*.

Jones and his father rarely speak. Roy Sr. refuses to attend his son's fights and leaves the house whenever he visits. "Once you break the plate at my table you can never eat there again," Roy Sr. tells friends who try to get him to make up with his son. Jones has given up on trying to get back together. "Deep in my heart, I'll always love him," Jones confessed in *Sports Illustrated*. "But I won't ever talk to him again."

OUT OF THE RING. Jones lives on a farm near Pensacola. He loves to play basketball and has hinted he might want to try out for an NBA team some day. Jones opened a community center and gym in Pensacola and works with young kids. He loves to visit schools and appear at charity events.

Jones has not let fame go to his head. "They can shine a light so bright on your face, you can't even see what you're standin' on, and then one day the light goes off and you look down and see you were standin' on nothin'," Jones explained to *Sports Illustrated*. "Sure, I'll do some showboatin' in the ring—I'm the only true performer in the ring today. But not outside of it. People assume every boxer wants to live the fast life. That's an escape, not a life. I want a person-to-person life."

Sources

GQ, June 1995.
New York Times, June 22, 1995; June 24, 1995; June 26, 1995.
Sports Illustrated, May 24, 1993; November 28, 1994; June 26, 1995; July 3, 1995.

WHERE TO WRITE:
C/O INTERNATIONAL BOXING FEDERATION,
134 EVERGREEN PL., 9TH FLOOR,
EAST ORANGE, NJ 07018.

Shawn Kemp

1969—

"He really gets airborne."
—NBA star Shaquille O'Neal

Shawn Kemp is one of the most exciting players in the National Basketball Association (NBA). His twisting, turning dunks are regular features on sports highlight shows, and no one finishes on an alley-oop pass like the Seattle Supersonics forward. Although Kemp is only 26 years old, he is a veteran of six NBA seasons. That is because he is one of only six players who have entered the NBA without ever playing a game in college. Though this decision worked out for Kemp, he says he wishes things had been different and would not recommend that anyone else go directly from high school to the pros. A member of "Dream Team II," which won the World Basketball Championships in 1994, Kemp has overcome his mistakes to become one of the best basketball players in the world.

Growing Up

FAMILY AFFAIR. Shawn T. Kemp was born November 26, 1969, in Elkhart, Indiana. His mother, Barbara, raised Kemp.

Kemp credits his mother with giving him his competitive fire and says even today she is the boss. "Whatever my mom wants she usually gets," Kemp revealed in *Sport* magazine. "I might mess with some players in the NBA, do my thing. But with her? No way." Kemp learned how to play basketball from his sister, Lisa, when he was eight years old. His sister, who is three years older, beat him all the time in one-on-one. "Lisa kept pushing me to be better and better," Kemp explained in *Sports Illustrated for Kids.*

Kemp had grown to six feet two inches tall by the time he was 14 years old. He was the star of his eighth-grade team, and college coaches began recruiting him to come to their schools. His high school coach, Jim Hahn, remembers seeing Kemp for the first time. "I said to myself," Hahn recalled in *Sports Illustrated for Kids,* "'I think my team will be pretty good [when we get Kemp] next year.'"

PRO PROSPECT. When Kemp was in tenth grade at Concord High in Elkhart, NBA scouts came to his games. By his senior year he began to recognize the faces of the professionals in the stands watching him play. Kemp led his team to the Indiana state high school title as a senior, and he gave much of the credit to Hahn. "He got it into my head that to be good at something, you really have to go out and give it your all every time," Kemp recounted in *Sports Illustrated for Kids.*

WILD WILDCAT. Kemp finally decided to attend the University of Kentucky, home of one of the most famous college basketball powerhouses in the nation. The Indiana newspapers labeled Kemp a traitor for leaving his home state. Kemp chose Kentucky because he did not agree with the philosophy of Bobby Knight, basketball coach at Indiana University.

Kemp had a hard time at Kentucky. He was academically ineligible to play his freshman season because he could not

---

SCOREBOARD

ONE OF ONLY SIX PLAYERS TO MOVE DIRECTLY FROM HIGH SCHOOL TO THE NBA.

MEMBER OF "DREAM TEAM II" SQUAD, WHICH WON WORLD BASKETBALL CHAMPIONSHIPS IN 1994.

THREE-TIME NBA ALL-STAR (1993-95).

KEMP HAS OVERCOME MISTAKES IN HIS LIFE TO BECOME ONE OF THE MOST EXCITING BASKETBALL PLAYERS IN THE WORLD.

Kemp slam dunking during the 1994 World Basketball Championship.

achieve high enough scores on the Scholastic Aptitude Test (SAT). "It's my own fault for ignoring academics," Kemp admitted in *Sports Illustrated*. "My mother was on me all the time about it, but I didn't listen. I'm not dumb; I'm not stupid. But I just didn't push myself. I didn't take school seriously enough, and that will always bother me."

BIG MISTAKE. Kemp had difficulty adjusting to living away from home. Soon he began to hang out with the wrong crowd. One of his friends stole a necklace from the son of Kentucky coach Eddie Sutton, and police caught Kemp trying to sell it. The incident made Kemp leave Kentucky without ever playing a game. Sutton stated in *Sport* magazine that the press made too much of the incident: "Everybody made Shawn

Kemp out to be some kind of criminal. That couldn't be further from the truth."

SONIC BOOM. After leaving Kentucky, Kemp enrolled at Trinity Valley Community College in Athens, Texas. He practiced with the team but could not play because the coach did not let players join the squad in midseason. At this point the Seattle Supersonics drafted Kemp in the first round of the 1989 NBA Draft. At age 19, he made the Sonics team. Kemp became one of only six players to ever go right from high school to the NBA without playing a college game. (The others are Moses Malone, Darryl Dawkins, Joe Grabowski, Bill Willoughby, and, most recently, Kevin Garnett.) "I was scared," Kemp confessed in *Sports Illustrated for Kids*. "I was scared of having to deal with the fans, the money, and the media. But I knew I could go on the court and play against the NBA players."

Kemp averaged only 6.5 points per game his first two professional seasons. He often turned the ball over and tried to dunk every time down the court. Kemp played mostly as a substitute and needed to work on basketball basics. "[Because] he didn't have any college as a base, he needed to work on the fundamental parts of the game," the Supersonics' coach, K. C. Jones, explained to *Sport* magazine. "When to drive. When to shoot. That's all experience. Patience. Those are all things he has to learn."

STARTING FORWARD. Players and coaches alike agreed that Kemp had the potential to be a superstar. "Shawn has a great combination of skill and creativity," Michael Jordan explained in *Sport* magazine. "He is very similar to the way I was when I was younger." No one worked harder than Kemp to improve. He spent his summers at basketball camps and spent countless hours in the gym practicing. Then, in 1990,

PREPS TO THE PROS

Four players before Kemp moved directly from high school to the NBA. The most successful has been Moses Malone. He won the NBA Most Valuable Player Award twice (1982 and 1983) and led the Philadelphia 76ers to an NBA championship in 1983. Through the end of the 1993-94 season, Malone had averaged 20.9 points and 12.3 rebounds per game in 20 seasons. Darryl Dawkins played 14 seasons in the NBA, averaging 12 points and 6.1 rebounds per game. Basketball fans remember Dawkins best for naming his dunks and his nickname, "Chocolate Thunder." Bill Willoughby averaged only six points and 3.9 rebounds per game in eight NBA seasons, and Joe Grabowski played 13 seasons from 1948 to 1962. Grabowski averaged 11 points and 8.1 rebounds per game.

Kemp got his chance. Seattle traded forward Xavier McDaniel, allowing Kemp to step into the starting lineup. "At the time I didn't know if I was ready for it," Kemp confessed in *Sport* magazine.

Kemp made the most of his opportunity. He averaged 15 points, 8.4 rebounds, and 1.5 blocked shots his first season as a starter. More important, his amazing moves drew rave reviews. Kemp displayed the rare ability to jump quickly and move and hang in the air. "I've never seen anyone jump as high as Kemp," Shaquille O'Neal said to the Associated Press. "He really gets airborne." Kemp has been a finalist several times in the NBA's Slam-Dunk competition but has never won.

Superstar

NEW COACH. George Karl took over as coach of the Sonics in 1992, and the team has been one of the NBA's best ever since. Western Conference coaches chose Kemp for the NBA All-Star team for the first time in 1993, a season in which he averaged 17.8 points and 10.7 rebounds per game. "You're kidding yourself if you don't think Kemp is in the top five [in the NBA]," Karl exclaimed in *Sport* magazine. The league named him to the All-NBA second team.

Seattle finished the 1993-94 season with the NBA's best record, and Kemp once again made the All-Star team. He averaged 18.1 points and 10.8 rebounds during the season. The Supersonics faced the Denver Nuggets in the first round of the NBA play-offs. The Nuggets had barely qualified for the postseason, and everyone expected an easy Seattle victory. Unfortunately, Denver had other ideas. The series went all seven games, and the last few seconds of Game Seven decided the outcome. Seattle trailed by a point and Kemp had two free throws. He missed both of them. The Nuggets had pulled off one of the biggest upsets of all time. The loss disappointed Kemp, but he tried to handle it like a professional. "We have nothing to be embarrassed about," Kemp told the *Orlando Sentinel.* "It just didn't end the way we wanted." Kemp scored only 14.8 points per game in the series.

TRADE RUMORS. During the summer Seattle considered trading Kemp for All-Star forward Scottie Pippen of the Chicago Bulls. Seattle fans rushed to Kemp's defense, forcing the Supersonics to call off negotiations. In 1994 the NBA recognized Kemp as one of the league's best players by naming him to the "Dream Team II" squad, which won the World Basketball Championships in Toronto, Ontario, Canada. Kemp starred on the team that demolished the best competition the rest of the world had to offer. He averaged 9.4 points and 6.8 rebounds in just 15.9 minutes per game. The International Basketball Federation named Kemp to the championships All-Star team. "Shawn's talent, speed, size, and ability to rebound are just awesome," Karl said in *Sports Illustrated for Kids*.

TALLEST SANTA

Kemp brightened the Christmas season for the children at the Yesler and Ranier Beach community centers in Seattle when he played Santa at their Christmas party in December 1994. The center had trouble finding a Santa suit that would fit the 6'10", 245-pound Kemp but eventually located one. "I got a lot of strange looks," Kemp recalled in the *Sporting News*. "But it was well worth it because it put smiles on the kids' faces and that made me feel good."

POTENTIAL. Many experts believed that Kemp and the Supersonics failed to live up to their potential during the 1994-95 season. Seattle won 57 games and finished second in the NBA's Pacific Division. For the third straight season, however, they lost in the first round of the play-offs.

Kemp, as the team's superstar, received most of the blame for the Sonics' early defeat, despite averaging 24.8 points and 12 rebounds in the series against the Los Angeles Lakers. He averaged a career-high 18.7 points per game during the regular season, but experts expected more. "How good does Shawn Kemp want to be?" asked journalist Steve Kelley in the *Seattle Times*. "And how important is winning to him? By most standards [Kemp's] stats are impressive. But by superstar standards, the standards by which Kemp should be judged, they are disappointing. Style isn't everything. It don't mean a thing if you ain't got that ring."

OFF THE COURT. Kemp lives in Seattle. He works with charities to help buy wheelchairs and returns each summer to his former high school to run basketball camps. Kemp's childhood idol was Earvin "Magic" Johnson, and he is friends with another Seattle star, Ken Griffey Jr., of the Seattle Mariners. He began wearing number 40 on his elementary school football team and has worn it ever since. Kemp enjoys music and going to the movies.

Kemp still has a promise he has to keep to his mom. "When I came into the NBA, my mom and I agreed that, no matter what, I was going to go back to college to get my degree," Kemp told *Sports Illustrated for Kids*. Kemp attends Indiana University and is majoring in communications. He wants to own a radio station someday.

Kemp takes his duty as a role model seriously. "Helping kids, watching them smile, this makes me feel good about myself," Kemp admitted in *Sport* magazine. "I want kids looking up to me."

Sources

Chicago Sun-Times, August 11, 1994.
Chicago Tribune, June 30, 1994; July 1, 1994.
Cleveland Plain Dealer, July 3, 1994.
Newsday, August 11, 1994.
News Tribune, July 30, 1994; June 31, 1994.
New York Times, April 24, 1994.
Orlando Sentinel, August 14, 1994.
Seattle Times, July 10, 1994; July 31, 1994; August 15, 1994; March 7, 1995.
Sport, March 1992; June 1994.
Sporting News, May 2, 1994; January 2, 1995.
Sports Illustrated, April 19, 1993.
Sports Illustrated for Kids, June 1993; December 1994.
Additional information provided by Seattle Supersonics.

WHERE TO WRITE:
C/O SEATTLE SUPERSONICS,
490 FIFTH AVE. N,
SEATTLE, WA 98109.

Nancy Kerrigan

1969—

Most people who watch Nancy Kerrigan skate think she looks like a fairy princess because she moves with such style and grace. What people do not know about her, however, is that she is a tough competitor willing to work hard to achieve her goals. In 1994 a vicious attack on Kerrigan almost knocked her out of the Winter Olympic Games in Lillehammer, Norway. Showing great determination, she delivered her best performance ever at the Olympics, proving once and for all that she was as tough an athlete as she was beautiful to watch.

"I always just wanted to compete."
—Nancy Kerrigan

Growing Up

FAMILY AFFAIR. Nancy Kerrigan was born October 13, 1969. Her father, Dan, is a welder, and her mother's name is Brenda. Kerrigan grew up in a two-story house in Stoneham, Massachusetts. The family, including Kerrigan's brothers, Michael and Mark, was very close.

SCOREBOARD

SILVER MEDAL WINNER
IN WOMEN'S FIGURE SKATING
COMPETITION AT 1994 WINTER
OLYMPICS IN
LILLEHAMMER, NORWAY.

BRONZE MEDAL WINNER IN
WOMEN'S FIGURE SKATING
COMPETITION AT
1992 WINTER OLYMPICS IN
ALBERTVILLE, FRANCE.

BRONZE MEDAL WINNER IN
WOMEN'S COMPETITION AT
1991 WORLD FIGURE SKATING
CHAMPIONSHIPS.

KERRIGAN OVERCAME A VICIOUS
ATTACK TO SKATE THE
PERFORMANCE OF HER LIFE AT
THE 1994 WINTER OLYMPICS.

Kerrigan was always especially close to her mother, who is legally blind. Brenda Kerrigan has limited sight in her right eye and is completely blind in her left eye. A virus caused her blindness. "My mom was always there for me," Kerrigan revealed in *People* magazine.

STARTS SKATING. Kerrigan began skating at age seven on a neighborhood ice rink. Her brothers both played ice hockey and Nancy watched their games. Once Kerrigan's parents realized that their daughter had talent, they enrolled her in lessons. She entered her first competition at age nine and quickly won local and regional competitions.

The Kerrigans were not wealthy people. From the beginning, Nancy's training was very expensive. To make ends meet, Dan Kerrigan worked odd jobs and took out loans for thousands of dollars. "Since Nancy started skating," he told one reporter, "the family hasn't been on a real vacation. We go to skating events."

Training was difficult for Kerrigan. She practiced with her coaches, Evy and Mary Scotvold, before going to class at Stoneham High School, getting out of bed at 4 A.M. When she learned a new routine, she did it for her parents in the family living room. "I do it on the floor in the living room, with my arm movements, everything, so my mother can see it," Kerrigan said in *People* magazine.

THE BIG THREE. Kerrigan established herself as one of the top skaters in the United States at age 19 when she won the National Collegiate Championships. At the time, she was a year out of high school and a student in the business program at Emmanuel College, an institution near Kerrigan's home in Stoneham. In 1991 Kerrigan finished third at the U.S. Figure Skating Championships, behind Tonya Harding, who finished first, and sec-

Kerrigan acknowledges the applause after a performance.

TOUGHING IT OUT

Sometimes the Kerrigans did not have enough money to purchase Nancy a new pair of skates. She would outgrow the ones she had and her feet hurt. When she complained to her mother, however, she was told to "suffer in silence." Kerrigan soon learned that her parents did the best they could, but sometimes they could not afford to buy her everything she wanted or needed. Now she appreciates all the sacrifices her parents made for her. "I feel like everything they did was for me," Nancy told in *People* magazine. "It's scary when [you] are spending so much money and you don't know what you will get for it."

ond-place finisher Kristi Yamaguchi. Her performance earned Kerrigan the right to compete at the 1991 World Figure Skating Championships in Munich, Germany.

At the world championships, the U.S. team pulled off a first when all three Americans won medals. Yamaguchi, who had only recently started skating in singles competition, won the gold, Harding won the silver, while Kerrigan took the bronze. Kerrigan fell once during her long program but skated well enough to move past an injured Midori Ito of Japan into third place. (In the long program, skaters choose which jumps and maneuvers they want to attempt.)

OLYMPIC EXPERIENCE. Kerrigan earned the right to represent the United States at the 1992 Winter Olympics in Albertville, France, when she finished second at the U.S. Figure Skating Championships. Yamaguchi won the competition, and Harding finished third. The three skaters made up one of the strongest American Olympic teams in history.

"I want to skate clean at the Olympics," Kerrigan told in *People* magazine before heading for France. Brenda Kerrigan traveled with her daughter and followed her Olympic performance on a large television screen set up for her use. Brenda Kerrigan put her face right up to the screen to see her daughter skate. "I can't see someone's features unless I'm practically kissing them," Brenda Kerrigan explained to the same magazine. "I get right up close to the monitor, and I know if Nancy does a jump. But I don't know what kind of jump."

Kerrigan had the flu her first three days in Albertville. She had to work hard to get back into shape once she felt better. Her skating partner, Paul Wylie, won a silver medal in the men's competition, and Kerrigan attended the competition. "What I did made her feel like anything was possible," Wylie stated in *Sports Illustrated.*

WINS MEDAL. Kerrigan and Yamaguchi roomed together during the Olympics, and the two roommates battled for the gold medal. The two Americans skated flawlessly in the short program and finished with Yamaguchi in first and Kerrigan in second. (The short program requires skaters to successfully complete certain jumps and maneuvers.) The long program would determine the championship. Yamaguchi went first and skated beautifully except for a fall trying to land a triple-loop jump. Kerrigan then skated, and she too made a mistake, touching her hand on the ice after a jump.

When the public address announcer read Kerrigan's scores, she realized she had won the bronze medal. "This is overwhelming, really," Brenda Kerrigan explained to *Sports Illustrated*. "I don't know how this happened. I had her in fourth. When I hugged her I said, 'I love you, you did great. But, oh, Nancy, I didn't think you did it.'" Yamaguchi won the gold medal, Midori Ito of Japan won the silver, and Harding finished fourth.

BEST IN U.S. When Yamaguchi turned professional after the Olympics, Kerrigan became the top-ranked American female figure skater. In 1993 she won her only national title, taking first place at the U.S. Figure Skating Championships in Phoenix, Arizona. The *Boston Globe* called Kerrigan "America's ice queen and poster girl." "Nancy's the girl next door," her friend Wylie told *People* magazine.

CRACKS UNDER PRESSURE. Despite her success, Kerrigan had problems during practice. In training she skipped jumps and rarely completed her program on the practice rink. Kerrigan's problems cost her at the 1993 World Figure Skating Championships in Prague, Czechoslovakia. She won the short program and led the competition going into the free skate. Disaster struck during her long program when Kerrigan made a mistake and let it bother her, causing her to completely fall apart. "I guess I felt more pressure than I admitted," Kerrigan confessed in *People* magazine. She finished ninth in the long program and dropped to fifth in the final standings. Kerrigan broke out in tears after her performance and told television commentators, "I just want to die."

Superstar

HARD WORK. Despite her disastrous performance at the world championships, experts still made Kerrigan a favorite to win a medal at the 1994 Winter Olympics in Lillehammer, Norway. To prepare for the most important competition of her life, she trained with fierce intensity. "She's never worked this hard," Evy Scotvold stated in *Sports Illustrated*. "She's never done the run-throughs she's doing now. Double run-throughs. Going for perfect run-throughs. She's in fantastic shape. Her power is incredible. When she skates, she looks like she needs a bigger ice surface."

The hard work paid off. Kerrigan won two major international competitions at the end of 1993—the Piruetten in Hamar, Norway, and the AT&T Pro Am in Philadelphia, Pennsylvania. She entered the 1994 U.S. Figure Skating Championships in Detroit, Michigan, as the overwhelming favorite to defend her title. Harding was her closest competition, but judges tended to like Kerrigan's artistic style more than Harding's more physical performances. The competition between the two skaters was intense, and Harding resented that she could rarely beat Kerrigan.

WHY ME? Before the national competition began, while Kerrigan was on her way to practice at Cobo Hall, a man jumped out and hit her on the right knee with a metal bar and ran away. "Why me? Why now? Help me! Help me!" Kerrigan called out for help seconds after the attack. She feared that her Olympic dream had ended.

At first the attack puzzled Kerrigan and the police. Her injury was serious enough to knock her out of the national championships, but doctors hoped she would be ready to skate in the Olympics. Harding won the U.S. championship, and teenager **Michelle Kwan** (see entry) finished second.

NAMED TO TEAM. Because of the circumstances of the attack, the U.S. Figure Skating Association decided that Kerrigan would skate at the Olympics, if physically able, rather than Kwan. Usually only the first- and second-place finishers at the national championships make the Olympic team. The attack had injured Kerrigan's kneecap and the muscles right above her knee. Only hard work and physical therapy would get her ready in time for the Olympics.

Kerrigan, who had planned to have her best performance ever at the U.S. championships, was disappointed. The media surrounded her parents' home in Stoneham, with some reporters camping out in the driveway. The attention made it difficult for Kerrigan to train or have fun at the Olympics. She could not go out without a bodyguard, and everyone wanted to ask her about the attack. "Everyone would be looking at me like I was some sort of freak," Kerrigan told *Sports Illustrated.*

CRACKING THE CASE. Soon the police investigation focused on friends of Kerrigan's archrival, Harding. Her former husband, Jeff Gillooly, figured if he could knock Kerrigan out of the way, Harding would stand a far better chance of winning the U.S. and Olympic competitions. Gillooly hired two men—Derrick Smith and Shane Stant—to attack Kerrigan. The two men had followed her to different events looking for their chance before finally carrying out the assault. Soon Gillooly, Smith, and Stant admitted their roles in the incident. The U.S. Figure Skating Association allowed Harding to skate in the Olympics because police could not prove that she had been involved in the attack. The news made Kerrigan and her family very angry.

Experts and fans wondered what effect the attack would have on Kerrigan. She had developed a reputation after the 1993 world championships for not handling pressure very well and not being tough enough to win big competitions. Determined to make all her hard work pay off, Kerrigan set out to prove her critics wrong. "Nancy Kerrigan's not a victim," Cindy Adams, Kerrigan's sports psychologist, explained to *Sports Illustrated.* "That's not how we're going to look at this. She doesn't understand what's happened or why, but she's not going to let this get in the way of what she's set out to do. She's going to be a little cautious around people for a while, but we all should be a little cautious. Nancy's not a worrywart. She's a strong individual, and she is loved a lot—and that helps a great deal."

BEST PERFORMANCE. Kerrigan's main rival in the Olympic competition was 17-year-old Oksana Baiul, the 1993 world champion, from Ukraine. The second-to-last skater to perform, Kerrigan turned in a nearly flawless performance, winning the short program. "I felt a little too calm," Kerrigan explained in *Sports Illustrated.* "I had tell myself, All right, this is it. This is the Olympics." Baiul, also skating well, came in second. Harding, who was out of shape and nervous from the media attention, finished tenth in the short program.

Despite winning the short program, many experts still expected Kerrigan to fall apart in the long program like she had at the 1993 world championships. "Prague was the biggest motivator of all this year," Evy Scotvold stated in *Sports Illustrated.* "More than Detroit. She knows what can happen if you're not ready to be the leader." During practice for the long program, Baiul collided with Tanja Szewczenko of Germany and needed three stitches to close the cuts on her leg. She also injured her back.

The 1994 Olympic Winter Games women's long program was one of the most widely watched athletic competitions in U.S. television history. To start, Harding broke a lace during warm-up and couldn't find a substitute. She was late getting on the ice for her performance, and judges nearly disqualified her from the competition. Unable to skate with her broken lace, Harding stopped her long program and asked for a chance to reskate. She came back on the ice and finished her program and moved up to eighth in the final standings.

Kerrigan took the ice for her long program and within minutes made a mistake, turning a triple jump into a double jump. Unlike during the world championships, however, she did not let the mistake get to her. *Sports Illustrated* described her performance this way: "She was nearly flawless: strong and fast and angular and increasingly animated as it became clear to her and everyone else that this was the best long program she had ever skated in competition.... This beauty had more than a small measure of grit and fight and moxie in her."

SETTLES FOR SILVER. Baiul skated after Kerrigan and turned in a nearly flawless performance of her own. She did stumble once, landing a jump with both feet on the ice. The voting for the gold medal was extremely close, but in the end five judges voted for Baiul and four for Kerrigan, giving the Ukrainian skater the gold medal. Baiul won by one-tenth of a point, the smallest possible margin in figure skating. The loss disappointed Kerrigan and her family, but soon they accepted the outcome. "It's not right what the judges did, but they did us a favor," Brenda Kerrigan admitted in *Sports Illustrated*. "The silver medal will give Nancy back her normal life quicker. Nancy, you know, never liked being special."

TURNS PRO. Kerrigan turned professional after the Olympics. She also signed with 26 different companies to do endorsements. A study showed that Kerrigan was second only to Michael Jordan in popularity. She made millions of dollars from doing commercials, workout videotapes, and ice shows.

Soon, however, the media began to criticize Kerrigan. They called her a sore loser for complaining about the scoring at the Olympics. She also received criticism for calling a parade she participated in at Walt Disney World "the most corniest thing I've ever done." The criticism hurt Kerrigan, who had a hard time living up to the fairy princess reputation the media created for her during the Olympics. "Everything was blown up so big before the Olympics that everyone rushed to let out the air after the Olympics," Brenda Kerrigan

TONYA AND NANCY

After the Olympics, Harding admitted that she found out about the attack soon after it occurred. The U.S. Figure Skating Association banned her from participating in the 1994 World Figure Skating Championships. Gillooly, Smith, Stant, and another man, Shawn Ekhardt, all pleaded guilty in the attack and are serving prison sentences. Television networks made several movies about the incident. Kerrigan says she hopes that now she can put the whole incident behind her.

explained in *Sports Illustrated*. "Nancy wasn't what they made her out to be before she skated, and she isn't what they make her out to be now."

OFF THE ICE. Kerrigan earned an associate degree in business from Emmanuel College. She gets a lot of fan mail and tries to answer it all. On September 9, 1995, Kerrigan married Jerry Soloman, her agent. Soloman had helped her get over the pre-Olympic attack. "We were at the Olympics," Kerrigan recalled in *Sports Illustrated*. "The whole time, after Detroit, everything had been talk about me. I was so sick of talking about me. I started asking about him. That was where we really started talking, to get to know each other. My parents hadn't arrived yet. I couldn't go anywhere because of all the stuff that was going on. We were there together every day."

Kerrigan told *Sports Illustrated* why she put herself through the hard work to compete at the 1994 Winter Olympics: "I always just wanted to compete."

Sources

Newsweek, March 2, 1992.
People, February 3, 1992; May 5, 1993; January 24, 1994; November 28, 1994; June 25, 1995.
Sports Illustrated, May 25, 1991; March 2, 1992; February 1, 1993; January 17, 1994; February 14, 1994; February 28, 1994; March 7, 1994; March 14, 1994; December 5, 1994.
Time, February 10, 1992.

WHERE TO WRITE:
PROSERVE, 1101
WILSON BLVD., SUITE 1800,
ARLINGTON, VA 22209.

Jason Kidd

1973—

If a basketball team were an army, then the point guard would be the general. His job is to run the team's offense and make sure his teammates get involved in the game and play to the best of their abilities. Nobody in the National Basketball Association (NBA) today does this better than Jason Kidd of the Dallas Mavericks. A star since eighth grade, Kidd has made a name for himself by making other players look good. Although his statistics are not always spectacular, they were good enough in his first NBA season to make him Rookie of the Year.

Growing Up

BORN SPECIAL. Jason Frederick Kidd was born March 23, 1973, in San Francisco, California. His father, Steve, is a supervisor with Trans World Airlines. His mother, Anne, is a bookkeeper at a bank. He also has two younger sisters, Denise and Kimberly. "I was different from the day I was

"I get a thrill out of seeing someone else score."
—Jason Kidd

SCOREBOARD

NATIONAL HIGH SCHOOL PLAYER OF THE YEAR (1992).

LED NATION IN ASSISTS (9.1 PER GAME) FOR UNIVERSITY OF CALIFORNIA (1994).

NBA ROOKIE OF THE YEAR (1995).

ONE OF THE BEST PURE POINT GUARDS IN THE NBA, KIDD GETS HIS KICKS BY MAKING HIS TEAMMATES BETTER.

born," Kidd told the *Sporting News*. "Dad is black. Mom is white. I had two different cultures and two different backgrounds to learn from. I think that helped me to be special."

Kidd's family was always close. "I never thought of him as a superstar, he was just a brother," his sister, Denise, recalled in the *Mavericks Press*. "I hung out with him and the guys all the time. Yeah, he picks on me, too." His parents say they tried to raise all their children the same way. "[We raised our children] to treat everybody like you want to be treated," Kidd's dad said. "All of our kids are like that. They'll help you any way they can."

SOMETHING SPECIAL. Kidd grew up playing basketball in his hometown of Oakland, California. Playing with older kids most of the time, he learned early that the best way to fit in was to help his teammates score. "Everybody wanted to score baskets," Kidd remembered in *Sports Illustrated for Kids*. "I would get picked [for teams] a lot because they knew I wouldn't shoot." By the time he reached junior high, Kidd was a basketball hero. People wanted his autograph when he was in eighth grade. "Everybody started saying how great Jason was," his dad recalled in the *Sporting News*. "We were flattered, but afraid to accept it. I guess by high school we started believing he might be something special."

Kidd was a high school sensation. He led his Saint Joseph of Notre Dame High School team to two consecutive California state titles with records of 31-3 and 32-3. Experts named Kidd state player of the year both seasons, and he finished his career as the assist record holder for high school players in California (1,155 assists). He averaged 25 points, ten assists, seven rebounds, and seven steals as a senior. In honor of his achievements, Kidd won the Naismith Award as the nation's top high school player (1992). "Our 800-seat gym couldn't handle the crowds," Saint Joseph's coach Frank

LaPorte told the *Sporting News,* "so we eventually had to play in the Oakland Coliseum."

Kidd also played soccer and baseball in high school. A baseball center fielder, Kidd only reluctantly gave up the game in college. "I loved the challenge of the one-on-one, just the pitcher against you," Kidd explained in the *Mavericks Press.* He batted .333 his senior season. Kidd's football career ended in sixth grade when he ran into a mailbox while playing in the street. During the summer, Kidd played basketball with college and professional players, further sharpening his skills.

BEAR CUB. Kidd wanted to go out of state when the time came to choose a college. His parents wanted him to stay close to home. Eventually, his parents won out. Kidd chose the University of California, only minutes from his family's home. "I want to be near my friends," Kidd said, explaining his decision. The Golden Bears were 23-33 in the two seasons before Kidd arrived. Kidd was ready for the challenge. "I think the transition from high school to college is not that great for me as it might be for some players," he explained in the *Sporting News.* "Playing with the pro players and college players in the summer, I have an idea of what it's going to take."

Kidd started as a freshman for the Golden Bears during the 1992-93 season. California replaced coach Lou Campanelli at midseason, and new coach Todd Bozeman opened up the team's offense to match Kidd's skills. He averaged 13 points, 7.7 assists, and 4.9 rebounds per game. These numbers were good enough to earn Kidd All-Pacific 10 (PAC-10) honors and several Freshman of the Year awards. Kidd led the Golden Bears to a 21-9 record and into the National Collegiate Athletic Association (NCAA) Basketball Tournament. There they upset two-time defending champion Duke University. Kidd had 11 points, 14 assists, eight rebounds, and four steals in the upset.

Getting used to college schoolwork was an adjustment for Kidd. "I didn't really know what to expect as a college student until the first couple weeks," Kidd admitted to *Sporting News.* "After that, I knew what kind of time I had to put in for school. It was really no big surprise, but I can't say I knew what college was all about before I started."

ALL-AMERICAN. In his sophomore season (1993-94), Kidd led the nation in assists (9.1 per game), set a career school record in steals, and averaged 16.7 points per game. He also averaged almost seven rebounds a game, an incredible number for a point guard. Kidd's honors included the PAC-10 Conference Player of the Year award and a spot on the first-team All-American team. He was a finalist for both the prestigious Naismith and Wooden Awards, given annually to the best player in college basketball. "When it comes time for the game to be won, he'll win it," Bozeman told *Sports Illustrated*. "He's one of those players who can dominate a game without scoring."

Superstar

MAVERICKS PICK. Kidd decided he was ready for the NBA following his sophomore season and declared himself eligible for the 1994 draft. He entered a draft that already included **Glenn "Big Dog" Robinson** from Purdue and **Grant Hill** from Duke (see entries). The Dallas Mavericks, who held the second pick in the draft, were anxious to have Kidd and picked him when they had the chance. It turned out that Kidd had always had a special Mavericks memento, a cap that he kept in the back of his mother's car. "I liked it because green is my favorite color, but I also saw myself playing in Dallas for some reason," Kidd admitted following the draft.

The Mavericks had been a terrible team but were on the upswing in 1994. Kidd joined shooting guard Jimmy Jackson and small forward Jamal Mashburn to give Dallas a potent attack. Kidd averaged 7.7 assists (tied for ninth in the NBA) and 1.91 steals (seventh in the NBA). He led the NBA with four triple-doubles. (A triple-double is awarded when a player earns double figures in points, rebounds, and assists in one game.) "[He] sees things other people don't see," Mashburn told *Sport* magazine about his new teammate. An injury to Jackson's ankle in February ended his season and crushed the

Mavericks' play-off hopes. Kidd took on more of the team's scoring burden, but Dallas fell short of a play-off berth.

ROOKIE OF THE YEAR. Kidd won the 1994-95 NBA Rookie of the Year award, tying with Grant Hill of the Detroit Pistons for the honor. He was also the only unanimous choice to the NBA All-Rookie team. In order to improve, Kidd must develop a more consistent outside shot. He shot only 38 percent during his rookie season. "I know my shot needs work, but I also know that when we need a big basket, I want the shot—and I usually make it," Kidd told *Sports Illustrated.*

Kidd must also learn to stay out of trouble. During his rookie season, he crashed his dad's car and left the scene of the accident before the police arrived. A judge ordered Kidd to pay $1,000 and teach basketball to kids at a Boys' and Girls' Club. "When you do something bad, something good can come out of it," Kidd confessed in *Sports Illustrated for Kids.* "What I went through will help me mature a lot faster."

OFF THE COURT. Kidd's favorite actor is Robert DeNiro, and his favorite actress is Julia Roberts. He is a big fan of rhythm and blues music, and his favorite musicians are the Isley Brothers and Chante Moore. In school, Kidd always liked math, maybe to add up his statistics. In his free time Kidd likes to play golf, and he hopes someday to get a hole in one. He has a Rottweiler dog named Mia, and his favorite thing to eat is Chinese food.

Kidd donated money to churches in Dallas and Oakland to help buy basketball floors following the signing of his first contract with the Mavericks. He also purchased a set of 30 seats to Mavericks games for "Kidd's Kids," seats he gives to underprivileged children. Kidd also maintains the Jason Kidd

THE NEW MAGIC?

Many experts compared Kidd's game during his rookie season to that of all-time great Earvin "Magic" Johnson. Kidd takes that as a compliment, and says that Johnson is his role model. "I will probably always pattern my game after Magic Johnson," Kidd admitted. "He was a total player. He always had fun on the court but at the same time he took care of business and he made everybody better around him. He brought his team to another level." Johnson is also a Jason Kidd fan. "[Jason] is the NBA's best point guard at making his teammates look good," Johnson said.

KIDD'S CARD COLLECTION

Kidd loves to collect baseball cards. He started when he was a kid. "I would buy packs with my best friend," Kidd recounted in *Sports Illustrated for Kids.* "We tried to collect all the players in the major leagues." Kidd has now expanded his collection to include baseballs, bats, and pictures. He also collects basketball memorabilia, including basketballs and shoes. Kidd's most prized possession is a Ken Griffey Jr. baseball card. "Junior is the best in baseball," Kidd told *Sports Illustrated for Kids.* "My goal is to be the best in basketball."

Foundation, a charitable organization, and the Jason Kidd Basketball Scholarship Fund at the University of California.

NBA Scouting Director Marty Blake best summed up Kidd's game when he said, "Point guards are born and not made. He's the kind of kid who will start and finish the play, and make people around him better."

Sources

Mavericks Press, Vol. 7, No. 4.
Sport, April 1995.
Sporting News, November 30, 1992; November 29, 1993; July 11, 1994; October 3, 1994.
Sports Illustrated, March 21, 1994; August 1, 1994.
Sports Illustrated for Kids, July 1995; September 1995.
Additional information provided by Dallas Mavericks.

WHERE TO WRITE:
C/O DALLAS MAVERICKS,
REUNION ARENA,
777 SPORTS ST.,
DALLAS, TX 75207.

Betsy King

1955—

Betsy King always liked sports. From the time she was a child she played whatever game she could, with basketball being her favorite. A knee injury, however, forced King to make a career out of one of her least-favorite sports—golf. The rest is history, as King went on to earn induction into the Ladies' Professional Golf Association (LPGA) Hall of Fame in 1995. A fierce competitor on the course and a devoted Christian in her private life, King has worked hard throughout her life to keep her priorities straight.

Growing Up

SPORTS IN HER GENES. Betsy King was born August 13, 1955, in Reading, Pennsylvania. She grew up in Limekiln, Pennsylvania. Her father, Weir, was a doctor. Both of King's parents were athletes. Helen King played basketball and field hockey at the University of Rhode Island. In 1987 the school inducted Helen into its Athletic Hall of Fame, honoring her as

"I tell all my students to look at Betsy King, the unemotional and classy way she handles herself. That's the way to be a consistent winner."—Ed Oldfield, pro golf teacher

SCOREBOARD

INDUCTED INTO LPGA HALL OF
FAME IN 1995.

THREE-TIME WINNER OF LPGA
PLAYER OF THE YEAR AWARD
(1984, 1989, AND 1993).

WON THREE OF WOMEN'S GOLF'S
MAJOR CHAMPIONSHIPS—THE
NABISCO DINAH SHORE WOMEN'S
OPEN (1987 AND 1990),
THE LPGA CHAMPIONSHIP (1992),
AND THE U.S. WOMEN'S OPEN
(1989 AND 1990).

KING BALANCED A COMPETITIVE
FIRE AND STRONG RELIGIOUS
BELIEFS TO REACH THE TOP OF
WOMEN'S GOLF.

the best all-around athlete of the class of 1940. Weir played baseball and football at Dickinson College.

ALL-AROUND STAR. King excelled in the classroom and in athletics. She loved to read as a youngster and wrote 60 book reports in the third grade. In high school, King qualified for the National Honor Society. She also played clarinet in the high school band and enjoyed ballet and tap dancing.

When it came to sports, King played everything. "All I can say is our household was the only one where the father relinquished [gave up] the sports section to his daughter," Helen King explained in the *New York Times*. King loved to swim, but had to quit because of her poor eyesight. She also liked to run, racing down the family's half-mile driveway with her father timing her.

KING OF THE COURT. Most of all, King loved team sports. Her favorite was basketball, and she starred on the Exeter Township High School team. The coach of the team, Jean Frey, was King's role model at school. "She had an excellent jump shot from 15 to 18 feet," Frey recalled in *Golf Digest*. King was the first female player in Exeter Township to dribble the ball behind her back. She also played field hockey and softball. King batted .480 her senior year and committed no errors at shortstop.

PALADIN PLAYER. King attended Furman University in Greenville, South Carolina, to study physical education. Her goal at the time was to become a physical education teacher and basketball coach. King continued to play several sports for the Furman University Lady Paladins. Her favorite was field hockey, but she hurt her knee making a sharp turn during a game. She played the rest of the game, but the knee swelled up the next day. King worked hard through physical therapy

to get her knee back into shape. Unfortunately, shortly after that she tore the ligaments in her knee playing for the Lady Paladins basketball team. The injury limited the sports King could play.

TURNS TO GOLF. Her bad knee forced King to take golf more seriously. "The knee injury was very fortunate," Weir King stated in the *New York Times*. King took her first lesson at age ten and played with her older brother, Lee, and his friends. "She and her brother also used to hit golf balls toward the house," King's father recounted in the same newspaper. "One time, from upstairs, I could hear her brother saying, 'I hit the house with a 4-iron today.' I was on them pretty good after that. I told them to keep it on the course." King liked golf, but not as much as other sports. In 1972 she reached the semifinals of the 1972 United States Golf Association Junior Girls' Championship.

In 1976 King teamed with Beth Daniel to lead Furman to the 1976 National Collegiate Athletic Association (NCAA)

King watches her shot during the 1994 U.S. Women's Open.

Women's Golf Championship. She also shot the best score for an amateur at the U.S. Women's Open, finishing in a tie for eighth. Her college success convinced King to join the LPGA tour in 1977.

EARLY STRUGGLES. King struggled on the LPGA tour, averaging 74.26 strokes per round in her first four years. Her best finishes were two second places—in 1978 at the Borden Classic and in 1979 at the Wheeling Classic. "For a lot of reasons, it's hard for me to remember my first few years on Tour," King admitted in *Golf* magazine. "But I do recall that I reached a point where I thought I might never win a tournament. I think I'd even begun to come to terms with that. I thought, well, I'm going to be the best non-winner who's ever been out there."

BIG CHANGES. In 1980 King decided to change her golf game and her personal life. To improve her game, she worked with teaching pro Ed Oldfield. "What I saw wasn't pretty," Oldfield recounted in *Golf* magazine. "Betsy's game was at the bottom of the barrel. Frankly, I don't know how much longer she could have gone on that way."

The idea of changing her game made King nervous. "I told her that her game would have to be rebuilt from top to bottom," Oldfield told *Golf* magazine. To try to calm her nerves, King went out and hit some balls with her father before her first lesson. "We found a deserted playground," Weir King recounted in *Sports Illustrated*. "She was hitting balls, and I was chasing them—and a cop came and chased us. I think that was the low point in her career. But that afternoon Ed [Oldfield] told me that she was going to be one of the five best players in the world."

King spent the winter working with Oldfield, and he overhauled her swing. "It was pretty drastic," King remembered in *Sports Illustrated*. "Ed pretty much breaks down your whole swing." Oldfield warned King that her game would get worse before it got better. "Most pros probably couldn't handle changing their swing altogether," Oldfield confessed to *Golf* magazine. "It takes an exceptional person. I quickly realized that Betsy King was that person. She was so patient, so trusting, so sincere. I'd never seen anyone who wanted to be the best player in the world more than Betsy King. She was willing to do whatever it took."

FINDS RELIGION. The biggest change in King's personal life involved her religious faith, which had not been very strong before. At Furman other students invited her to Bible study classes, but she turned them down. King devoted her life to Christianity after attending a Fellowship of Christian Athletes conference. "The speaker talked about making difficult choices, choosing the narrow path, having a personal relationship with God," King recalled in *Golf* magazine. "Around me were people like [fellow touring pro] Donna White and I saw how well they handled the pressure of life on the Tour. I suddenly knew I'd discovered truth. Truth with a capital T."

Christianity helped King get control of her fierce competitiveness. "In the past I tended to compare myself too much to other people," King admitted in *Golf Digest.* "I used to resent people who would beat me. I'd want to win at everything, if it was just playing cards. I just always had that. I don't know why."

MOVING UP. King improved steadily, lowering her scoring average from 73.96 in 1981 to 71.77 in 1984. She won her first LPGA tournament in 1984, the Women's Kemper Open. During 1984 King won two more tournaments, led the LPGA in earnings, and won her first Player of the Year award. She also won two tournaments in 1985 and 1986.

King was in contention for another LPGA Player of the Year award in 1987, battling Ayako Okamoto and Jane Geddes. She took a break from the tour to fulfill a commitment to Habitat for Humanity, a Christian organization that uses volunteers to build houses for the poor. The time away from the tour cost her the championship, which Okamoto won. King did win her first major tournament—the Dinah Shore Women's Open. She sank a shot from a sand trap for a birdie on the third-to-last hole to tie Patty Sheehan. King went on to win the tournament in a sudden death play-off. She also won her first Vare Trophy, given to the player with the LPGA's lowest scoring average. (The Vare Trophy is named after Glenna Vare, a women's golf pioneer who won a record six U.S. Women's Amateur Championships in the 1920s and 1930s.)

Superstar

TOP OF HER GAME. King had her best season ever in 1989, winning six tournaments. Her biggest win came at the Indianwood Country Club, host of the 1989 U.S. Women's Open. King led the tournament by four strokes entering the third round but finished with a bogey, double bogey, and bogey on the last three holes to fall into a first-place tie with Patty Sheehan. Her collapse made King nervous, but Oldfield told her not to worry. She played well in the fourth, and final, round to win the tournament by four strokes. King won a then record $654,132 in prize money in 1989, and experts ranked her as the world's best player. From 1984 through 1989 King won an amazing 20 tournaments.

King defended her U.S. Women's Open title in 1990 in Duluth, Georgia. Patty Sheehan led the tournament by nine strokes entering the final round, only to lose the tournament. At one point King trailed by 11 strokes, but she did not give up. "They're not gonna know what happened down the road," King admitted in *Sports Illustrated* following the tournament. "They'll see the winner's name and won't know what occurred." King also won the Nabisco Dinah Shore Women's Open for the second time.

MAKING CHANGES. Despite winning two tournaments in 1991, King again felt the need to take stock of her life and career. She realized that she had few close friends and only found golf and religion interesting. "It helped me put golf in perspective," King admitted in *Sports Illustrated*. "I realized I needed to develop other relationships and other outlets." King opened a beauty shop, Betsy K's Salon, in Phoenix, Arizona. The business struggled, so King became more active in its day-to-day operation.

To improve her game, King decided to change her swing and coach. She worked with Bob Dickman, a teaching pro from Illinois. Dickman changed her swing, but the results were disastrous. King had a number of disappointing tournaments to start 1992, so she again switched coaches. Finally, she went back to Oldfield, begging him for help. He straightened out King's swing and got her back on the winning track.

LPGA CROWN. King made a mini-comeback by winning the 1992 LPGA Championship at the Bethesda Country Club. She trounced the rest of the field, winning by 11 strokes. King became the first player in LPGA history to shoot four consecutive rounds in the 60s in a major tournament. "Experience is important in majors," King told *Sports Illustrated,* explaining her victory over the much younger golfers competing against her. "Veterans usually come to the fore."

PUTTING THINGS IN PERSPECTIVE

In November 1993 King and four other LPGA golfers traveled to Romania to pass out food and candy to orphaned street children through a program called Alternative Ministries. "I went from celebrating an incredible win and season to extreme sadness," King recalled in *Sports Illustrated.* "I was so happy, and then it all became very, very clear. I said to myself, How important is golf, anyway? We were standing in snow, freezing, dealing with young children who live under a train station. It gave me perspective that has changed my life. The whole country is so poor. It's sad to think about the children we left behind."

BACK ON TOP. In 1993 King won her third LPGA Player of the Year award. She won the award after birdieing the last hole of the Toray Japan Queen's Cup, the last tournament of the year. King shot a final-round 67 to seal a one-stroke victory. For the year she earned more money than any other player on the LPGA tour ($595,992) and earned her second Vare Trophy. She just missed out on winning the du Maurier Ltd. Classic, the only major tournament she has not won, when Brandie Burton beat her on the first hole of a sudden death play-off.

HALL OF FAMER. The final goal for King was induction into the LPGA Hall of Fame. She needed 30 tour victories to qualify but did not win a tournament in 1994. Nine times King held the lead in the final round of a tournament but could not win. The pressure to win her thirtieth title hurt King's game. "I know people mean well and try to encourage you, but a lot

HALL OF FAMERS

In 1995 King became the fourteenth player to earn induction into the LPGA Hall of Fame. Induction is based on a combination of total tournament wins and victories in the major championships of the LPGA. Following is a list of the LPGA Hall of Famers and the year they earned this prestigious honor.

Player	Year
Patty Berg	1951
Betty Jameson	1951
Louise Sugga	1951
Babe Didrikson Zaharias	1951
Betsy Rawls	1960
Mickey Wright	1964
Kathy Whitworth	1975
Sandra Haynie	1977
Carol Mann	1977
Jo Anne Carner	1982
Nancy Lopez	1987
Pat Bradley	1991
Patty Sheehan	1993
Betsy King	1995

of people were asking about it and mentioning it," King explained in *Golf* magazine. "There's been a lot of prayer on my part to keep perspective and I haven't always done well with that. I did feel it was unfair that anytime I was close to the lead, people were saying if I didn't win, I lost it. I used to count the days that went by when someone didn't mention the Hall of Fame. Those were few and far between the last two years."

King's slump lasted 20 months. Finally, in 1995, King won at the ShopRite LPGA Classic, her thirtieth career victory. She became the fourteenth player to earn induction into the LPGA Hall of Fame. "The pressure's off," a relieved King told in the *New York Times*. The Hall of Fame inducted King on November 11, 1995. At the end of the 1995 season, King led the LPGA in career earnings with $5,374,022.

TOO MEAN? Fans sometimes mistake King for being mean because she concentrates so hard on the golf course. "I put on my game face because that's what I need to do to win," King told *Sports Illustrated*. Other players have come to know the real King. "Betsy is maybe the most misunderstood person out here," Meg Mallon explained in *Golf* magazine. "People say she is nice, as though that were a fault. But beneath that calm exterior is a remarkable person who has the courage of her convictions. For what it's worth, she might be the most competitive person out here. She's only invisible to the press because she doesn't fit the model of what they think a champion should be."

King finds it difficult to deal with what fans think about her. "I think sometimes people think you're cocky or standoffish because you're shy," King stated in *Golf Digest*. "I have a hard time handling the people coming up. I've never felt my job is to make sure I give 5,000 autographs every week. It's scary in a way, when people put you on a pedestal. I feel like right away it limits any kind of relationship you can have."

OFF THE COURSE. King lives in Scottsdale, Arizona. She likes playing basketball and says she might want to coach someday. In 1993 King worked as an assistant basketball coach at the Scottsdale Christian Academy. "Boy, when she was coaching she was a different person," Head Coach Sandy Austin told *Golf Digest*. "I almost had to put a seat belt on her. She nearly got a technical."

King's favorite board game is Monopoly. "She loves to have money," fellow pro Barb Thomas told the same magazine. She also enjoy concerts and the theater. And, of course, King loves all sports.

King is a very devout Christian. She attends weekly Christian fellowship meetings where players study the Bible and pray together. King does not drink or smoke. "I've never really been that wild," King admitted in *Golf Digest*. "I've been drunk maybe three or four times in my life. I never liked beer, so that was no great hardship." King enjoys Christian music and attends Christian athletic camps. "She's as good a Christian as she is a golfer," Bill Lewis of the Fellowship of Christian Athletes told *Sports Illustrated*. "I've never met a superstar athlete with so much humility." King donates her time and at least 10 percent of her earnings to charity.

King is a good role model on the course and in her private life. "I tell all my students to look at Betsy King, the unemotional and classy way she handles herself," Oldfield told *Golf* magazine. "That's the way to be a consistent winner."

Sources

Golf, July 1991; September 1995.
Golf Digest, September 1994.
New York Times, July 13, 1995.

Sports Illustrated, February 12, 1990; July 23, 1990; August 27, 1990; May 25, 1992; December 27, 1993.

Additional information provided by Ladies' Professional Golf Association.

 WHERE TO WRITE:
LADIES' PROFESSIONAL GOLF ASSOCIATION,
2570 VOUSIA ST., SUITE. B,
DAYTONA, FL 32114.

Michelle Kwan

1980—

Figure skating is fast becoming one of the most popular sports in the United States. One of the best American figure skaters is Michelle Kwan, a 15-year-old teenager who has skated her way to the top. Kwan began skating when she was five and dreamed of someday winning an Olympic gold medal. One of the youngest world-class skaters ever, she is working hard today to make that dream come true at the 1998 Winter Olympics in Nagano, Japan.

"Just do what you want to do, work hard, and that's all you can hope for."
—Michelle Kwan

Growing Up

LITTLE KWAN. Michelle Wing Kwan was born July 7, 1980, in Torrance, California. Kwan's father, Danny, came to the United States from Hong Kong in 1971. Her mother, Estella, followed in 1975. Danny Kwan is an administrative supervisor for Pacific Bell Telephone, and Estella Kwan is the manager of the Golden Pheasant, a family-owned restaurant. Kwan, whose nickname is "Little Kwan," is the couple's third child.

WON WOMEN'S SINGLES COMPETITION AT 1996 U.S. FIGURE SKATING CHAMPIONSHIPS.

FINISHED SECOND IN WOMEN'S COMPETITION AT BACK-TO-BACK U.S. FIGURE SKATING CHAMPIONSHIPS (1994 AND 1995).

FINISHED FOURTH IN WOMEN'S COMPETITION AT 1995 WORLD FIGURE SKATING CHAMPIONSHIPS.

KWAN IS THE BEST U.S. HOPE TO WIN A GOLD MEDAL IN THE WOMEN'S COMPETITION AT THE 1998 WINTER OLYMPICS.

EARLY LEARNER. Kwan discovered skating at the age of five when she went to watch her brother, Ron, play hockey. Kwan and her sister, Karen, skated after her brother's practice. They both liked skating so much they began taking figure skating lessons. "My first skating memory is from when I was six," Kwan recalled in *Sports Illustrated for Kids*. "I was wearing rental skates and eating Nerds candy."

Kwan was great right away. She entered her first competition when she was six years old. Kwan won. She decided to take the sport seriously after watching Brian Boitano win the men's gold medal at the 1988 Winter Olympics. Her dream was to win a gold medal for herself. "I thought, 'Okay, tomorrow I'll go to the Olympics,'" she recounted in *Sports Illustrated for Kids*. It would not be that easy, however.

LEAVES HOME. Kwan's parents hired coach Frank Carroll to work with their daughters in 1990. Both Michelle and Karen Kwan went to live and train at the Ice Castle International Training Center in Lake Arrowhead, California. The center was only two hours away from the family's home in Torrance, California, and Kwan's mother went to live with her daughters. Even though both sisters skate against each other competitively, they say there is no sibling rivalry. "We're really good friends," Karen explained in the *Christian Science Monitor*. "I don't think we have any of that rivalry stuff." Kwan made many new friends at Lake Arrowhead. The students often went shopping and played sports together.

PASSES TEST. Kwan began to move up the ladder in U.S. figure skating. She finished ninth at the 1992 U.S. Junior National Championships. To qualify for the 1994 Winter Olympics, Kwan would have to move up to the senior level. To do that, she would have to pass a test. Kwan wanted to take the test, but Carroll said no. He thought she needed more experience.

Kwan skating during a 1993 competition.

Kwan decided to take the test anyway and picked a day when her coach was out of town. She passed. Carroll was mad when he heard what his student had done, Kwan told *People* magazine. "I knew I might get in trouble, but I just had to do it."

The decision to take the test turned out to be the right one. Kwan won the women's singles competition at the 1993 U.S. Olympic Festival in front of the biggest crowd to ever watch a figure skating competition. She landed six triple jumps during the competition and became the youngest champion in the history of the Olympic Festival. Kwan also won three other major competitions in 1993 and finished sixth in the 1993 U.S. Figure Skating Championships.

PRESSURE COOKER. The pressure of competing as a teenager at such a high level was hard on Kwan. In 1992, while Kwan was preparing for the national junior championships in Orlando, Florida, her father tried to help her deal with the pressure. "I had been telling her about the competition, not to worry," Mr. Kwan remembered in *People* magazine. But then Mr. Kwan went into her room one night and found his daughter talking in her sleep, saying, "It's nothing, it's nothing" over and over. He asked himself, "What are you doing to her?"

Kwan placed a disappointing ninth in the competition. Mr. Kwan decided that he and his daughter needed a change of attitude about the sport. "I went to Michelle and I said, 'You are my daughter. Skating has cost a lot of time and money and worry to your parents. But when I see you get too stressed out like this, I think it's time to quit,'" Mr. Kwan continued in *People*. "I told her I just wanted her to have fun, to enjoy skating."

Superstar

NATIONAL SPOTLIGHT. Kwan unintentionally became a star in January 1994 at the U.S. Figure Skating Championships in Detroit, Michigan. Before the competition began, two men injured skater **Nancy Kerrigan** (see entry) by hitting her knee with a metal bar. Kerrigan, the favorite to win the competition, was unable to skate after the attack. With Kerrigan out of the competition, Tonya Harding took first place and Kwan finished second.

As the second-place finisher, Kwan would have normally been guaranteed a spot on the U.S. Olympic team set to compete at the 1994 Winter Olympics in Lillehammer, Norway. However, since Kerrigan probably would have won the competition in Detroit if not for the attack, the U.S. Figure

Skating Association decided to put Kerrigan on the Olympic team instead of Kwan. Although disappointed, Kwan showed good sportsmanship in dealing with the decision. "It's a bummer for me, but I was kind of hoping Nancy would be able to go," Kwan admitted in *People* magazine. "She deserves it."

GOES TO OLYMPICS. Investigations into the attack on Kerrigan led police to believe that Harding, or friends of hers, had been involved. The attackers believed injuring Kerrigan was the only way for Harding to defeat her longtime rival. The U.S. Figure Skating Association decided to send Kwan to Norway with the Olympic team. She would skate if police could prove that Harding had been involved with the crime. "I don't quite know when we're going or where we're going; all I know is that we're going," Carroll told the *New York Times*. "We're going there as an alternate unless things change. And then she will be put on the ice." Kwan tried to put the whole incident out of her mind. "I try not to think about it," Kwan said of Harding's troubles. "I just skate."

WATCHES OLYMPICS. Kwan's role at the Olympics disappointed her. She was not allowed to live in the Olympic village, train at the Olympic rink, or participate in the opening ceremonies. "It didn't feel like an Olympic experience," Kwan admitted in *Sports Illustrated for Kids.* "I never really got to see the ice rink. I never got to see the Olympic village." Kwan made the best of her situation, however, and in a statement she released to the press before leaving for Norway she said, "As the first alternate, I have to keep training and stay focused, in case I'm asked to compete. The only thing that's changed is that now I'll get to go to Norway, and that will be fun."

The U.S. Figure Skating Association allowed Harding to skate at the Olympics because police had no firm evidence against her. As a result, Kwan spent her first Olympics in the stands. She would have been the youngest U.S. Olympian ever if she had been allowed to compete.

WORLD COMPETITION. Kwan returned to the United States after the Olympics. She went back to her regular training schedule in preparation for the 1994 world championships in Chiba, Japan. Kwan became the highest-ranking female amateur figure skater in the United States after the U.S. Figure Skating Association banned Harding from competition. Harding admitted after the Olympics that she had been told about the attack after it occurred. Kerrigan announced her retirement from amateur skating shortly after her silver medal Olympic performance. The change at the top placed additional pressure on Kwan. She had to finish in the top ten at her first World Figure Skating Championships or the American team would not qualify to compete at the same competition in 1995.

Kwan got off to a rocky start in the women's competition. She finished eleventh in the short program, the part of the competition where all skaters have to complete the same moves and jumps. Kwan would have to deliver in the long program, where skaters design their own routine. She met the challenge. Kwan's program, which included several triple jumps, moved her up to eighth in the overall standings.

UPSET. Figure skating experts expected Kwan to become the youngest champion ever at the 1995 U.S. Figure Skating Championships. "I think she was a little star-struck last year by the other big names," Carroll explained to the Reuters News Agency. "But since then she has been on tour with them [skating stars] and she is much more comfortable now." Carroll admitted, however, that there was more pressure on his young skater: "I think she was too young to be intimidated last year. At 13, there is no fear. As you get older, it gets tougher."

Experts were shocked when both Tonia Kwiatkowski and Nicole Bobek finished ahead of Kwan in the short program. Kwan still had a chance to win the title when she took the ice as the final skater during the long program. She would have to have a flawless performance. Unfortunately, Kwan stumbled during the landing of a triple loop jump and fell trying to do a triple lutz. Bobek, on the other hand, completed a virtually perfect free-skate program to take the title. "I skated well," Kwan explained in the *Philadelphia Inquirer.* "I don't think the pressure got to me. But I was disappointed that I fell because I had been skating very well before that."

Kwan tried to not let her defeat bother her. "I'm fine," Kwan revealed to the Reuters News Agency. "I don't look back. There is no more or no less pressure on me then if I had won. You don't get pressure from anyone else, you get it from inside yourself." Karen Kwan, Michelle's sister, finished a respectable seventh in the competition.

WORLD CHAMPIONSHIPS. Both Kwan and Bobek qualified to participate in the 1995 World Figure Skating Championships in Birmingham, England. Bobek won the short program, and Kwan finished fifth. Both Americans were in contention, and the long program would decide the championship. Bobek fell twice during her long program. Kwan landed seven triple jumps during her program, and many experts thought her performance would move her past Bobek and into third place. That would be good for a bronze medal.

The judges, however, did not think Kwan had done enough to overcome Bobek's lead. "Maybe they [the judges] thought I was too young," Kwan said in the *Los Angeles Times*. "I think that has a lot to do with it, but I don't really care. It wasn't up to me. It's up to everybody else to decide whether I'm first or last. I did my best and I was excited afterward and I didn't care where I finished." Chen Lu of China won the title, and **Surya Bonaly** (see entry) of France finished second.

NATIONAL CHAMP. Figure skating experts made Kwan and Bobek the favorites to win the women's competition at the 1995 U.S. Figure Skating Championships in San Jose, California. Kwan took the early lead, winning the short program. Tonia Kwiatowski finished second and Bobek third. Just

PEGGY FLEMING

The youngest champion ever at the U.S. Figure Skating Championships was the legendary Peggy Fleming. She won the competition in 1964 at 15 years old. Fleming won the women's figure skating gold medal at the 1968 Winter Olympics in Grenoble, France. She wore costumes sewn by her mother during the competition. Fleming became one of the sport's most popular champions following her Olympic victory and still skates professionally today.

TOO YOUNG?

Many skating experts worry that skaters like Kwan are being forced to do too much too soon. To win major competitions, skaters must learn difficult triple jumps and practice seven days a week. "To get that body in the air and make three turns, I'm afraid you've got to start them very young," Kwan's coach, Frank Carroll, told the *Christian Science Monitor.* "If you wait until they're 16 or 17, it's too late." Kwan does not attend public school, and all her friends are other skaters. She must also worry about gaining weight. Kwan's parents try to help their daughters, both of whom are world-class skaters. "I make it a point to talk to both of my daughters about life, not skating," Mr. Kwan explained in the New Jersey *Record.* "We watch them very carefully. I tell them that life is not fair and you must take what you have been given, make the most of it, and be prepared for things to change. You get prepared by not expecting too much. And the bottom line is, that what my wife and I expect from them is not a gold medal but for them to have a happy life always." Kwan does do many things kids do. She went trick-or-treating as Fred Flintstone and carries a teddy bear knapsack. Kwan says she is having fun. "I am not feeling pressured or made crazy by the attention," Kwan revealed in the same newspaper. "I do normal things. I'm having fun."

before the long programs were to begin, Bobek announced that she had to withdraw from the competition because of an injured ankle.

Bobek's injury opened the way for Kwan to win her first national title. Kwan skated beautifully in her long program to the music of the Richard Strauss opera, "Salome." She landed seven triple jumps and showed improved artistic skating ability. Kwan became the second-youngest U.S. champion in history. (Peggy Fleming was three weeks younger than Kwan when she won the national title in 1964.) Kwiatowski finished second and 13-year-old Tara Lipinski took third place.

THE FUTURE. Kwan continues training and will undoubtedly be a major force in international figure skating for years to come. Her routine includes three hours of training a day, seven days a week. Five days a week Kwan studies her schoolwork with a private tutor.

Kwan usually does a very difficult free-skating routine, including six or seven triple jumps, the most difficult moves to successfully complete. She is practicing what she hopes will be the jump that will win her the Olympic gold medal: the triple axle. Only two women have successfully completed the move in competition: Tonya Harding and Midori Ito of Japan. "She does seven triples," Carroll told Reuters News Agency. "She is up there with any of them in terms of difficulty. She has all the tricks." Kwan also plans to work on her artistic performance, as important in figure skating as athletic ability. "You can always make yourself more artistic," Kwan admitted in the *Los Angeles Times*.

THE DREAM. Kwan has a sticker above her dresser that says "Nagano 1998," reminding her of her dream of winning a gold medal at the 1998 Olympics in Nagano, Japan. "In my dreams, I'm crying because I'm happy and I have the gold medal," Kwan told *Sports Illustrated for Kids*. "Then I wake up and think, 'Oh, darn!'"

OFF THE ICE. Kwan collects troll dolls and has almost 30 in her collection. "They bring me good luck," Kwan told *Sports Illustrated*. She also has three pets, a cat named Spike and two cockatiel birds. Kwan likes to play basketball but admits she is not very good. "I can barely make a shot," she confessed in *Sports Illustrated for Kids*. Kwan also likes to read and watch movies.

Kwan is a good student, earning mostly As in school. She is learning French and is trying to learn Mandarin, a dialect, or type, of the Chinese language. "I can say 'I'm very hungry' and 'I'm very tired' in Mandarin," Kwan told *Sports Illustrated for Kids*. Kwan stated her philosophy in the *Christian Science Monitor:* "Just do what you want to do, work hard, and that's all you can hope for."

Sources

Chicago Tribune, February 12, 1995; May 28, 1995; January 15, 1996; January 21, 1996.
Christian Science Monitor, March 10, 1995.
Detroit Free Press, February 10, 1995.

Los Angeles Times, March 28, 1995.
Newsweek, February 13, 1995.
The Oregonian, February 12, 1995.
People, February 14, 1995.
Philadelphia Inquirer, February 11, 1995.
Record (New Jersey), February 10, 1995.
San Diego Union-Tribune, February 10, 1995; February 11, 1995.
San Jose Mercury News, January 21, 1996.
Sports Illustrated, February 20, 1995.
Sports Illustrated for Kids, February 1995.
Time, February 27, 1995.
Transpacific, April 1994; June 1994.
Additional information provided by Reuters news wire, March 7, 1995, March 10, 1995, and March 11, 1995.

WHERE TO WRITE:
PROPER MARKETING ASSOCIATES,
322 VISTA DEL MAR,
REDONDO BEACH, CA 90277.

Index

H

R

Rahal, Bobby *2:* 498

Raines, Tim *2:* 192

Randy Johnson Rule *2:* 192

Rawls, Betsy *2:* 240

Reagan, Ronald *2:* 175

Recchi, Mark *2:* 177

Reebok *1:* 91, 174, 431, 532

Reese, Wayne *2:* 89

Reeves, Dan *1:* 123, 125

Retton, Mary Lou *1:* 384-385; *2:* 52, 316, 320-321

Rexford, Bill *2:* 130

Reynolds, Butch *2:* 186

Rheaume, Manon *2:* **398-405**

Rice, Glen *2:* 329

Rice, Jerry *1:* 400, **446-452**; *2:* 169, 543-544

Rice, Jim *2:* 507

Riley, Dawn *2:* 299, 301

Riley, Pat *1:* 138, 241, 243; *2:* 329

Ripken, Cal, Jr. *1:* 153, **453-459**

Ripken, Cal, Sr. *1:* 453, 456

Roberts, Robin *2:* 119

Robinson, David *1:* 430, **460-466,** 499

Robinson, Frank *1:* 195, 457, 532

Robinson, Glenn *2:* 160, 230, **406-412,** 514

Robinson, Jackie *1:* 32; *2:* 507

Robitaille, Luc *2:* 116

Rod Carew on Hitting *1:* 116

Rodriguez, Ivan *1:* 169

Rookie of the Year, Baseball
    Alomar, Sandy, Jr. *1:* 26
    Nomo, Hideo *2:* 340-341, 346
    Piazza, Mike *2:* 370, 375
    Ripken, Cal, Jr. *1:* 455

Rookie of the Year, LPGA
    Lopez, Nancy *1:* 340

Rookie of the Year, NASCAR
    Earnhardt, Dale *2:* 72, 74
    Gordon, Jeff *2:* 127

Rookie of the Year, NBA
    Bird, Larry *1:* 53
    Ewing, Patrick *1:* 137
    Hardaway, Anfernee *2:* 151

    Hill, Grant *2:* 155-156, 161, 231
    Johnson, Larry *1:* 251
    Jordan, Michael *1:* 256
    Kidd, Jason *2:* 227-228, 231
    Mourning, Alonzo *2:* 327
    O'Neal, Shaquille *1:* 431
    Robinson, David *1:* 464
    Webber, Chris *2:* 513, 519

Rookie of the Year, NFL
    Marino, Dan *1:* 370
    Sanders, Barry *1:* 498
    Smith, Emmitt *1:* 517
    White, Reggie *1:* 558

Rookie of the Year, NHL
    Lemieux, Mario *1:* 319

Rose, Jalen *2:* 157, 513, 515

Rose, Pete *1:* 192; *2:* 135

Ross, Bobby *2:* 428-429

Round Mound of Rebound (See Barkley, Charles)

Roy, Patrick *2:* **413-421**

Rudolph, Wilma *1:* 202; *2:* 489

Russell, Bill *1:* 55, 424, 426; *2:* 327

Rutgers University
    Lalas, Alexi *2:* 282

Ruth, Babe *1:* 100, 152-153, 531; *2:* 14

Ryan, Buddy *1:* 559-560

Ryan Express (See Ryan, Nolan)

Ryan, Nolan *1:* 2, 24, 97, 116, 345, **467- 473;** *2:* 189, 194, 196

Ryder Cup
    Faldo, Nick *1:* 142, 144

S

Sabatini, Gabriella *1:* 178-180; *2:* 384

Safe Passage Foundation *1:* 35

Sampras, Pete *1:* 11, 90, 107, **474-479;** *2:* 523

Sampson, Ralph *1:* 111, 422, 423

Samuelsson, Ulf *2:* 334

San Antonio Spurs
    Robinson, David *1:* 463

Sanchez Vicario, Arantxa *1:* 93, 179, **480- 486,** 511; *2:* 379, 386-387, 526